GV
875
.N4
T73
1995

Trachtenberg, Leo.

The wonder team.

21918

$29.95

DATE			

The Wonder Team

The Wonder Team:
The True Story
of the Incomparable
1927 New York Yankees

Leo Trachtenberg

Bowling Green State University Popular Press
Bowling Green, OH 43403

Sports and Culture

General Editors
Douglas Noverr
Lawrence Ziewacz

Other books in the series:

The Sports Immortals: Deifying the American Athlete
Peter Williams

Hunting and Fishing for Sport: Commerce, Controversy, Popular Culture
Richard Hummel

Cricket for Americans: Playing and Understanding the Game
Tom Melville

Baseball in 1889: Players vs. Owners
Daniel M. Pearson

The Kid on the Sandlot: Congress and Professional Sports, 1910-1992
Stephen R. Lowe

Lines of poetry quoted from "Sports of the Times," by John Kieran, April 17, 1927. Copyright © by The New York Times Company. Reprinted by permission.

Copyright © 1995 by Bowling Green State University Popular Press

Cover design by Gary Dumm

Library of Congress Cataloging-in-Publication Data

Trachtenberg, Leo.
    The wonder team : the true story of the incomparable 1927 New York Yankees / Leo Trachtenberg.
        p.   cm. -- (Sports and culture series)
    Includes bibliographical references and index.
    ISBN: 0-87972-677-6 (cloth). -- ISBN 0-87972-678-4 (paper)
    1. New York Yankees (Baseball team)--History.   2. Ruth, Babe, 1895-1948. 3. Gehrig, Lou, 1903-1941. I. Title. II. Series.
GV875.N4T73   1995
796.357'64'097471--dc20   95-14665
                                                                          CIP

Dedication

For Danny, who got me started.

Contents

Acknowledgments

I wish to thank the following persons and organizations who helped me during the writing of this book: Scott Mondore of The Baseball Hall of Fame and Museum Research Library; Tom Bannon, director of the New York Yankees publications department; Gregg Mazzola, editor of *Yankees Magazine*; Dave Szen, former publications director of the New York Yankees, and now Yankees traveling secretary; The New York Historical Society; The New York Society Library; The Society for American Baseball Research; and The Cincinnati Historical Society. Also, Michael Anton, Bill Burdick, Tom Carwile, Bill Deane, Milt Gaston, Debbie Gobert, Dave Gould, Cliff Kachline, Frank Kendig, Jim Kreuz, and Vita Trachtenberg.

The reminiscences of the following were invaluable for information about the personalities and accomplishments of the 1927 Yankees: the late Pete Sheehy, Yankee clubhouse manager; the late Ken Smith, 1920s sportswriter; deceased Yankee players George Pipgras, Mark Koenig, Joe Glenn, Ray Morehart, Bots Nekola, Oscar Roettger, Whitey Witt, and Ed Wells.

1927 Yankees

Photo courtesy of the New York Yankees.

1927 New York Yankees Management

Colonel Jacob Ruppert, Owner
Edward Grant Barrow, Business Manager
Miller James Huggins, Manager

1927 New York Yankees Player Roster

Walter Beall P
Benny Bengough C
Pat Collins C
Earle Combs CF
Joe Dugan 3B
Cedric Durst OF
Mike Gazella 3B
Lou Gehrig 1B
Joe Giard P
John Grabowski C
Waite Hoyt P
Mark Koenig SS
Tony Lazzeri 2B

Bob Meusel LF
Wilcy Moore P
Ray Morehart 2B
Ben Paschal OF
Herb Pennock P
George Pipgras P
Walter Ruether P
Babe Ruth RF
Bob Shawkey P
Urban Shocker P
Myles Thomas P
Julian Wera 3B

1927 New York Yankees Staff

Paul Krichell, Scout
Art Fletcher, Coach
Charley O'Leary, Coach
Doc Woods, Trainer
Eddie Bennett, Batboy
Pete Sheehy, Gofer

Introduction

It was 1927. Calvin Coolidge was president, Prohibition was the law of the land, Lindbergh had just flown to Paris, and the movies were still silent. But none of this mattered to me, a nine-year-old sitting with his father in Yankee Stadium watching my first major league baseball game. I don't remember who the Yankees played that radiant summer afternoon before a crowd of tumultuous fans, a day when the grass on the field seemed greener than it ever would again. Nor do I recall who pitched for either team, or who won the game. What I do remember is a barrel-chested, skinny-legged man in a pinstriped uniform who stepped up to the plate in the first inning.

"That's Babe Ruth," my father said. "Watch. He could hit a home run."

I don't recall the count or if I had my fingers crossed, but the prodigious swing of Babe's bat, the sharp crack as it met the ball, and the roar of the immense crowd remain etched in my memory. High into the air soared the ball, a white dot ascending with extravagant and splendid velocity towards the right field bleachers where it dropped into a forest of outstretched hands. I watched excitedly as the Babe circled the bases, touched home, and tipped his hat to the adoring fans. At that moment I became, then and forever after, a fan of baseball, the New York Yankees, and George Herman "Babe" Ruth.

"Does he always hit home runs?" I asked my father. "No, not always," he said, laughing, "but plenty of times. More than anybody."

I was to see the Babe hit other home runs, and I've been lucky enough during 60-plus years as a Yankee fan to see the likes of Joe DiMaggio, Mickey Mantle, Reggie Jackson, Yogi Berra and other pinstriped sluggers whack the ball into the stands. But none compared to the homer Babe hit that afternoon in 1927—for me.

A few months later, on October 8, Yankee second baseman "Poosh 'em up" Tony Lazzeri stood at that same Stadium home plate. It was the fourth game of the 1927 World Series (the Yankees had taken the first three games from the Pittsburgh Pirates), the bottom of the ninth with the score 3–3 and two out.

On third was Yankee center fielder Earle Combs. Pirates hurler John "Big Serb" Miljus got the signal and loosed an errant pitch towards home. The ball flew past the desperate grasp of Pirate catcher Johnny Gooch's outstretched mitt, 60,000 fans erupted when Combs scuttled in from third, touched home, and a legend was born.

1

2 The Wonder Team

The ball club that won the 4–3 game that October day, completing a four game sweep of the world series, was the 1927 Yankees, judged by many as the greatest of all teams in the long and splendid history of professional baseball. In the 60-some years since those "Murderers' Row" Yanks shattered the opposition with prodigal skills and awesome power they have become the recognized model of singular baseball achievement. A few excellent teams preceded them, others followed, but none were quite their equal.

Scarcely had the series tumult died away when James R. Harrison, a sportswriter not easily given to overstatement, wrote in the *The New York Times* of October 9, 1927, "They must not be far wrong who assert that these Yankees are the greatest team in the more than fifty years of baseball history."

H.I. Phillips, writing in the *New York Sun* of October 10, 1927, with no trace of Harrison's small equivocation, stated, "Their original ideal that they (the Pirates) might win a game from what is beyond doubt the greatest team of all time was definitely and finally snuffed out when...pitcher Miljus threw a ball at an invisible catcher." The Yankees, he wrote waggishly, "are the first team in history to have magicians, miracle men, jinns, a Beowulf and a couple of Thors on it." Then, in a moment of insight and divination he added, "It is a team out of folklore and mythology."

Phillips was on to something. For the remarkable ball club that had swaggered through baseball and taken the measure of the best in both leagues has in fact become part of our American folk tradition. And though years have passed, and admirable ball clubs have come and gone, the sovereign reputation of the 1927 Yankees remains undiminished. Indeed, in the recent years of profound changes in our national pastime—expanded leagues, night ball, the designated hitter, pool table playing surfaces, indoor stadiums, a ball so juiced up that homers are commonplace instead of feats of special accomplishment—that reputation has taken on added luster with each passing season.

In the May 1951 issue of *Sport Magazine,* Paul Gallico, who began his prominent writing career as a sports reporter and columnist, called the '27 Yanks "the greatest all-around baseball team ever to trot up the dugout steps onto the diamond—and unquestionably the greatest collection of assassins of pitchers."

The same magazine, in an October 1962 article by Josh Greenfeld, quotes Wilbert Robinson, a charter member of that famous gang of diamond depredators, the Baltimore "Old Orioles." Said Robinson, "This Yankee team would have murdered the old Orioles. We never saw the day we could make runs like Huggins' mob."

And though you'd think that by 1963 some other ball club would be jostling the '27 Yanks in the contest for all-time supremacy, that year 84 out of 100 sports editors voted the 1927 Yankees number 1. Reporting these results in the *Sporting News* of June 8, 1963, veteran sports writer Dan Daniel stated: "They'll never be matched." Today, with the twentieth-century waning, Daniel's prediction stands unchallenged.

Of course, other great ball clubs have come on the scene since the departure of the 1927 Yankees, notably Connie Mack's 1929–31 Philadelphia A's, Joe McCarthy's 1936 Yankees, and Sparky Anderson's "Big Red Machine" Cincinnati Reds of the 1970s. You can crunch their numbers in approved Quanto-History style, examine their virtues and acclaim their eminence; but, significantly, hardly ever do we hear them selected as the "greatest," in the history of the game. That accolade, at least until now, has been reserved for the 1927 Yankees, a golden team for a golden time.

Who were the 1927 Yankees, the team of "Five O'Clock Lightning" and Babe's epochal 60 homers? What sort of men were those supremely gifted, irresistibly confident athletes who dominated baseball like some colossus casting a shadow beyond its time? Who brought them together for that glorious season? And what exactly did they accomplish in the climactic year of the 1920s, that time between the great wars when the unemployment rate was 3.2 percent, taxes were low, optimism high, we were sure of ourselves as a nation and a people, and sports thrived in its first Golden Age? Looking back at that time of cheerful expectations and high confidence, it's small wonder that historian Paul Johnson, in his book, *Modern Times,* dubbed the 1920s "The Last Arcadia."

Six of the 1927 club are in the Hall of Fame in Cooperstown, New York: Babe Ruth, Lou Gehrig, Tony Lazzeri, Earle Combs, Waite Hoyt, Herb Pennock. So are Miller Huggins, their great manager, and Ed Barrow the business manager who wheeled and dealed to bring superb players to New York.

The most famous, of course, was their right fielder, the lusty, roistering child/man George Herman "Babe" Ruth, a player gifted beyond the reasonable, a force of nature responding to the crowd as no other ballplayer before or since.

Patrolling center field was Earle Combs, the Bible-reading "Kentucky Colonel" from the Cumberland, swift, graceful, the best leadoff man ever. Bob Meusel, with his icy stare and surly disposition, the picture swing and rifle arm, was the left fielder.

The Yankee infield was equally gifted. Playing first base was the strapping, even-tempered "Iron Man," Lou Gehrig, a true baseball immortal who with Ruth comprised the most devastating one-two punch the game has ever known. "Poosh 'em up," Tony Lazzeri, a take-charge fielder and slashing hitter, the first of a long line of brilliant Italian-American Yankees, covered second. Mark Koenig, the man sportswriters once said would never make it in the majors, played short and found immortality on the great team. "Jumping Joe," Dugan, nearing the end of his playing days, yet still peerless at the hot corner, picked 'em at third. Joe Collins, Benny Bengough, and Johnny Grabowski, all sterling catchers, shared the assignments behind home plate.

The pitching staff was top rank, a manager's dream. The ace righty was the free-spirited "Schoolboy," Waite Hoyt. Herb Pennock, the wily, brainy, Quaker countryman with a wicked curve and fine control, was their dominant lefty hurler. Rookie Wilcy Moore was there, the Oklahoma dirt farmer with steady nerves and a bewildering sinker. So was that most courageous of pitchers, Urban Shocker, winning eighteen while slowly dying of heart disease. Rounding out the staff was George Pipgras, finally coming into his own after discouraging years on the bench, and Dutch Ruether, ending his major league career as a winning hurler. On the strong Yank bench were sterling backups—Mike Gazella, Cedric Durst, Ben Paschal, Ray Morehart—men lost in time whom few recall, who never had the slightest chance of winning a plaque in Cooperstown yet found themselves, through the benign touch of fate, of a piece with true greatness.

Not least, there was Miller Huggins (manager), Edward Grant Barrow (business manager), Colonel Jacob Ruppert (owner): three men who came together to form a management alliance that was made in some baseball heaven. Who, in the apogee year of a beguiling decade—before the Great Depression, Hitler, World War II, and the nagging anxieties of the nuclear age—saw their '27 Yanks triumph with an exuberance that mirrored the time.

The word "great" is defined in my Webster's as "remarkable in magnitude, degree, or effectiveness," a definition that surely fits the 1927 New York Yankees. For they were a remarkable ball club in every way by which superior achievement is judged in baseball. Brought together and attaining a kind of radiant perfection in that one magnificent year, their accomplishments will continue to resonate as long as the game is played.

One of the dwindling number who saw those '27 Yankees play, I have carried with me the luminous memory of the ball club that came into my life that summer afternoon. Now, in remembrance of joyous days in the company of Babe, Lou, and their memorable teammates, I invite you to join me in playing baseball with the 1927 New York Yankees.

Leo Trachtenberg
January 15, 1995
New York City

1

Spring Training, 1927

Babe gets into shape, so do Yankees.

During the winter of 1927, while snow covered the diamond at Yankee Stadium, George Herman Ruth, under the firm hand and critical eye of physical trainer Artie McGovern, worked hard to shed the accumulated suet of a winter's gourmandising and prodigal bibulousness. Now at the top of his career, this spring Babe was determined to be in shape when the ump hollered that most inspiring of sounds to his ear, "Play ball!"

The news of Babe's Spartan regimen was carried to Yankee owner Jake Ruppert, manager Miller Huggins, and the millions of the Bambino's admiring fans, which included most of the nation's population. As of February 22 the glad tidings were that the six-feet-two-inch Ruth was down to a muscular 224 pounds and still dropping. His waist measured a svelte 38-3/4 inches, his sturdy calf 16, his robust forearm 12-1/2.

For Babe's single-minded devotion to physical training, and in appreciation of his achievements in seasons past, Colonel Jake offered him a contract of $52,000 for one year—the same sum Ruth earned in 1926 when he whupped the ball at a thunderous .372 clip and slammed 47 homers. Ruth promptly and politely returned the contract unsigned, accompanied by a letter stating why he was worth $100,000 per.

Nobody was surprised, certainly not the press, and surely not the Colonel, for this salary negotiation was a late winter ritual, its moves as predictable as a grand quadrille. To New Yorkers still ankle-deep in slush, it was a clear sign that spring couldn't be far off, not with the Babe and the Colonel hassling out a contract at the Yankee front office and in sports pages the country over. Editors, of course, were delighted. Indeed, it was almost a principle of journalism that if on any given day a man wasn't biting a dog, the press could count on Babe for diverting copy.

At one point, feigning high dudgeon and low spirits, Ruth announced that rather than settle for a sum more befitting a plebian wage slave than the Sultan of Swat, he might renounce baseball to open a chain of physical culture salons with McGovern as partner. Among baseball's legion of followers this droll piece of news was good for more laughs than the antics of clowns or the tabloid comic sections.

5

Commenting on the salary burlesque, W.O. McGeehan wrote in the *New York Herald Tribune* of February 26, "Congress could come to the aid of Colonel Ruppert...and save the situation for that harassed sportsman." Then McGeehan proposed that the solons in Washington amend the Prohibition law so that the beer-brewing Ruppert could afford to pay his impecunious slugger. "And if the net income of the brewery was not sufficient...[Ruth] might be induced to accept some of the salary in kind...for with both the brewery and Babe Ruth idle...the outlook for the summer is far from pleasant." Fortunately such drastic measures weren't necessary.

After the expenditure of enough newsprint to fell a small forest, Babe and the Colonel cut a deal. Ruth got a total of $210,000 over three years, a princely sum for those halcyon days; Colonel Jake got his magnetic, larger-than-life star slugger; the public got its fill of preseason diversion.

Of course, though you would never know it from the sports pages, there was more to the '27 Yankees that late winter than the eminent George Herman Ruth. To be precise, there were eight other positions to be filled in the lineup.

By late February a phalanx of Yankees was in St. Petersburg, Florida, ready to face the scrutiny of Miller Huggins. Nine years earlier, Huggins, known affectionately as "Hug," had moved to New York from St. Louis where he had managed the Cardinals for five seasons. In his nine seasons as a Yankee, Hug led New York from a perennial second division status—they had never won a pennant since their inception in 1903—to four pennants (1921–23, 1926), and one world championship (1923).

Skinny, dyspeptic, a gritty little master of baseball, Huggins was born in Cincinnati on March 27, 1879. He learned to play ball in the rough-and-tumble days of the game: the time of the dead ball, the legal spitter, scraggy fields, and hardscrabble salaries. From playing semipro ball he went to St. Paul in the American Association, then to Cincinnati in 1904. After six seasons with the Reds he moved to the St. Louis Cards as a player and, for five of those seasons, as manager.

Hug was a slick second baseman with good range and sure hands. An excellent leadoff man adept at drawing walks, he was also a fine bunter. His mind was analytical, his character tough, and he knew, as did few others, that arcane element of our sports culture, "inside" baseball. With players of only ordinary skills Hug had managed the Cards from deep in the second division to contender status. And—no small achievement—while playing ball he earned a law degree at the University of Cincinnati.

But Hug never practiced law. For baseball and its inimitable strategies and competitive nature, the ballpark atmosphere of challenge, and the pleasure of playing a game for a living, became the true center of his life.

Ruppert's decision to sign him to manage was crucial to the establishment of the first Yankee pennant-winning dynasty.

In 1926 the Yankees won the pennant, but lost the series to the Cardinals in seven rousing games. Still, as always in baseball, there was next year. When next year arrived and Miller surveyed his ball club in St. Pete, what he saw gladdened his heart and pacified his vulnerable nervous system.

The Yankee infield that spring—Gehrig (1B), Lazzeri (2B), Koenig (SS), and Dugan (3B)—was slick, agile, and could hit with power. By season's end these four infield regulars would have a combined batting average (BA) of .309. Of that bunch of grounder-grabbers, the illustrious Gehrig and the take-charge Lazzeri are in the Hall of Fame. In batting average, run production, and run scoring they were the best ever. And though, in the long history of the game, they were surpassed by other clubs in fielding statistics and other performance criteria, still, the 1927 Yankee infield was of prime quality.

The outfield was top-rank; indeed, the Ruth, Combs, Meusel aggregation was arguably the best ever. Combs covered the far and wide reaches of center field like a bounding deer. Only his arm was ordinary; as a fielder he was the peer of such as Tris Speaker and Joe DiMaggio (who came to the Stadium nine years later and whom Combs coached). Left fielder Bob Meusel, swift and untypically hustling that year, had a rifle for an arm. As for Ruth—well, he was the Babe, so enough said.

And that outfield was baseball-smart, not given to the common inanities that drive managers to strong drink, and fans to jeering and despair (e.g., throwing to the wrong base, stumbling into each other, musing on the state of the world while waiting for a fly ball to arrive). And—a fact not easily grasped in our time of overnight hype when hitters of only middling skills have instant eminence conferred upon them—the combined BA of the outfield was an astonishing .349.

The catching was merely very good. Pat Collins, Johnny Grabowski, and Benny Bengough expertly handled the Yank hurlers, and in '27 dependably hit .275, .277, and .247, respectively. Today, catchers like that, in the artful clutch of agents and barristers, would have owners falling over each other in a stampede to create three more instant millionaires. But money, as philosophical types know, isn't everything. Collins, Grabowski, and Bengough, while earning enough of Colonel Jake's bucks to stay out of the poorhouse, wore the pinstripes on a surpassing ball club. And in the fateful design of history, that was its own reward.

Also in St. Pete that spring was a gaggle of talented rookies who may have been born to play ball, perhaps in Elmira or Sioux Falls, but not with the New York Yankees of 1927. Baxter Williams, George Davis, and Henry

Johnson were among those who didn't make the team. Nor did a 20-year-old fantast from Brooklyn named Joe Bruno, who paid his way down hoping to land a pitching slot on the roster. The intrepid Bruno came and went quickly, but his optimism was an admirable reflection of the American Dream. In years to come, as the legend of the '27 Yankees flourished, these rejects could tell their grandchildren that they had once played on the same field with the great ones, a wistful footnote to history.

Dan Howley, the rookie manager of the St. Louis Browns, was there too. After scouting Hug's team, Dapper Dan Howley told the assembled press on March 2, "The winner of the American League pennant will be the team that beats the Yankees." And which might that be? the diligent scriveners pressed him. "The Athletics maybe. The Indians have a chance. Possibly the Senators." As for his own team, Howley predicted without fear of rebuttal, "They are not going to win every day...but they are going to hustle every day."

Then Dapper Dan departed to join his band of Browns, with no inkling of the dread happening that would befall St. Louis that season, when Howley's club lost the first 21 out of 22 to the Yanks, a doleful record they hold to this day.

Not that Miller Huggins was thinking of winning 21 out of 22 from anyone that spring. While contemplating his roster, Hug confided to the press vexing doubts about his hurlers. "The Yankee pitching staff has reached the stage where I must gamble," grumbled Hug on March 6 as he ruminated on graybeards like Pennock (33), Ruether (33), Shocker, and Shawkey (both going to seed at 36).

Some writers concurred with Hug's misgivings. Richards Vidmer, a reporter with a discerning eye, wrote in *The New York Times* of March 31, "The Yankees aren't any stronger than they were a year ago and they will have stronger opposition.... Their weakness lies in their pitching staff." And on April 5, John Kieran, featured columnist for the same paper stated that "the Yankees are the hardest team in either league to 'dope'.... The team is practically the same as last year, with perhaps a slight flavor of age in the pitching staff."

When Huggins told the press that he intended to use kids like Pipgras (he did), rookie Chesterfield (he didn't), and Myles Thomas (he did), there were sagacious nods from the fourth estate, and sympathy for Hug's predicament. Sure, he had Hoyt and the slightly suspect Pennock, but who else could he depend on? After all, hurlers like Hoyt and Pennock didn't show up like spring swallows in your ballpark every year. But Miller needn't have fretted. Stats buffs will note that the aforementioned oldsters would account for a won-lost mark of 52–23 in 1927—not bad for a bunch of dodderers.

Miller did have one promising rookie pitcher on hand. Not quite in the superannuated class, Wilcy Moore was a husky, balding, 29-year-old, an unexpected hunk of rare ivory from Greenville in the South Atlantic (Sally) League. Although Moore had been 30–4 with Greenville, with 31 of his 34 starts complete games, some were skeptical about his stuff. This country boy off an Oklahoma dirt farm had knocked around the minors a long time, and where the hell was Greenville anyway? After opening day the doubters would eat their words.

In training Wilcy showed a baffling sinker and pinpoint control, valuable assets he carried into the season to become the relief stopper for Hug. He would last only seven years in the majors, except for 1927 all of them mediocre, but that first year he proved to be the best short-term investment in a ballplayer business manager Ed Barrow ever made.

As always, when the Yanks assembled, it was Ruth who was the focus of press and fans' attention. When Babe arrived in training camp on March 7, the rest of the team might as well have been in another town playing tiddlywinks. With his carefree lifestyle, his kid's ebullience, his penchant for performing baseball's grand gesture, the wallop into the stands, Babe was a gift to the public appropriate to the time. With public divertissements in perennial demand in a prosperous era, nobody filled that need quite like Babe Ruth. On the field, in the press, he was stage center in an ongoing public theater.

Five days earlier, on March 3, Artie McGovern had paraded Babe around his New York gym like a blooded horse at a Keeneland auction. The Babe, Artie pointed out to a clutch of reporters ignorant of matters physically cultural, had a 40-inch chest, not unusual in large men. But, said Artie significantly, when expanded the Ruthian chest billowed to a remarkable 47 inches. "It means that his upper chest is very powerful," Artie told the assembled envoys of the fourth estate. "Babe's seven-inch expansion shows why he can get such a swing into his drives and hit the ball so far." Then Artie, surpassingly proud of his winter's oeuvre, added, "His upper body muscles are wonderful."

Solemnly, the Bambino concurred, and the next day he appeared at the Ruppert brewery to sign his new and bountiful contract, as Colonel Jake smiled jovially for the cameras. And why not? A ball player with a seven-inch chest expansion didn't show up at the home of near beer every day.

As it went that day at the brewery, so it would go all that spring. Miller Huggins would have 25 men on his roster, but the centerpiece of the Yankee story was unquestionably Babe Ruth. Each day that spring, Ruthian news disseminated northward to Babe-oriented editors in New York and its environs. Each day, it was devoured by millions of readers hungry for glad tidings about their prodigious idol.

"Hit me, hit me as hard as you can," said Ruth to a gaggle of newspapermen at St. Pete. An obliging correspondent slammed his fist into Ruth's belly, but according to *The New York Times* of March 8, "G. Herman merely smiled contentedly and went on breathing in a natural way." The assault on the Ruthian gut dutifully reported, readers were treated to a description of Ruth's line drives, a practice trot around the bases, a turn at pitching (a skill George Herman was proud of to his dying day—and rightfully so).

Meanwhile, Hug—reflective, pinch-faced, a chaw of tobacco in his cheek, the light of cautious optimism in his eye—watched his team shape up. He looked hard at his rookies, counseled his regulars, instructed and hectored.

"Look at young Flickinger out there. Throws without stepping out with his right foot. I'll have to tell him about that." To onlooking writers, Hug confided that Gehrig was weak going to his left: "Now Lou, play further off the bag towards second and see if you can stop them on your left," he coached Gehrig.

And with the memory of costly bobbles in the '26 series still rankling, Hug declared, "I'm going to start working on Koenig next week. Any shortstop who can't go to his left with one hand is not a great shortstop.... Koenig will have to learn how to do it."

The computer and its adjuncts—the spate of numbers, the printouts, the mathematical profiles that can never give us the heart and soul of a player, or predict his hunger to win when the chips are down—were unknown in Huggins's time. All he had was his sharp judgment and experience to go by; as with all great managers this was sufficient. They told him, for the most part, to stand pat with his 1926 pennant winner.

The Yanks won their share of grapefruit league games, the annual exercise that means nothing in the standings but is an ordeal for aspiring rookies. Coaches Art Fletcher and Charley O'Leary instructed, goaded, hollered it up.

Fletcher, recently liberated from managing the National League Phillies—then a baseball Siberia—was an aggressive ex-Giant shortstop. A rowdy jaybird in the coaching box, a hassler of umps, Fletch was an ideal assistant to the quieter, cerebral Huggins. As for the smart, diminutive O'Leary, he was a lively ex-shortstop who came up with the White Sox back in 1900, a close friend of Huggins and, like Fletcher, a seasoned baseball man.

When the Yankees broke camp and headed north on the evening of March 30, 1927, there were still qualms about their pitching, even though Miller had swapped the aging Sam Jones with the Browns for young Joe Giard (with outfielder Cedric Durst thrown into the deal by St. Louis). The consensus was that the Yanks were a good team, but no one—not the sportswriters, or the most admiring Yank boosters—thought they were destined to become the greatest of all ball clubs.

Since the early days of baseball, teams moved north at the end of spring training, like flocks of birds following the sun. That journey was part of the green promise of April, in which the sharp crack of a bat against a ball, and the thump of a ball in a mitt, merged in rhythm with the animating sweep of warm wind and a quickening of the blood. A climax to spring training, the barnstorming journey northward was a happening dating back to the 1880s, when "Cap" Anson first brought his Chicago Nationals to train in Hot Springs, Arkansas.

Today ball clubs go from here to anywhere at 600 miles per hour at 30,000 feet. The terrain below them slips past, impersonal and distant. What is missing in this jet-lagging journey is a closeness to the land, its towns and people. In baseball's past days that proximity was avidly displayed by fans and players when trains rolled into small cities, and renowned big leaguers stopped to whip the ball around the infield, or bust it into the rickety stands.

Before the broadcasting of games, before the advent of the dominant icon of our time, the 21-inch tube, those appearances on the hometown ball fields bestowed an abiding memory to baseball fans in towns like Knoxville, Montgomery, and Chattanooga. In 1927 the Yankee trip north by rail was a movable feast of baseball, eight full courses played with their 1926 series conquerors, the St. Louis Cardinals.

Great crowds turned out to see them. On April 1, in Jacksonville, Florida, where the Yankees beat the Cardinals 3–2, Richards Vidmer wrote in *The New York Times,* "The throng overflowed the new grandstand, perched on the bleachers roof, swarmed along the foul lines, and basked in the outfield."

In Savannah, Georgia, on April 2, where the Cards blasted the Yanks 20–10, "there was an outpouring of...kids from the bleachers, the stands, the boxes, and probably the knotholes in the fence," wrote Vidmer. "They swept...across the playing field and Ruth had to wade through them...in order to reach the bench." Said Babe, grinning, "I wish they were all mine."

On April 5, as the Yankee train passed through the little town of Etowah, Tennessee, the entire population turned out at the train station in a driving rain. There was a man on board named Ruth, and it seemed that a glimpse of him would brighten their humdrum lives. Who passes through Etowah today? Is there a train that does? Is there a station?

Moving north, the Yanks split eight games with the Cards, arrived in New York, promptly knocked off the Brooklyn Dodgers twice at Ebbets Field, and prepared to open the season's festivities on April 12 by playing the Philadelphia Athletics at Yankee Stadium.

12 The Wonder Team

Around the American League there would be pitchers battles, bases pilfered, phenoms coming up and veterans departing, the whole robust display of baseball action that has been part of America since well back in the nineteenth century. It would be entertaining, exhilarating, a welcome respite from daily labor, passing afflictions, and living in a rut. And if a few prescient observers suspected that Hug's athletes were no ordinary ball club, their intuitions would be confirmed in the coming weeks.

2

April

Yanks win six straight, a portent of things to come.

A sellout crowd of 70,000 filled Yankee Stadium on a balmy opening day, April 12, 1927, to see the Yankees take on Connie Mack's Athletics. A preseason poll of baseball writers had picked the A's to win the pennant, but the Yanks either did not read the poll or decided it had small relevance to how baseball should be played. Heaving his blazing fastball, the great Lefty Grove struck out Ruth, Gehrig, Combs, and Lazzeri in the early innings. An unlikely feat, still, there it is in the record. But in the fifth the Yanks scored 4, and another 4 in the sixth sending Grove and his zinger to the showers—and won the game 8–3. Yankee pitcher Waite Hoyt went the full nine to earn his first win of the season. At sundown Hug's team ended the day in first place, a slot they would enjoy for many pleasant months to come.

Ruth didn't get a hit, but the festivities weren't without compensation for the "Big Fellow." For reasons still something of a mystery, New York's playboy chief executive, "Gentleman Jimmy" Walker, awarded Babe a three-foot-high silver loving cup, lending a decorous touch to a splendid day.

On April 13 the Yanks won 10–4, in the process inducing Connie Mack to use four pitchers, all to no avail. The following day the score was tied 9–9, when darkness descended on the Bronx and the game was called. Night baseball didn't come to Yankee Stadium until the end of World War II; a tied game had to be played again.

Connie Mack, lanky, lean, pennant-hungry, attired as always in dark civvies, his bony throat encased by a stiff collar, diamond strategies gyrating in his canny head, had eight future Hall of Famers on his club—Ty Cobb, Zach Wheat, Al Simmons, Lefty Grove, Mickey Cochrane, Jimmy Foxx, Eddie Collins, plus Mack himself—but they were not enough in that opening series. In the final game, on April 15, Hug's men fortified their message to the American League by winning 6–3 for a sweep. It's safe to say that Connie and his luminaries were happy to leave the Bronx ballpark after the disastrous proceedings.

14 The Wonder Team

Babe Ruth hit his first homer of the season in that series with the A's, off Howard Ehmke, on the 15th. And Mark Koenig went 2 for 3 in the opener, fielded brilliantly, and hit 5 for 5 in the second game. It was a gratifying and redeeming start for the Yank shortstop, who, only a year before, had struggled to prove to the world that he could really play like a big leaguer.

Mark Anthony Koenig arrived in New York at the end of the 1925 season, a plague year for the Yankees. It was the year when Ruth, after gorging on food and beer, suffered the most celebrated bellyache (and emergency surgery) in history. To add to Ruth's troubles, he was fined $5,000 by Huggins, and suspended for insulting behavior and breaking club rules. It was also the year when the Yankees, for the only time under Huggins's leadership, toppled into the second division to finish a hapless seventh. But to young Mark these were small matters, for finally he was in the big leagues.

Koenig's professional career began in 1921, at the age of 17, in Moose Jaw, Canada, which was like playing no place. To make matters worse, in mid-season Moose Jaw and the league containing it collapsed like a bad soufflé, and Koenig began a journey through the minors. He finally made it to the high minor league AAA St. Paul Saints, where he starred in the 1924 Little World Series, caught the knowing eye of Yankee scout Paul Krichell, and was bought by the Yankees. In the spring of 1926 Miller Huggins chose the switch-hitting, righty-throwing Koenig to play alongside another rookie, a second baseman named Tony Lazzeri. That plan occasioned doubts among sportswriters and baseball cognoscenti.

Sure, the skeptics said, this kid might hit big league pitching, but he was erratic in the field and wouldn't make it. Still clear minded at 83 and eager to talk, Koenig recalled his rookie year troubles.

"I had some bad days and...the sporting writers got on me.... They said, 'Koenig will never last.'" But the critics didn't reckon with Hug, a man noted for nurturing talent. "Huggins," Mark said, "used to call me into his office and say, 'I'm running this club, not the sportin' writers. And as long as I want you in there, you're gonna stay in there.' And that gave me a lot of confidence."

Koenig had a powerful arm, but he insisted he wasn't a great glove man. "I had such small hands, and the gloves weren't the size they are now. They got butterfly nets now." Koenig could have used a butterfly net in the final game of the 1926 World Series when he won goat horns for booting a double-play ball that gave the Cards the game and the championship. Mark had a nightmare or two about that bobble, but it was just an unseemly prelude to enduring fame. For though not born to

Mark Anthony Koenig   *Photo courtesy of the New York Yankees.*

greatness, as some of his illustrious teammates were, Koenig had fame thrust upon him as a 1927 Yankee regular.

"I was ordinary, a small cog in a big machine," he told *Sporting News* writer Dave Newhouse on July 5, 1980. "The Yankees could have had a midget at shortstop," and still won the pennant. Hardly. Koenig's self-disparagement is overstated. You don't win pennants with bungling shortstops, and nobody knew this better than Huggins. With the take-charge Lazzeri steadying him, Koenig played a very good short. And by batting a healthy .285 for the season, between Combs at leadoff and Ruth at No. 3, he gave pitchers his share of fits and agitations.

Koenig's sensational play early in the '27 season campaign moved John Kieran of *The New York Times* to consult his muse on April 17, 1927, and come up with the following balladry.

> And now we'll make the welkin ring,
> And now young Mark Koenig's praises sing.
> For he can throw like anything,
> And how that boy does play.
> He puts the pitchers in a fright,
> With steaming singles left and right,
> Who talked of benching him? Good night!
> He's on the job to stay."

That morsel of poesy isn't Keats or Robert Frost, but the sentiment is heartfelt. Koenig surely savored reading it after the censure he took from the press. Not only was his solid shortstopping critical to the exalted reputation of the club, but he carried his talents into the 1928 championship season.

The Yanks took their sixth pennant of the decade in 1928, finishing three games ahead of a rebuilt Philadelphia A's club. Then they walloped the Cards for their second straight World Championship, four games to none. In that stellar year Koenig sparkled at short and hit a lusty .319 in what was his, and the Yankees', farewell to the 1920s.

New York finished second to the Athletics in 1929, and though Koenig hit .292 and fielded well, a time of troubles was upon him. When he developed a seemingly chronic eye problem, the Yankees dealt him to Detroit in mid-season of 1930. In an absurd move the Tigers tried turning him into a pitcher, something Mark never could be. He was born to hit a baseball, not curve it at the corner of the plate. The experiment failed: Koenig was waived from the majors in 1931.

He landed with the San Francisco Missions of the Pacific Coast League (PCL), his career headed for an inglorious ending. But whoever had examined Koenig's eyes must have been looking through the wrong end of his instrument, for a San Francisco eye specialist successfully treated him, and in 1932 the ex-Yank was fielding well, and hitting up a storm for the Missions. Then Fate stepped into his life in the guise of a lady with a gun.

On July 6, 1932, a Miss Violet Popovich, suffering from unrequited love, and flaunting an excess of pique and a pistol, confronted Chicago Cubs shortstop Billy Jurges in his hotel room. When the passion and madness was over Jurges had been shot twice, benching him more effectively than any manager could. What to do?

Chicago looked to San Francisco where Koenig was bludgeoning baseballs at a .333 clip, and sweeping them up at short. "Grab him," ordered Cub president Bill Veeck, Sr. So Koenig came to the Cubs, where, for the next 33 games he played like he had for the Yankees in 1927. He fielded well, lambasted pitchers, and insured the Cubs the flag. For Koenig's superlative efforts, in a display of avarice Scrooge would have admired, the Cubs players voted him only a one-half share of the series swag. They soon regretted their parsimony.

Chicago's opponent in the 1932 series was the Yankees, and Koenig's old buddies didn't spare the vitriol at game time. Led by Babe Ruth, who called the Cubs penny-pinchers, misers, and less printable epithets, the Yankees racked up Chicago in four straight games for their fourth World Championship.

It was in the third game of that series that Ruth, as every baseball zealot knows, did or didn't call his now legendary "called homer."

Koenig was asked about the call in a December 26, 1984, interview with the author. "Well, it's a question," he said. "There's pros and cons. He raised his right arm, but whether he actually pointed to centerfield, I doubt it.... Root, the pitcher, he denies it up and down that he pointed. But I got to give [Ruth] credit. He was a great hitter and did some remarkable things."

Koenig played eighty games as a Cub infielder in 1933, moved to Cincinnati in 1934, and ended his major league career with the Giants in 1935 and 1936. That last year he appeared in his fifth series, which the Giants lost to the Yankees four games to two. Koenig didn't like Giants manager Bill Terry, but Terry called him a valuable player on his pennant-winning club. That overload of praise didn't do Koenig much good. Next year he was back in the minors; at the end of 1937 he hung them up.

Mark Koenig never again was connected with organized baseball; though he stayed in touch with some of his old Yankee teammates, he became something of a recluse in his old age. But as the 1920s Yankees died off, he was repeatedly tracked down by writers for stories about Ruth, Gehrig & Co.

Looking back on his playing days, he said of the famous team and players of his era: "Naturally I'd favor them. I think the old timers were a lot better than these young guys now. It seems to me there are an awful lot of crybabies now. I never saw so many guys sittin' on the bench, they're injured, so many pitchers...they can't pitch nine innings. And the ball is livelier now. If Ruth were playing today he'd hit a hundred and two home runs."

Not likely, but who wouldn't bet that Ruth could break 60? As for the old shortstop, who could fault him for his extravagant views? After all, he was a 1927 Yankee.

Mark Koenig—last survivor of the legendary team—died on April 22, 1993.

On April 16 the Yanks defeated the Red Sox 10–6 at the Stadium. On the 17th they crushed Boston 14–2 as Gehrig homered twice. And the rest of the lineup didn't do badly either. The way they hit Boston's hapless pitchers that day showed how Yankee power was distributed.

Gehrig made three hits; Lazzeri singled and tripled; Meusel smacked three singles; Koenig had two singles; Combs doubled and singled; Ruth singled and was on base three times; Mike Gazella came off Hug's strong bench to sub for Dugan and doubled; catcher Pat Collins had three hits and walked once. How appropriate for 1927, that year of joyous excess.

The Yankee bats were comparatively quiet on the 18th but Miller's boys won anyway, 3–0, as the game was played in a brief one hour and 29 minutes—a pleasant afternoon for the ballplayers, though unprofitable for the purveyors of hot dogs. Hoyt, Pennock, and other hurlers were often going the distance, a not uncommon event for Yank pitchers that year but a discouraging portent for the rest of the league.

The next day, after winning their first six games, the Hugmen finally lost one, 6–3, to Boston; Bob Shawkey was the loser. An ace Yankee righty for 13 years, Bob had little left in his last pro-ball season. On Hug's first string of pennant winners in the early '20s, Shawkey had four 20-or-more game-winning seasons, and would finish his career with a lifetime 196–150 and a 3.09 earned run average (ERA). In his 15th year in the majors, though he would go only 2–3 while hurling a mere 43 innings, it was gratifying that he finished playing ball as part of the great club.

On April 20, in Philadelphia, the Yanks dropped their second in a row, 8–5, as Shocker was relieved by Moore in the seventh. And on April 21, when the Yanks beat the A's 13–6, Moore came in to relieve for the third day in a row, squelched a three-run A's rally, and made Yankee business manager Ed Barrow look like a genius. Which, as a baseball man, he was.

Before Dave Righetti, before Sparky Lyle and Goose Gossage, before Fordham Johnny Murphy, fireballing Joe Page, and the rest of the fraternity of Yankee firemen, there was a 30-year-old righty named William Wilcy Moore. He had guile, the nerves of a safecracker, and a confounding, elegantly controlled sinker that made batters reflect that they'd be better off in another league, in another town. In moments of high crisis Wilcy's pitching made infielders chortle, the starting pitcher happy, the manager a wizard. A key player on the 1927 Yankees, Moore was one of the first of baseball's great relievers.

He began his pro career at 24—an advanced age for a beginner in organized baseball—with Fort Worth of the Texas-Oklahoma League. In those days an extensive network of minor league clubs brought baseball to small towns and cities.

Eastern Shore, Western, Appalachian, South Atlantic, Pacific Coast, Tri-States, Cotton States—these and a host of other leagues recall a time when America was younger and perhaps more innocent; a time when baseball was played in the sun, and the odious notion of playing our national pastime on a leg-fatiguing carpet made from oil gunk and chemicals had not yet occurred to anyone. It was in those minors that Wilcy Moore learned his trade, for six years hurling a pretty good fastball in the outlands of Fort Worth, Ardmore, Okmulgee, and Greenville.

Wilcy might have continued his minor league wandering, his fastball losing its zip, his body lapsing into superannuation, if his salary arm hadn't been fractured by a batted ball one fortuitous day in Greenville in 1925. When Moore returned to the Greenville lineup late in the 1925 season, he found it hard to throw overhand. So he switched to sidearm, giving the ball a novel gyration, and lo!, an incredible sinker was born. That pitch drove South Atlantic batters to distraction in 1926, and was Wilcy's passport to the majors.

One day, late in 1926, Yankee business manager Ed Barrow read in the *Sporting News* that a pitcher named Moore had won 30 games for Greenville in 1926, lost only four, and had a 2.86 ERA. More sleuthing disclosed that he won his first start, lost the second, reeled off a nifty 17 in a row, and at one point had won 27 out of 29. True, Greenville was in the low minors, but the canny Barrow decided that whoever belonged to those stats was worth a close look.

"I sent [scout] Bob Gilks to find out about him," wrote Barrow in his autobiography, *My Fifty Years In Baseball.* Gilks must have scouted the wrong pitcher, for he reported to Barrow, "He can't pitch, and anyway he says he's thirty, but he must be forty." Barrow would have none of Gilks's quibbles. On a hunch he paid Greenville $3,500 for Moore—peanuts for a

William Wilcy Moore   *Photo courtesy of the New York Yankees.*

ball player even in 1926—and Cy, the strapping, balding, supposedly antiquated country bumpkin became a '27 Yankee.

His salary was $1,800—not for a week, for the season. Even a cagey operator like Barrow couldn't have been certain that his $3,500 roll of the dice, and the less than bountiful stipend, would turn out to be gilt-edged pennant and World Series insurance.

With future Hall of Famers like Hoyt and Pennock, and skilled hurlers like Shocker, Ruether, and Pipgras available, the 1927 Yankee staff was the best in baseball. But when the going got rough for any of these aces, having Wilcy around meant the difference between a race and a runaway. In that one season the rawboned rookie with the pitching smarts, a respectable fastball, a decent curve, and above all a nefarious dipping pitch, was the Yankees' bread and butter.

A good sinker, artfully placed, is one of baseball's more subtle pleasures, earning maledictions from batters and—in our era of largess—fat paychecks. It is the "out pitch" par excellence, when adroitly controlled, the certain consequence of gravitational force. Not that Wilcy thought much about Newtonian physics; he was a high school dropout, and analyzing nature's laws was not his strong point. But gravity surely worked for him on the mound.

Back in the 1920s starting pitchers were expected to finish: compared to today's hurlers they completed a surprising number of games. By July 19, 1927, Yankee pitchers had gone the route in 45 games, 40 of them wins. By season's end Hoyt had completed 23 games, Pennock 18. And that year there were pitchers in the majors who topped those numbers for completions. But even 67 years ago hurlers suffered from malaise brought on by a long night on the town, or by unexplainable manias for issuing walks and giving up hits. In such perilous situations the summons for a reliever went to the bullpen.

Nowadays we have short relievers, middle relievers, and relievers for the relievers (guys who come in to pitch to only one batter). This state of affairs is due to the steady pace of specialization: righties who only pitch to righties, lefties who only pitch to lefties, and that abomination that has so changed baseball strategy, the designated hitter. Baseball didn't indulge itself in such doubtful luxuries in the 1920s.

No matter what inning, when Huggins gave Moore the ball Cy and his sinker generally stayed the course and usually won. He performed so expertly that by the time what passed for the pennant race was over Moore had won 19 while losing only seven. And to show he was a man of parts, he started six games and won four. All told, Moore appeared in 50 games in 1927, allowed just 54 earned runs in 213 innings, and had a 2.28 ERA.

For his sterling 1927 performance, Moore, at the urging of Huggins, received a bonus. The $2,500, a meager sum under the circumstances, was a painful example of Ed Barrow's sometimes shabby behavior with a buck. But Wilcy did pick up another $300 in a droll wager with Babe Ruth.

Moore was a terrible hitter. His 1927 batting average is a laughable .080, his lifetime BA is .102. During spring training, Ruth—who tended to break up when Moore batted—bet Cy $300 to $15 that he wouldn't get three hits all season. On August 26, in Detroit, Wilcy got his third hit, a dinky roller along the third base line that three Tiger infielders left undisturbed hoping it would roll foul. Perversely, it didn't.

Said Wilcy to the press as Babe paid up the $300, "This is just an easy park to hit in."

For good measure he got three more that season, the last one a homer into Ruth's favorite target, the right field stands. It was the only homer of his big-league career; but that home run and the bet gave writers material for droll copy for years to come. With part of the $300 Cy bought two mules, which he named Babe and Ruth, a christening that gave him great pleasure, and lots of laughs for the folks back home.

Moore closed out the great season with outstanding performances in the World Series against Pittsburgh. In Game 1 he relieved a weakening Hoyt in the eighth to save a 5–4 victory. In the final of the four-game sweep, at Yankee Stadium, he started and went all the way to win 4–3.

For the Yankees it was the end of a glorious season; for Wilcy it was a prelude to hard times. Never again was he the exceptional pitcher he had been in his rookie year. Arm trouble plagued him in 1928 (4–4), and in 1929 (6–4). In 1930 he missed the entire season with a bad arm. Dealt to the Red Sox, he had a losing season in 1931 and most of 1932. Then, in August 1932, the Yankees brought him back to the Stadium.

To the delight of manager Joe McCarthy and Wilcy's old Yank chums, he won two and lost none. In the fourth and final game of the 1932 series, against Chicago, after Johnny Allen was bombed for four runs in the first, Wilcy came in to squelch the Cubs, holding them with his revived sinker until the seventh as the Yankees caught up and went ahead. And— no doubt with a grin in Ruth's direction—Cy singled in the fourth. In poetic justice, Herb Pennock, whom Moore had occasionally relieved, took over to finish the 13–6 Yankee win.

Wilcy's series record now stood at 1.000 (two games, two wins), with a series ERA of 0.56. It was his last moment of glory in the bigs. After a 5–6 season with the Yankees in 1933, he was through in the majors—but not in organized baseball.

Moore and his sinker moved around the minors for seven more years. By the time he retired to full-time farming, and the permanent company of Babe and Ruth, he had spent 13 of his 20 ball-playing years in the minors.

After retiring, Wilcy farmed and attended occasional Old Timers games, where he was welcomed by former teammates and later generations of Yankee fans and players. Though he had been a Red Sox, and traveled the minors until age 43, he was always remembered as the ace reliever of the 1927 Yankees.

Wilcy Moore died at home in Hollis, Oklahoma, in 1963 at the age of 65.

April 21 saw the Yanks beat the A's again, this time by a score of 13–6, as A's pitchers wilted under a blistering assault.

Lou Gehrig put New York ahead in the sixth with a three-run shot off the upper tier in left field. Lazzeri also hit one into the stands, Meusel tripled and doubled, and their free-swinging cohorts weighed in with the rest of 15 hits. Babe didn't homer that day, but during batting practice he amused the customers by smacking five balls literally out of the park. One landed on the roof of a building, three soared into the street, and one dented a telegraph pole beyond the center-field fence.

On April 22 it rained, giving writers a chance to think deeply on the state of Huggins's team. "Ruether, Pennock, Hoyt, and Shocker are all right as far as they go, but they don't go far enough," wrote James R. Harrison in *The New York Times* on April 23. "It may be that Wilcy Moore will develop into a fifth starter.... Pipgras must show something now or go back to the minors to stay." After further rumination Harrison stated, "Dugan is old and brittle.... There is always the possibility that Lazzeri may be shifted to third and Ray Morehart put in at second." If Hug recalled that fulsome analysis at the end of September it must have been with a smile, even a touch of smugness.

Ruether, Pennock, Hoyt, and Shocker chalked up 72 wins among them in 1927. Pipgras won another 10 and was a big leaguer through 1935. Lazzeri remained at second for most of the season, where he played spectacularly. And Dugan, the breakable 30-year-old, though spelled by reliable "Gazook" Gazella when a bad ankle or Joe's bum knee acted up, picked 'em at third as gracefully as he did when he first came to the Yanks in 1922.

On April 29 the Yanks slammed Boston 9–0 as Koenig, Gehrig, Meusel, and Collins, in a private match of follow-the-leader, all tripled. For Dutch Ruether, obtained from Washington in mid-1926, it was his second shutout of the year, with another still to come.

William Henry "Dutch" Ruether had been around the majors since 1917 when he came to the Chicago Cubs, where he won two and lost none. He then went to Cincinnati and won 19 games in 1919. It was there, in the infamous 1919 World Series against the crooked Chicago White Sox (Black Sox), that he pitched and won the opener 9–1 on a six-hitter.

That win turned out to be a delusion. For a year later, when the news broke that the Sox, with Cicotte hurling, had thrown the game, Dutch was furious.

"I beat them easily," he was quoted in a *Sporting News* obituary in 1970. "What hurt me was the disclosure...that they were merely fooling around. It's hard to believe. I really thought I had worked a tight game."

Before coming to the Yankees Ruether spent four seasons with the Brooklyn Dodgers, and all of 1925 plus part of 1926 with the Washington Senators. His 18–7 mark with Washington was a major factor in helping them win their second pennant. Unfortunately, his superior numbers with Washington didn't offset his night-roaming habits and reputation as a drinker. Despite a 12–6 won-lost in midseason of 1926, the Senators dealt him to the Yankees where he found congenial company and continued to pitch well.

But the 1927 season was Ruether's last in the majors. He went out with a bang, not a whimper, sporting a 13–6 won-lost for the Yankees, a .684 percentage (PCT), a 3.38 ERA, achievements suitably in rapport with the rest of the club's.

Dutch played eight more years after leaving the majors, mostly with clubs in the Pacific Coast League. He managed Seattle of the PCL for three years, then scouted for the Cubs and Giants. Dutch Ruether died at 76 in Phoenix, Arizona, on May 16, 1970.

The Yanks dropped the last game in April, to the Red Sox, 3–2, when the Sox scored on a wild pitch by Wilcy Moore. At the end of the month the Yankees and the Athletics were tied for first place in the American League, each with a won-lost of 9–5 and a PCT of .643, while Chicago at 9–7 was running a close third in what still looked like a contest.

William Henry "Dutch" Ruether

Photo courtesy of National Baseball Library, Cooperstown, N.Y.

May 1, 1927

AMERICAN LEAGUE

STANDING OF THE CLUBS.

	Won.	Lost.	P.C.
New York	9	5	.643
Philadelphia	9	5	.643
Chicago	9	7	.563
Washington	7	6	.500
Detroit	6	6	.500
St. Louis	6	6	.500
Cleveland	7	9	.437
Boston	3	11	.214

3

May

Hug says his club is much better than last year. Jake Ruppert and Ed Barrow smile, count the gate, and agree.

On May 1, 1927, the Yanks faced the Philadelphia Athletics with the American League lead on the line. Serving up spitters and other quaint and mystifying pitches was 44-year-old Jack Quinn, who had broken into the majors in 1909 when Ruth was in a reformatory and Gehrig barely out of kindergarten. (Quinn would pitch for another six years, finally retiring from the Brooklyn Dodgers at 50.) Pennock hurled for the Yankees. What the fans saw was a 7–3 New York win, though their vaunted power was restricted to a paltry five hits.

Unhappily for the A's, three of the hits were homers: two by Babe, one by Lou, both with Koenig on base, adding up to five runs. Quinn gave up only two hits before he was replaced in the sixth, but both were homers (one by Ruth, the other by Gehrig). The A's reached Pennock for 12 hits, but they were good for only three runs, thanks to brilliant Yankee fielding. Skillful, guileful Herb Pennock, an artist on the mound, hung tough to go the nine and keep the Yankees in first.

Herbert Jefferis Pennock was a country gentleman in a game amply endowed with boors and louts. Dubbed the "Squire of Kennett Square," Pennock bred silver foxes, raised chrysanthemums, rode to the hounds, and won ball games. Born a Quaker on a farm in the lush countryside southeast of Philadelphia, young Herb attended Cedar Croft Prep school because it had a ball team. There the coach discovered that brainy, skinny, Pennock threw befuddling curves, not always around the plate yet near enough to strike out batters. When he whiffed 19 in one game, Herb caught the eye of one of Connie Mack's scouts.

To hide Pennock from other covetous eyes, Mack steered him to the Atlantic City club of the semipro Seashore League, a collection of college kids playing under assumed names so they wouldn't be charged with the heinous moral offense of professionalism. Pitching against Cape May,

Herbert Jefferis Pennock   *Photo courtesy of the New York Yankees.*

Pennock won his first outing, but soon after that the league folded. That didn't discourage young Herb: playing ball for a living was what he wanted to do.

The ambiance was pleasant, the hours short, the money—if he made it to the majors—ample. So Pennock stayed with the now independent Atlantic City club to play against other semipros, one of them an esteemed black team, the St. Louis Stars. When he tossed a no-hitter against the Stars, Connie Mack promptly brought the 18-year-old lefty to the Philadelphia Athletics in 1912.

The A's, riding on back-to-back World Championships, were loaded with starters, so Herb went to the bullpen. Two days later the kid heard the great Connie call out, "Boy, warm up."

Pennock recalled that day to writer Harry Brundidge in a February 13, 1930, *Sporting News* article. "The Chicago White Sox had scored five runs...in five innings. I think the toughest experience of my life was that walk from the bullpen to the mound.... I was badly frightened." Who could blame him for his case of the jitters, a kid who had previously hurled for a boarding school and a bunch of pickup nobodies?

Herb didn't disappoint. Chicago won 7–0, but he held them to one hit and one run in four innings, a respectable showing. That first year Pennock relieved in 17 games, won one and lost two—hardly a portent of the great years to come. Still, he was a major leaguer learning his trade from hurlers like Eddie Plank and Chief Bender, both eventually in the Hall of Fame. And to Herb it was preferable to hitting the books in college, where it was doubtful that a professor could teach him to throw a screwball.

By 1914 Pennock was an ace pitcher on the A's, with a won-lost of 11–4 and an ERA of 2.79. You'd think Connie Mack would keep a kid with an arm like Pennock's—and brains to boot—but that didn't happen.

The A's won their third straight pennant in 1914, but were whipped by the famous Boston "Miracle Braves," an aroused bunch of overachievers who went from last place on the Fourth of July to first by season's end. This humbling debacle, and the prospect of plentiful cash, prompted Mack to sell off his team of veteran stars plus—in a moment of classic masochism—the gifted but outspoken Pennock.

Herb had disobeyed instructions one day, and, according to Dan Daniel writing in the February 11, 1948, *Sporting News,* the angered Connie snapped, "Young man, so far as I'm concerned you can sit on the bench all season and never pitch another ball." Boldly Pennock answered, "If you don't care for my pitching why don't you trade me or sell me?" Which Mack did, shipping Herb to the Red Sox in 1915, and regretting it for the rest of his long life.

Boston also had an abundance of good pitchers, so Pennock was sent to the minors where he spent the better part of two years. In 1917 he returned to Boston where he went 5–5 before enlisting in the U.S. Navy, where he was assigned to a destroyer. Then, on somebody's happy brainstorm, he was transferred to London to pitch for the Navy against an all-star Army team.

On July 4, 1918, before 60,000 people, including King George and the Prince of Wales, neither of whom understood what was happening on a field unlike those at Eton and Oxford, Pennock hurled a famous 10-inning 2–1 victory over the Army. The encounter had nothing to do with fighting a war, but it was a lot more fun than heaving on a tin-can destroyer, or dodging German shells in a bloody muddy trench.

After the so-called war to end all wars, Herb rejoined the Red Sox, and in 1919 pitched an impressive 16–8. He continued as a mainstay on a club that was being systematically depleted of their best players by their chronically impecunious owner, Harry Frazee. Babe Ruth, Carl Mays, Waite Hoyt, and Wally Schang—top-flight players who would help the Yankees become a pennant winner were among those sent to New York. In 1923 an elated Pennock followed them.

Boston got $40,000 for Herb and three players whose names nobody remembers—a larcenous coup by Ed Barrow, but a fitting destiny for an outstanding pitcher. Pennock was a superb 19–6 in 1923, for a .760 PCT, as the Yanks won their third straight pennant, and met the Giants in the third consecutive New York City subway series. McGraw's club had taken the first two series: that they didn't win the third was to a large measure due to Pennock.

The Giants took the first game 5–4, when, with two out in the ninth and the score tied, Casey Stengel, the once and future "old perfessor" himself, with two out in the ninth, smacked his celebrated inside-the-park homer into the nethermost corner of Yankee Stadium. But the next day, Pennock, with timely help from two Ruth homers, pitched an adroit nine-hitter at the Polo Grounds for a 4–2 victory. In the third game the inimitable Casey hit another homer, giving the Giants a 1–0 win. And that was it for the McGraw men. Casey had run out of vitality and homers.

The Yankees won the fourth game 8–4, with Pennock relieving Bob Shawkey in the eighth to squelch a menacing rally. After the Yanks took the fifth game 8–1, Herb won his second series game 6–4, giving the Yankees their first World Championship. For the graceful 29-year-old hurler it was a stellar performance, the first of what would be 11 splendid seasons as the lefty ace of the Yankees.

Pennock lacked an overpowering fast ball, but his curve was a dandy, his control perfect, his change-up confounding. He threw with an easy, rhythmic motion. To innocents like Detroit's "Fat" Fothergill, he seemed easy to hit.

Fat murdered left-handers. A strong hitter with an ample girth and minimal fielding skills, Fothergill has a robust lifetime BA of .326. Bob Broeg wrote in the *Sporting News* of April 24, 1971, that while watching Pennock warm up one day, Fothergill licked his chops at the prospect of batting against the frail-looking lefty. Then he went 0 for 4.

"I can't understand it," moaned Fat to his roomie, the great Harry Heilman (lifetime .342, Hall of Famer, and aficionado of pitching). "What the hell happened?"

"You didn't face a left-hander," answered Heilman, "you faced Herb Pennock."

Herb never stopped studying batters. Joe Williams, writing in the *New York World-Telegram* of February 8, 1933, recalled Yankee coach Charley O'Leary saying, "If you cut that bird's head open the weaknesses of every batter in the league would spill out." Pennock was a master of that prime weapon of the brainy hurler, the calculated psyche-out. On the mound the cagey Herb deliberately exasperated batters to disturb their concentration. He'd tug at his cap, finger the ball as if it were a rare objet d'art, hitch his belt, look around at his fielders, stare at the batter, again adjust his hat. Then, the batter suitably galled, Herb threw—usually exactly where he wanted the pitch to go.

His canny fidgeting drove batters to distraction. The short-fused Ty Cobb was known to holler at Pennock, "Come on, you son of a bitch, pitch the ball!" Eruptions like that pleased Pennock. The fidgeting continued, he took even more time before throwing. Let the great Tyrus gripe and stew. In 1927 Herb's won-lost was an excellent 19–8, his ERA 3.00, his PCT .704. If the Yankees were pennant bound from opening day, Herb Pennock deserved a good share of the credit.

Here are Pennock's ten commandments of pitching, as listed by Bob Broeg in *Sporting News* on April 24, 1971. It's a decalogue young hurlers aspiring to the majors would do well to heed.

1. Develop your faculty of observation.
2. Conserve your energy.
3. Make contact with the players, especially the catchers and outfielders.
4. Work everlastingly for control.
5. When you are on the field always have a baseball in your hand, and don't slouch around.
6. Keep studying the batters for their weak and strong points.
7. Watch your physical condition and mode of living.

8. Always pitch to the catcher and not to the batter. Keep your eye on that catcher, and make him your target before letting the ball go.

9. Find your easiest way to pitch, your most comfortable delivery, and stick to it.

10. Work for what is called a rag arm. A loose arm can pitch over-handed, side-arm, three-quarters, underhand—any old way to suit the situation at hand.

Pennock added an 11th for good measure. "Don't beef at the umpire, control yourself as well as the ball. Fury is as hard on you physically as emotionally." That the commandments from Kennett Square aren't universally obeyed is probably why many naturally talented pitchers fail.

Though Pennock was 7–4 at the close of the 1933 season, he was obviously nearing the end of his career and the Yanks released him. Nonetheless, the New York baseball writers named him Player of the Year, an honor usually bestowed on players at the top of their game. Herb spent 1934 with the Red Sox where he went 2–0 and quit, a winner to the end.

He coached for the Red Sox for several years, then supervised their farm system. In 1944 he became general manager of the Phillies where his baseball savvy laid the groundwork for the 1952 Phillies' pennant-winning "Whiz Kids." Sadly, he didn't live to see his creation take the flag. While attending the 1948 National League winter meeting he passed away from a stroke. Later that year he was elected to the Hall of Fame.

A complete pitcher, Herb Pennock is remembered in Yankee history as an athlete who combined intelligence and skill to become one of the premier hurlers of his era, and, not least, the lefty ace of the 1927 Yankees.

On May 2, the Yanks beat the Senators in Washington, 9–6, with a 17-hit attack, including Lazzeri's homer, triples by Dugan and Grabowski, and sundry doubles and singles by other Yanks. Every one of the starters got at least one hit. Waite Hoyt, who got two hits, was the winner with help from Cy Moore in the ninth. "Murderers' Row" was cranking it up. And smiling Eddie Bennett, the Yankee batboy, hex artist, and guarantor of good luck and winning streaks, was once more basking in the reflected glory of a winner.

To hear Eddie tell it, a pennant was a sure thing if he was the batboy/mascot of your ball club. Of course, it helped to have a couple of guys named Ruth and Gehrig in the lineup, but according to Eddie ball games weren't won by brawn and brains alone. Harmonizing with inscrutable powers was what put the lock on first place. Considering the young man's personal history, who would dare contradict him? By the time Eddie arrived at the Yanks in 1921, his fame as a talisman had preceded him.

Eddie was born in the Flatbush section of Brooklyn, probably in 1904. He was a hunchback, the result of a fall from his baby carriage. Perhaps. Maybe. Nobody ever knew much about Eddie's past that could be authenticated. Who raised him? Where did he grow up? How did he survive? Eddie was self-advertised, a mystery, the creation of his imagination and audacity. But his supposed occult powers were never in doubt, at least not to superstitious ballplayers, which means almost all of them.

Bennett began his sorcery in 1919 by smiling fixedly and continually on White Sox center fielder Oscar "Happy" Felsch from the Polo Grounds bleachers where the Sox were playing the Yanks. (That year the Yankees played their home games at the Polo Grounds, their own ballpark having burned down.) Eddie's wide, infectious grin, so fraught with covert meaning, must have soothed Felsch's secret, well-founded anxieties and buoyed his batting average. He told White Sox pitcher Ed Cicotte about the smiling hunchback kid, Cicotte told manager Kid Gleason, and Eddie was hired as the Sox batboy.

Which was great for Eddie, the White Sox, and Happy's state of mind; but what Felsch, Cicotte, and six other guys on that blighted team really needed in the coming months was a flock of cagey lawyers. That the Sox won the pennant in 1919 is indisputable. What is also beyond question is that Felsch, Cicotte, and six co-conspirator Chicago players threw the 1919 series to the Cincinnati Reds, igniting a scandal that rocked baseball. And though Eddie didn't beg Sox star Shoeless Joe Jackson to "Say it ain't so," he was sufficiently distressed to abandon the malodorous team when the corruption hit the front pages.

Eddie Bennett took his esoteric powers to the Brooklyn Dodgers in 1920, and of course the Dodgers, confounding many experts, won the pennant. How could they not win with Eddie Bennett taking care of the bats, letting ballplayers rub his back for good luck, (who can fathom the arcana of wizardry?), and putting the Flatbush hex on the rest of the National League? But the Dodgers tempted fate in the subsequent World Series with the Cleveland Indians, and in so doing learned a bitter lesson in the importance of generosity and not trifling with the occult.

After Brooklyn took the first two of three games in Ebbets Field, the Brooklyn management, pleading unanticipated poverty, refused to scrounge up the money to take Eddie to Cleveland. So Eddie appealed to the players, who told him in a rash and unbecoming manner to get lost.

Eddie Bennett   *Photo Courtesy of the New York Yankees.*

Greed had displaced prudence in the borough of Brooklyn, so, naturally, the penny-pinching Dodgers lost the series. Among other indignities, they were victimized by the first grand-slam in series history (by Indian Elmer Smith), and the only unassisted triple play in series history (by second baseman Billy Wambsganss).

Said Eddie, "I put the jinx on them."

According to Waite Hoyt, he came across Eddie in February 1921 in Prospect Hall, in Brooklyn, at a pro basketball game between the New York Celtics (the team, or at least the name, hadn't yet migrated to Boston), and the Brooklyn Visitations. Bennett was mascoting for the Celtics, and picking up a shower of change from the crowd after regaling them between halves with a slick foul-shooting exhibition. The take must have been pretty good, because Bennett had several assistants helping him pick up the money. It wasn't major league baseball and big-time hexing, but it was a living of sorts.

After collecting the money, the nervy Eddie approached Hoyt. "Eddie was strong in pointing out the potency of his magic charm," said the Yankee pitcher. "If we could get him the mascot job with the New York Yankees, he was sure the Yanks would win their first pennant. Would we intercede for him?" Hoyt talked to Miller Huggins, Hug talked to Ruppert and Barrow, and sure enough, Eddie got the job.

And in 1921 the Yanks won their first pennant, and in 1922 they won another, and in 1923 another. Counting his seasons with the White Sox and Dodgers, that made it five straight for Eddie Bennett, the magical mascot.

The word "mascot" is derived from the Latin word "masca," meaning "witch." Eddie Bennett was no witch, but obviously he could have taught witches a thing or two about the black arts. He remained a Yankee batboy/mascot with the great clubs of the '20s and '30s, a friend to star players, the envy of kids throughout the city.

Only Eddie was permitted to handle the bats of certain players: to break that rule would tempt bad luck. Wilcy Moore preferred to throw his first warm-up ball to Eddie. When one of the Yankee sluggers socked one into the seats, Eddie was at the plate to shake hands with him. He was a favorite of Miller Huggins and Colonel Ruppert. In the team picture of the 1927 Yankees, Eddie sits in the bottom row center, on the ground in front of Huggins.

"Eddie never grew in height, although he did fill out a bit," recalled Hoyt. "He retained the face and features of a boy as he advanced in years, so it was always difficult for players to realize the little hunchback had grown to the mental proportions of an adult." During the winter Eddie worked in the Yankee office; come spring he went south with the club.

There was no penny-pinching nonsense about leaving him behind; for the orphaned kid from Flatbush it was fantasy come to life.

Until, in 1932, Eddie ran into hard times. He was badly hurt in a cab accident, needed crutches to walk, and—a shattering consequence—had to give up his batboy/mascot job. Colonel Ruppert kept Eddie on the Yankee payroll with a sum sufficient to sustain him. Unfortunately, said sustenance included large quantities of booze. "Eddie's companions," said Hoyt, "were not teaching Sunday school."

Alcoholic, crippled, his singular gifts gone forever, his baseball life behind him, Eddie Bennett died alone in a West 84th Street Manhattan rooming house on January 16, 1935, at the age of 31. When the cops and medical examiner arrived they found Eddie's room cluttered with baseball memorabilia, the remnants of his great Yankee days. Signed photos of famed ballplayers, autographed baseballs, a scattered collection of bats, score cards, gloves, surrounded Eddie as he lay on his bed, dressed, dead. On the wall behind him, barely visible in the darkened, cheerless room was a team picture of the 1928 World Championship Yankees.

The Yanks again victimized the Senators, this time on May 3, thanks to a tie-breaking hit by Gehrig in the eighth. But they lost to Washington two days later, as Senators hurler Hod Lisensbee (good pitcher that year, 18–9), squelched the Yankee hitters, and New York's fielding suffered an attack of shakes and tremors. Koenig, Ruth, Meusel, and Collins each made a bobble; Urban Shocker made two; Huggins came close to swallowing his chaw. But things looked up on May 6, though in uncommon circumstances.

How and why the Yankees detoured to Fort Wayne, Indiana, on May 6 to play an exhibition game with a semipro club called the Lincoln Lifes is something of a puzzle. But they did, and an amusing game it was, with Babe playing first base, and Lou patrolling right field, before 35,000 customers. The denouement of the performance was in grand style with, predictably, Ruth in the spotlight.

The Lincoln Lifes tied the score in the eighth, 3–3. So far so good for the valiant locals. Then, as if by preordained design, Babe was surrounded near the bench by hundreds of worshipful kids wanting to speak to the great man, perhaps to experience the ineffable by touching him.

The kids were dispersed from the field, the game resumed, but not for long. Babe came to bat, waved to the customers to go home, then slugged the ball over the right-field fence to end the festivities. As he rounded the bases, Mike Gazella ahead of him, a herd of idolizing youngsters swarmed onto the field. In a way that remains something of an enigma, Ruth's magnetism transcended today's electronic hype. A one-of-a-kind phenomenon, he was a ballplayer like no other before or since.

The sideshow over, the Yanks hopped a train to Chicago where they had more serious business with the surging White Sox. They cooled the Sox in the first two, 8–0 and 9–0, but lost the third game when Wilcy, with a man on second, adroitly fielded a bunt and threw to where he thought first base was. It wasn't, as Chicago scored the winning run.

Despite the loss the Yanks left Chicago for St. Louis with a 14–8 record, still the league leader. Detroit at 11–9 was in second place; Chicago at 13–11 was in third. Awaiting them were the St. Louis Browns, whose playing contributed liberally to Yankee eminence that year.

The Browns were not a bad team: they just looked hapless against New York in 1927. At first base they had George Sisler, unquestionably one of the great hitters in baseball history. Sisler batted .407 in 1920, an extraordinary .420 in 1922. In the outfield they had two other first-rate batters: Bing Miller, who hit .325 in 1927, and Ken Williams who hit .323. But against the Yankees that year, those averages just didn't matter. It's instructive, though not amusing to Browns rooters still among us, to examine the Yankee-Browns encounters that season.

On May 10 the Browns were ahead 7–6 in the top of the ninth with two out when Lou Gehrig singled, driving in two runs to put the Yankees in the lead, 8–7. The Brownies rallied in the bottom of the ninth, loading the bases on Herb Pennock who had come in to relieve Giard. With one out, Brownie Wally "Spooks" Gerber hit into a double play, Koenig to Lazzeri to Gehrig, and that ended it. In the next set-to, on May 11, 1927, as Babe doubled and smacked his eighth homer, the Yanks won 4–2. Shocker went all the way for New York.

On May 12, despite a great start by Browns ace "Sad Sam" Jones—he struck out Combs, Koenig, and Ruth in the first inning—Pennock still brought in the win, 4–3.

May 13 saw the Yankees add insult to injury as they took the fourth game 3–1, even though the Browns outhit them 10–9. Their sweep of St. Louis now history, the Hugmen bid a reluctant farewell to St. Louis and headed to Detroit.

It was below freezing in Detroit on May 16 but Yankee bats were hot. Gehrig hit his eighth homer, tying Babe, and Miller's boys beat the Tigers 6–2 to win their fifth straight. Bob Meusel stole second, then third, then home. Obviously, Long Bob was in a rut—and finally playing up to his potential.

If, as George Bernard Shaw has informed us, silence is the most perfect expression of scorn, Robert William Meusel, the left fielder of the 1920s Yankees was the most disdainful ballplayer to roam the outer reaches of Yankee Stadium. A cold fish, often surly, a loner, he was famously short on conversation, though, when the spirit moved him, long on playing ball.

Discerning baseball people agreed that Meusel was an exceptionally gifted athlete, a quintessential natural. He could hit, was fast, had a powerful right arm, and he was endowed with all the talent needed to make him great. Yet, there was about Bob Meusel a sense of heights never reached, a potential unfulfilled. Miller Huggins managed Meusel for almost his entire career. In the *Sporting News* obituary of Meusel, on December 17, 1977, Hug is quoted as once ruefully saying, "His attitude is just plain indifference."

The Yankee manager's estimate of Meusel reflected exasperation, even disdain. For when Miller was a second baseman covering his territory—and some extra—for the Cincinnati Reds, writers and fans dubbed him "Little Mr. Everywhere." A little guy among big men, a knock-down target for a take-out slide, Miller was the Charlie Hustle of his time. If Meusel, given his plentiful skills, had had some of his skipper's fierce drive to excel he might have been a star in the class of his two outfield cohorts, Combs and Ruth (well, anyway, with Combs). Instead, he was just a very good ballplayer.

Meusel was born in San Jose, California, on July 19, 1896. He was the younger brother of big league outfielder Emil "Irish" Meusel, who was shorter than Long Bob, had a deficient arm, and wasn't Irish. The Meusel boys were of German descent.

Bob began his career with Vernon of the Pacific Coast League where he compiled a three-season, eye-catching .341 BA, while limbering up a right arm that, to prowling scouts, bore a marked resemblance to a Winchester. The Yankees signed him in August 1919, beginning a mutually beneficial, if sometimes uneasy, relationship.

During spring training in 1920, Huggins said of his rookie that Meusel would be one of the most talked-about hitters in the country, a natural hitter with a perfect hitting swing. Hug was right. Meusel was a pleasure to watch as he stepped into the ball with a rhythmic picture swing. That first year he played in 119 games, mostly in the outfield, hit a healthy .328, and became the buddy of Babe Ruth.

With Babe and Bob in the lineup the Yankees had the first two members of what became the famed "Murderers' Row" of the powerful 1926–28 clubs. But there was an intrinsic difference between the two sluggers. Ruth murdered the ball because he loved to; with every swing of

Robert William Meusel   *Photo courtesy of the New York Yankees.*

his bat he aimed to send the ball beyond the reach of outfielders, preferably into the seats. But Meusel larruped the ball when the spirit moved him, which wasn't as often as Hug would have liked.

In the 1921 series against the Giants, Meusel hit only .200 (they played a five out of nine matchup that year), though his season BA was .318. That picayune batting average was the start of a pattern for him. In six World Series he reached .300 only once (1922), and well below his season average in the others. His lifetime series BA is .225, not what you'd expect from a slugger with a lifetime .309 BA.

At the end of the 1921 series Ruth and Meusel, tantalized by the aroma of easy money emanating from America's outlands, decided to barnstorm with a gaggle of semipros. But Commissioner Kennesaw Mountain Landis, a man as imperious as his name, would have none of this seemingly innocent endeavor. As the recently chosen lord and master of baseball, he forbade the journey.

But perversely, like headstrong juveniles, Babe and Bob shuffled off to Buffalo and Elmira and Scranton, a junket that brought them fewer dollars than they had reckoned on, and the back of the Commissioner's hand. In the aftermath of the still-festering Black Sox scandal, Landis staked out the high ground of baseball Czardom. A couple of mere ballplayers weren't going to defy him and get away with it.

On December 5, 1921, Landis suspended Ruth and Meusel for the first six weeks of the '22 season, and fined them their shares of the recent series. The two malefactors paid the fine and sat out the six weeks. To Ruth it was purgatory; to Meusel, who knows?

Certain outfielders go after a fly ball with the speed and grace that makes even the most difficult catch seem easy. Earle Combs and Joe DiMaggio were like that. So was Terry Moore of the '30s and '40s Cardinals, and the great Tris Speaker who played most of his career for the Red Sox and the Indians. But Meusel sometimes made easy catches look difficult by the casual way he played them. At times he gave the fans and his teammates the impression that he was doing them a favor by showing up at the ballpark.

Though fast (he was a good base stealer), the six-feet-three-inch Meusel would dawdle across the grass and turn routine catches into cliff-hangers. He would sometimes gallop in on a fly ball, then slow down and let it bounce in front of him. The extra effort dive was simply foreign to his nature. But there were exceptions to this behavior.

In the seventh game of the 1926 World Series against the Cardinals, discarding his notorious nonchalance, Meusel got under a crucial fly only to let the ball drop when he tried to throw before controlling it. Momentary passion had overwhelmed habit, and that led to disaster.

The Cards tied the score, and went on to win the game and the championship.

In the August 1926 issue of *Baseball Magazine* Meusel was quoted thus: "Hustling is rather over-rated in baseball...it's a showy quality that looks and counts for little." What his fellow Yankees said about that statement is probably unprintable.

But after all is said about this aberrant ballplayer, so detached, so remote yet so gifted, there is his record and fabled arm. Meusel hit over .300 in 7 of his 11 big league years. For the 10-year span 1920 to 1930 he drove in more runs than any other Yankee except Ruth. And—the most distinctive of his talents—he threw clothesline strikes to all bases, cutting down many a presumptuous runner. Knowledgeable baseball men rated his throwing arm as the best the game had seen.

"He had lightnin' on the ball," said Casey Stengel. He also had lightnin' in his gut on one memorable occasion.

On June 13, 1924, the Yankees were leading the Tigers in the ninth, in Detroit, when Tiger pitcher Bert Cole, having been pummeled for four runs in the eighth, vented his displeasure at the Hugmen with unbecoming behavior. First he threw at Ruth's head, upsetting not only Babe but his pal Meusel. After Ruth fouled out, the unregenerate Cole let fly at Meusel, whacking him in the ribs. Diffident Bob exploded.

Flourishing his bat, he went not after Cole but after Tiger manager Ty Cobb, who, Muesel believed, had ordered the offending pitches—Cobb of the lifetime .367 and sharpened spikes, a baseball immortal noted for superlative playing and an unmannerly disposition. Umpire Billy Evans promptly tossed out Meusel and Cobb, as thousands of fans poured onto the field and took part in a donnybrook involving players, cops, umps, and fans.

It was the worst disorder in modern baseball history up to that time, a dubious distinction which upset officials, owners, and sensible players and fans. The game was declared forfeit by Detroit—not exactly a gift to the Yanks, who were leading 9–0.

It is a paradox that this most colorless of players was a key regular on one of the most colorful teams in baseball history. Yet apparently the aura of brilliance and supremacy of the 1927 club did affect him: that year he performed like the great player he could have been throughout his career. Batting between Gehrig and Lazzeri, Meusel hit .337, intimidated runners with his throwing, and was dangerous in the clutch. Without doubt he contributed substantially to the runaway race in 1927.

Meusel was no ascetic: he paid a price for his extensive late-hours shenanigans. After the '27 season he lost a step or two, his BA tailed off to .297 in 1928, and he was let go by the Yankees at the close of 1929. Bob played for the Cincinnati Reds in 1930, then exited the majors. At the age of 34, nobody in the majors wanted him. He went to minor league Minneapolis in 1931, to Hollywood in 1932, then quit.

"Character is destiny," wrote Heraclitus (535–475 B.C.), one of those wise and ancient Greeks. Surely that was true of Bob Meusel. Call it attitude, or a temperament out of sync with the rest of the world, finally it was character that dictated what he was. A very good, sometimes superb, often difficult ballplayer who never became the star he could have been. But sometimes a bit of the old Yankee pride would surface in his later years.

When asked how the '27 club would have fared against recent championship teams, Meusel, according to Bob Broeg, writing in the July 20, 1979, *Sporting News,* answered, "A breeze. We'd win by twenty games or more, and then have another four game series."

Meusel spent his final working years as a guard at the U.S. Navy Base at Terminal Island, California. Presumably impassive and speaking no last words, he died on November 28, 1977.

On May 19, 1927, Wilcy Moore replaced Shocker in the second to save a 4–3 win over Cleveland. The accommodating Cy, a man of multiple talents, laid down a neat bunt in the ninth to squeeze Joe Dugan home with the winning run. Today, relieved from the taxing duty of hitting a baseball, American League pitchers are no longer required to perform that stratagem.

The Yanks faced the Indians on May 21, and the game was interrupted in the bottom of the seventh by the dramatic announcement that Charles A. Lindbergh had landed his tiny airplane in Paris, completing his epochal nonstop flight from New York. About 15,000 fans stood silently, heads bowed in prayer, as the band played the National Anthem. Then the Yanks lost to Cleveland, 5–4, in a 12-inning game that saw Huggins in the third-base coaching box, cheering his men on to no avail.

In the last week of of May the Yankees were still in first place; Gehrig was giving Ruth a close and surprising tussle in the homer derby, and tormenting pitchers with a league-leading BA of .408. On May 26 the club displayed its homage to flag and country by playing the Cadets at West Point. The game was not an artistic success (it was rained out in the second), but the visit was.

Before striking out in the first on three ludicrously out-of-reach pitches, Ruth presented an autographed ball to the best player of each of the 12 companies of cadets—baseballs most likely heirlooms of sundry aging grandchildren. In the mess hall the Yankees received a tumultuous ovation from the 1,200 cadets, a heart-warming tribute to the team and to our national pastime.

Home again on May 27, the Yanks split a doubleheader with Washington, and then blasted five Red Sox pitchers for 17 hits to win, 15–7, on May 29. A major contributor to the carnage, with four hits and a walk, was backup catcher Johnny Grabowski. Johnny, along with utility infielder Ray Morehart, came to the Yankees from the White Sox early in 1927 in exchange for aging second baseman Aaron Ward. Used sparingly but effectively by Huggins, Grabowski was part of the '27 club's strong bench. While his lifetime BA is a so-so .252, in keeping with Destiny's design he hit a sturdy .277 in 1927.

June 1, 1927

AMERICAN LEAGUE

STANDING OF THE CLUBS.

	Won.	Lost.	P.C.
New York	28	14	.667
Chicago	27	17	.614
Philadelphia. . . .	22	20	.524
Washington	19	19	.500
Cleveland.	20	23	.465
St. Louis.	19	22	.463
Detroit	18	22	.450
Boston	11	27	.289

On Memorial Day, May 30, 80,000 fans (40,000 in the morning, another 40,000 in the afternoon) watched the Yankees and A's split a doubleheader in Philadelphia. On the final day of the Merry Month, the Hugmen flailed Mack's team twice, 10–3 and 18–5, as Ruth hit No. 15 and No. 16.

On May 26, 1927, with the team comfortably in first place, and Yankee fans clicking through the turnstiles in record numbers, a happy Miller Huggins was quoted in the *Sporting News,* telling the world in a palpable understatement, "I have a much better club than last year." In the front office Ed Barrow was happy because the steamroller named the Yankees was largely his creation, and Colonel Ruppert was also happy because he loved to win and make money.

4

June

Yankees increase their lead, "Five O'Clock Lightning" strikes the American League, Babe and Lou contend for homer lead.

The Yankees opened June by beating the A's in Philadelphia, then took two from the Tigers in New York to stretch their latest streak to five. One of the wins over the Tigers, 2–0, took one hour and 31 minutes, an unheard-of playing time today, what with recurring caucuses on the mound, frequent pitching changes, and repeated throws to first to catch a plethora of larcenous runners. Looking over their shoulders the Hugmen saw the aspiring and threatening Chicago White Sox.

The White Sox had yet to lose in the East, and were only one game behind the Yanks, inducing visions of a pennant among the faithful in the Windy City. The pipe dream didn't last. On June 7 the first of four games went to the Yankees, 4–1, with Ruth, Gehrig, and catcher Pat Collins all homering, and Hoyt pitching a neat seven hitter.

June 8 saw inferior pitching on both sides, but a vivid and unnerving demonstration of Yankee power. Chicago scored on a homer in the second, the Yanks went ahead 2–1 on a homer by Lazzeri, with Cedric Durst (subbing for Meusel) on base. In the bottom of the sixth Chicago led 7–5, and Wilcy Moore replaced Ruether. Spitballer Red Faber still hurled for the Sox, his pitches spraying who knows what into catcher Buck Crouse's mitt and countenance. Lazzeri slugged another homer in the eighth, an inside-the-park job. In the ninth the embattled Sox tallied two more, the score was 11–6, and most of the 20,000 customers headed for home and hearth. It was a premature exit.

For in the Yankees' half of the ninth they tied the game by scoring five times, the *pièce de résistance* a third homer by their resident Italian, Signor Lazzeri. The 11th arrived, supper was waiting, the Yanks decided enough is enough. They nudged across the winning run on a sac fly by utility infielder Ray Morehart, scoring substitute outfielder Cedric Durst, 4 for 6 that day.

Durst, liberated from the Browns in late 1926, would play in only 481 games in seven major league seasons. One of those seasons was 1927, Durst's claim to a portion of baseball glory. As for the cannonading on

45

June 8, it was an entertaining example of what came to be known in Yankee baseball lore as "Five O'Clock Lightning."

The next day Chicago was ahead 3–2 in the sixth, but Yankee lightning struck again when six runs romped across the plate in the bottom of the seventh. The highlight of the inning was the diversely accomplished Ruth stealing home as Sox hurler Cole wound up as if he had the rest of the afternoon to deliver the ball. The final score was 8–3, the Yankee streak stood at seven. To spare themselves total despair, Chicago won the fourth game of the series, 4–2, on a tidy five-hitter by Ted Lyons, their future Hall of Famer.

"Losing three out of these four games means nothing to us," declared an undaunted Ray Schalk, the Chicago skipper, to Joe Vila, writing in *Sporting News* June 16, 1927, "Our team is in the fight to stay and we'll get better as time passes," he added, chin up, as the White Sox exited Gotham nursing their illusions, and muttering imprecations at Yankees in general, and Anthony Michael Lazzeri in particular.

New York City had seven million people in the 1920s, one million of them Italian-Americans. But not until the spring of 1926 did an excellent ballplayer of Italian origin grace the city, and the Yankees. When Tony Lazzeri arrived at the Stadium he was the first of a line of illustrious Yankees whose names ended in vowels: Lazzeri, Crosetti, Rizzuto, Berra, and of course, the great Joe DiMaggio. (Ping Bodie, nee Francesco Pezzolo, played briefly for the Yanks in the early 1920s, but he was a journeyman at best.)

Anthony Michael Lazzeri was born in the Cow Hollow district of San Francisco on December 6, 1903. A rowdy youngster in a roughneck environment, his formal education was minimal. "I was a pretty tough kid," he recalled to *Sporting News* reporter, Harry T. Brundidge, writing on December 11, 1930. "The neighborhood wasn't one in which a boy was likely to grow up a sissy, for it was fight or get licked, and I never got licked."

So adept with his fists was Tony that at first he wanted to be a prizefighter. Fortunately, he hit a baseball with the same gusto as he threw a haymaker. When he took up pitching, and later the infield, prizefighting lost a possible champ, but the national pastime gained a memorable ball player.

Tony was hardly a model young scholar. At 15, too much taken with fisticuffs, hell raising, and playing ball to study, the emotionally exhausted authorities requested that he exit the school. For which, Tony told Brundidge, "I voted all of them my thanks and good wishes." He joined his

Anthony Michael Lazzeri   *Photo courtesy of the New York Yankees.*

father at the boilermaker's craft, at the same time enhancing his baseball skills with the Golden Gate Natives, a good semipro team. "My pitching stood me in good stead," at boilermaking, he breezily said in the 1930 interview, "I could toss a rivet with the best of them."

By 1922 he was through tossing rivets: concentrating on his true metier, baseball, the Cow Hollow toughie caught on as an infielder with Salt Lake City of the Pacific Coast League. (Whether from sentiment or prudence, he kept his Boilermakers Union card throughout his baseball career.)

After moving around the minors Lazzeri became the regular Salt Lake City shortstop in 1925, and began smiting baseballs hard and often. It was in Salt Lake City that he got his celebrated nickname, "Poosh 'em up Tony," when Italian immigrant fans exhorted him with that fanciful phrase to wallop the ball into the stands, which he did, "pooshing 'em up" for a gaudy 60 homers in 1925.

Soon the ivory hunters descended on the Salt Lake club. Cincinnati scout Howard Doyle wrote to Reds president August Herrmann, on April 14, 1925, that Lazzeri "is one of the best looking ball players in the minor leagues. I hope that the Cincinnati Ball Club will make every effort to secure him." Herrmann must have been in a state of torpor or nursing an anemic bankroll, for nothing came of Doyle's recommendation. That was a break for the Yankees. They signed Tony, and in 1926 he arrived in New York sporting a .355 BA, and the well-publicized distinction of having slugged those 60 homers in AAA ball. He was a $65,000 beauty of a rookie at a time when that was a lot of money, even for generous Jake Ruppert.

But some doubted the wisdom of the purchase; one of those was hard-nosed Ed Barrow. His disquiet was based on elementary physics. In the thin air of the high Mormon city a well-hit baseball zoomed towards the stands like a hungry hawk after a toothsome quarry. Before signing Lazzeri and his suspect stats, Barrow, in his autobiography, tells us that he conveyed his skepticism to Yank scout Bob Connery. A trusted connoisseur of on-the-hoof diamond talent, Connery gave Lazzeri the once-over, and exhorted Barrow, "Buy him. He's the greatest thing I've ever seen."

Connery's judgment proved sound. From opening day 1926, Lazzeri and shortstop Mark Koenig were a strong combination up the middle. Koenig was erratic at times, but Lazzeri took over second as if born and raised there, steadying not only Koenig but Lou Gehrig, who was still learning the finer moves around first. And although Tony wasn't sending the ball into the seats as often as Ruth and Gehrig, by mid-May of '26 he was at .316, and a certified member of a Yankee wrecking crew that induced novel forms of neurasthenia in pitchers. Plainly, the negligible 70 feet above sea level in the Bronx was no hindrance to the kid from San Francisco. In his rookie year Lazzeri hit .275, slammed 18 homers, and drove in 114 runs. Only Ruth exceeded Tony's RBI mark for the Yanks that pennant-winning year.

Mention Tony Lazzeri to oldtimers, or knowledgeable younger fans, and chances are they'll smile knowingly. "Oh sure, Lazzeri," they'll say. "He's the one with that famous strikeout." Yes, Tony's the one.

The 1926 World Series—Yankees vs. Cardinals—was a rouser to the end of the tense seventh game. In the seventh inning of that last game, at Yankee Stadium, with the Cards ahead 3–2 and two out, Gehrig, Meusel, and Combs loaded the bases. When Lazzeri came to bat, Cards pitcher Jesse Haines was replaced by 39-year-old Grover Cleveland Alexander.

Arm weary after winning two of the Cards games, still reviving after a boozy night on the town, the great Alex (373–208 lifetime), hadn't expected to pitch again. Ambling to the mound, pitching artifice ingrained in his canny head, a chaw of tobacco lodged in his grizzled cheek, "Old Pete" faced the youthful, hard-hitting Lazzeri. Years later, the celebrated trauma behind him, here's the way Tony, in the 1930 interview with Brundidge, told what happened as he faced the wily Alexander.

> The first ball was a bad one, high and wide, and Alex, figuring I wouldn't swing at the next, grooved it, and the call was one ball and one strike. I fouled the third (a screaming shot into the stands, barely foul), and then made up my mind to crack the next one. The Old Master must have read my mind, for he tossed a tantalizing curve on the outside, and although I did my best to resist I was set to swing, and I did. I missed the ball by eight inches.

The Cards won the series when Ruth, with two out in the ninth, walked and was thrown out when he rashly tried to steal second. But the Cardinals' triumph isn't what is usually remembered about the '26 series. Lazzeri's immortal strikeout with the bases loaded, by the hung-over Alex, is what remained as the high point of the series. That whiffing conferred a certain negative eminence on Lazzeri—and was a prelude to 1927 when he hit .309, fielded splendidly, and held the infield together on the great team.

Recalling Lazzeri during a December 16, 1984, phone interview, his infield sidekick, Mark Koenig, said, "Tony was a nice kid. He didn't say much, but he was a Sicilian and he got a temper. You couldn't say anything against him. Once I was in infield practice and I called him a Sicilian. Boy, he got madder'n hell. He was gonna kill me." One memorable day in 1936 Lazzeri's explosive temperament was directed against Connie Mack's pitchers.

On May 24, 1936, in Shibe Park, against the Philadelphia Athletics, Lazzeri homered twice in one game with the bases loaded! That is one of baseball's rarest feats; it has been done only seven times in over 125 years of major league ball. Lazzeri was the first to do it. And his eleven RBIs in that game stands as the American League record. (Jim Bottomley holds the National and Major League marks with twelve, established in 1924.)

In that game, which the Yanks won by the bizarre score of 25–2, Lazzeri hit a third homer, mercifully for the A's with nobody on base. It was a great day not only for Lazzeri but for Joe DiMaggio and shortstop Frank Crosetti. Frankie slammed two homers in successive times at bat; DiMag hit a homer, and for good measure singled and doubled. All in all it was a memorable performance by the Italian-American Yankees, led by "Poosh 'em up Tony."

Lazzeri's Yankee career lasted from 1926 to 1937. He spent 1938 with the Cubs, 1939 with Brooklyn, playing only occasionally for each club. From Brooklyn he went to the Giants in 1939, and was released by the Giants on June 7, 1939. A short stint as manager with Toronto followed, then Tony quit baseball to run a bar and grill in San Francisco.

An epileptic, he never had an on-field seizure. When he was found dead on August 6, 1946, it was probably from a heart attack, though epilepsy might have been a contributing cause.

Lazzeri's glory days were with the Yankees. A first-rate hitter, a slick fielder, a smart player and leader, he had that decisive competitive edge that so often separates the outstanding player from the commonplace. He was elected to the Hall of Fame in 1991, an honor long overdue.

Cleveland came to town on June 11 to be greeted by the Babe with homers No. 19 and 20, the artistic centerpiece of a 6–4 win. The first soared towards the right center bleachers, and landed six rows beyond the 461-feet mark of the old Yankee Stadium fence. Taken with vexation and suspicion, Indians catcher Luke Sewell inspected Ruth's bat for evidence of foreign matter inserted into the bludgeon. He found none.

His next time up the indignant Babe slammed another into the bleachers, not quite as far as No. 19, perhaps to spare Sewell the need for further scrutiny. Sadly, the harried Luke suffered yet another spell of disquietude when Lazzeri hit a shot which, *The New York Times* reporter James Harrison reported, "landed beyond the cinder track and fled into the bull pen, hiding coyly under a green bench," as Tony touched every base including home.

The Yanks lost the next game, 8–7, but on June 13 they walloped the Indians 14–6 as Ben Paschal, subbing for the indisposed Meusel, homered twice. Dugan also homered, as did Lazzeri and Collins, in a display that bordered on ennui as the overabundance of runs scampered across the plate. Paschal added a double and triple to his home runs in his five at-bats.

Ben, the reserve outfielder par excellence, hit a solid .317 in 1927. Since joining the Yanks in 1924, he had been a robust righty hitter (his lifetime BA is .309), a reliable backup to the Yank outfield. On most other major league clubs Paschal would have been a regular. In 1925 it was Paschal who replaced Ruth when Babe gorged and caroused himself into the hospital. Taking over for Ruth on Opening Day 1925 Paschal homered. He further distinguished himself that year by hitting two inside-the-park home runs, the first American Leaguer to accomplish this. A Yankee through the 1929 season, he retired that year.

Dan Howley's Browns were the next to experience the Yankees taxing hospitality.

On June 16, 1927, in New York, the game was held up 25 minutes as teams and fans awaited the arrival of honored guest, "Lone Eagle" Charles A. Lindbergh. He didn't show, festivities commenced, and the Yankees won, 8–1. Ruth hit No. 22 and lamented, "I had been saving that homer for Lindbergh and then he doesn't show up." Gehrig also homered, but we have no quote from the more retiring Lou. An indication of how things were going for the spooked Browns was reported by droll reporter for *The New York Times* James P. Dawson.

When Gehrig hit a high fly to center, "The Browns held a district convention around the spot where the ball descended. They chatted about this and that and someone told a funny story and there was a discussion of the Russian situation. An argument arose as to which player should catch the ball, and it was a wonder one of them wasn't hit on the head." The ball dropped onto the beautiful Stadium greensward, the bases were filled, and dependable Benny Paschal singled home two runs.

Lindy finally arrived, with no excuse for his tardiness. No matter—in 1927 he could do no wrong.

The Yanks won 3–2 on June 17, 1927, as Urban Shocker pitched a masterful four-hitter against his old Browns teammates.

June 18, 1927, saw the Yankees win 8–4 as Gehrig homered twice, No. 16 and 17. For emphasis, he tripled. Lou was now leading the league with a .391 BA, Meusel was second with .377. Myles Thomas, a pitcher of pedestrian talents, won with help from Moore.

It rained on June 19, giving the Browns a chance to regroup, leave town, and contemplate with alarm their remaining 15 games with New York.

Unhappily mired in last place, Boston hosted the Yanks on June 21. Their ill-mannered guests took both games of a doubleheader, 7–3 and 7–1. Pennock pitched a six-hitter in the first game, Hoyt won the second with a five-hitter. Between games a delegation of ebullient Italians from Boston's North End presented Lazzeri with a jeweled ring. The grateful Tony responded with 2 for 4 in the first game, 2 for 3 in the second, and filled in at short for the indisposed Koenig. Utility infielder Ray Morehart, in his only Yankee year, in the last of his three-year career in the majors, covered second.

For the rest of his life the journeyman Morehart would be remembered for two things. Playing for the White Sox in 1926 he got nine hits in a doubleheader (a mark that has been tied but not broken), and he was a 1927 Yankee. "I get requests from all over the United States just because I was a teammate of Babe Ruth," he told Mike Mulhern, writing in the *Baton Rouge State-Times* of September 1, 1987, thus giving us a telling example of the enduring afterglow of reflected glory.

Persisting in excessive hospitality, on June 22 the Red Sox lost two more, 7–4 and 3–2. Babe, feeling at home in his old Boston playground, hit No. 23 and 24 in Game 1. Showing no compassion (a virtue notably absent on the diamond), on June 23 the New Yorkers again walloped Boston, 11–4, for a five-straight sweep.

Lou Gehrig busted three homers in the final, and went 4 for 5. By the end of June, Gehrig would lead the league with a whopping .392 BA, and tie Ruth with 24 home runs. Lou, a very great ballplayer, was making his unique, indelible mark on baseball and America.

He was born June 19, 1903, into a poor German immigrant family living at 1994 Second Avenue in Manhattan, and christened Henry Louis Gehrig. Of four children born to Christina and Heinrich Gehrig, he was the only survivor. Heinrich was a good but somewhat ineffectual man; it was Christina, a devoted, indefatigable woman, who anchored the family during hard times.

She did washing for other families, cleaned their homes, cooked their meals even as she made certain young Louis attended P.S. 132, did homework and—not least—was well fed. Some random bug might assail her son, but he'd never suffer from malnutrition. With Christina's hearty cuisine under his belt Lou grew into a husky kid.

Gehrig's fondness for his mother's cooking remained with him for all of his 39 years. George Pipgras, the old Yankee pitcher and Lou's teammate on the 1927 club, recalled in a December 10, 1984, phone interview with the author, "After the game he rushed home to Mama and a

Henry Louis Gehrig   *Photo courtesy of the New York Yankees.*

great German meal." Gehrig often brought several of his Yankee teammates with him, and Christina's scrumptious feasts became famous around the Yankee clubhouse.

Though a closely protected child, the future Iron Man was a happy and energetic kid in his poor but respectable New York neighborhood. He swam in the rivers surrounding Manhattan (they were cleaner then), and played baseball in the local parks. Dave Gould, a boyhood friend of Gehrig's, said in a 1987 phone interview with the author, "It was quite obvious at that age (around 14) that he had something the rest of us didn't have. He was an extremely outstanding ballplayer." And, recalled Gould, "He was looking forward not only to playing in high school, but I think he wanted to go straight to the majors without even thinking about Columbia College."

A good though not a brilliant student, Lou entered the High School of Commerce preparing—because Mama said so—to go to college and become an accountant or engineer. But one impressive and decisive fact put Christina's plans on hold: when her strapping son hit a baseball it traveled with astonishing speed towards the horizon.

At Commerce Lou starred in football and baseball and—of import to future Yankee Stadium fans—learned from his coach, Harry Kane, how to hit lefties. It was under Kane's aegis, too, that he took his first step towards baseball immortality. For in 1920, Commerce won the New York City high school baseball championship, and was invited to Chicago's Wrigley Field to play Lane Tech High, the Windy City's champs.

Years later Gehrig came to know that ballpark well, when, in the 1932 series with the Cubs he slammed the ball at a .529 clip and had a slugging average of 1.118. And in the 1938 series against Chicago, though his diseased body was rapidly deteriorating, he still hit a respectable .286. But stepping onto a big league ballpark in 1920 probably gave the 17-year-old Gehrig goose pimples, though it surely didn't unsettle his incredible batting eye.

"The game took on an atmosphere of a world series contest with two bands...motion picture cameras and photographers, cheer leaders and a crowd of more than 10,000," reported *The New York Times* on June 27, 1920. "Gherrig [*sic*]...who played first base...and who came here touted as the 'Babe' Ruth of the high schools, lived up to his reputation by driving the ball over the right field wall...for a home run with the bases filled."

That homer, with two out in the ninth, not only nailed down the 12–6 Commerce win, but it set off a sequence of events that dashed Christina's hope that her boy become a staid accountant. As for the antics of Louis's schoolmates, these must have bewildered her. So her son hit a ball over a fence in Chicago: very nice, but why all the fuss?

The public commotions, of course, were because nothing gets the American juices to running quite like a baseball championship victory. And Lou was now a certified New York hero due to his herculean clout at Wrigley Field.

Thousands of cheering people met the Commerce team at Grand Central Station. With a band in the vanguard the team and crowd headed up Park Avenue to 59th Street, where they were joined by the Board of Education, taking time off from trifling pedagogical concerns for a jubilant celebration at Commerce High. From that day on Lou Gehrig's destiny was settled.

Gehrig graduated from Commerce in 1920 to find two dozen colleges brandishing athletic scholarships at him. Lou chose Columbia. He was familiar with the school, he would be near his family, and how would he be able to eat Christina's cooking away from New York?

At Columbia he was a passable tackle on the football team, but a batting terror on the diamond. Giants manager John McGraw got wind of the college slugger and invited him to the Polo Grounds for a tryout. For the young and impressionable Lou that was like being invited to play on hallowed ground. McGraw saw a brawny kid who couldn't field worth a damn, but slammed the ball high and far, against the fences or into the seats. Unfortunately, as a college amateur Lou was unsignable, a detail that didn't faze the guileful Giant manager.

As a Baltimore Oriole McGraw had played baseball with the ethical disposition of a juvenile delinquent: he knew how to evade legalities. McGraw tried to hide his discovery by convincing Gehrig to go to minor league Hartford for the summer and play pro ball under an assumed name. It was O.K., said the persuasive McGraw; other college players did it to get experience and earn a few dollars, so could Gehrig.

The gullible Lou went to Hartford, and played 12 games under the moniker of Lou Lewis before Andy Coakley, his Columbia baseball coach, hustled up to Hartford and yanked Lou back to New York. For his misdeed Gehrig was barred from college baseball for one year. He never quite forgave McGraw for misleading him. But Gehrig wasn't exactly a fuzzy-cheeked lad: he should have known better than to let McGraw inveigle him.

While this hugger-mugger was going on, the astute Yankee scout, Paul Krichell, was eyeing Gehrig. According to Waite Hoyt, after seeing Lou hit for Columbia a euphoric Krichell told Ed Barrow, "'I've been watching another Babe Ruth.' Barrow, forever the tough realist, laughed. 'All right, go ahead laugh, but I still say, I saw another Ruth,'" insisted Krichell (Waite Hoyt Papers, Gehrig section 4).

In 1923 Heinrich was chronically ill, and doctor bills were piling up. So on June 23, Gehrig, who always felt responsible for the welfare of his parents, quit Columbia and signed with the Yankees for $3,000 and a $500 bonus. (How strange those sums seem today when applied to Lou Gehrig.)

Waite Hoyt, in his papers, has left us a vivid description of Gehrig's arrival at Yankee Stadium. "In June 1923...we Yankees were...taking batting practice. There was Ruth, Wally Pipp, Everett Scott, and Aaron Ward. From the direction of the Yankee bench marched two men.... The 'little guy,' walking with his toes turned outward, and in mincing steps, was Miller Huggins. The young, smooth-faced Atlas trailing him...who walked with an ungainly roll, was to become one of the greatest and most admired of all ball players."

Wally Pipp—of all people—was in the batting cage as "Huggins chirped, 'Hey Wally, let the kid hit a few.'" Not having a bat, Gehrig took one that was leaning against the cage. It was Ruth's 48-ounce bludgeon. Babe said nothing as Gehrig positioned himself in the cage.

"He missed a couple. He dribbled a couple of grounders in the infield." Then, "Lou cut at the next pitch—and wham, the ball took off— higher and higher, and long and far away. Into the section they called Ruthville, high over the railings of the right field bleachers.... Babe's eyes popped." After Gehrig socked a few more into the same area Hug said, "That's enough Lou. Let the bushers hit." He and Gehrig walked towards first base where they had serious business to attend to. The new kid had to learn how to play first base (Hoyt Papers).

Lou played his first Yankee game on June 15, 1923, when Huggins put him on first in the ninth inning. He handled one chance, a grounder putout to end the game. On June 18 he batted for Aaron Ward in the ninth and struck out. Hug then sent him to Hartford where manager Paddy O'Connor was told to play him at first base every day, no matter how tangle-footed he seemed. By the time he returned to the Yanks in September, Gehrig had a .304 BA, 24 of his hits were homers, and his fielding had improved.

Gehrig played in 134 games with Hartford in 1924, and amassed numbers that cheered the Yanks and distressed pitchers: a healthy .369 BA, 40 doubles, 11 triples, 37 homers. And though hardly graceful, Lou was beginning to look like a big league first baseman.

Ultimately he would play his position so well that wise old heads like McGraw and Connie Mack rated him among the best they had seen. And Joe McCarthy, who managed Lou from 1931 to 1939, considered Gehrig the greatest ballplayer he ever saw. As for Miller Huggins, his faith in the quiet, rather naive, gentlemanly rookie from Columbia never wavered. In 1925 Hug decided to keep Lou with the Yanks.

June 1925 was a month for streaks. Early that season the Yankee shortstop, Everett "Deacon" Scott, was benched after playing a record

1,307 consecutive games. His journeyman replacement, Pee Wee Wanninger (lifetime BA a puny .234), got streak-fever and hit in what was for him an improbable 13 straight games, until, on June 1, reality caught up with Pee Wee.

That landmark day he was 0 for 3 when Huggins lifted him for Gehrig—who didn't get a hit. But on June 2, 1925, Gehrig replaced the man who was suffering history's most famous headache, Wally Pipp, and went 3 for 5. However, stats-nuts (which means all true baseball fans) should be aware that Gehrig began his remarkable—and still a record—consecutive game playing streak of 2,130 games by pinch-hitting for Wanninger. Not, as is often written, as a replacement for Pipp.

Gehrig played in 126 games in 1925, and hit .295 while methodically making himself into a skillful first baseman. Setting a longevity record for games-played certainly never entered his mind that year, but surely he wouldn't have reached his astonishing mark without becoming at least an adequate first baseman.

According to Hoyt, when Gehrig first came to the majors he was weak on play-making. "He had the bad habit to run to the bag when the ball was hit off to his right. He could not grasp the fact that the pitcher would cover the bag while he went after the ball" (Hoyt Papers 9).

And he was negligent on cutoff plays. In a 1925 game with the Tigers, Gehrig goofed on a cutoff play that eventually allowed Ty Cobb to score. "Lou," snapped the exasperated Huggins, "You gotta make that cutoff play. After this it will cost you." The abashed Gehrig didn't answer. Later he "said to the utter amazement of us all, 'I know you'll think I'm dumb, and maybe I am, but what the hell was Huggins talking about?'" Writes Hoyt, "We didn't think we'd heard right—but we had. We had to explain it." Gehrig listened, practiced, and he "was never caught that way again" (Hoyt Papers 10). Indeed, Huggins said of Gehrig that he was the kind of player who once he learned something never forgot it.

Gehrig's average was .313 in 1926, and though his homer total was a modest 16, he led the league with 20 triples and hit .348 in the 1926 series. By the 1927 season the Iron Horse had solidified his hold on first base, was batting cleanup in the Yankee lineup, and was one of only five big leaguers who played in every game in 1927.

That standout year he batted .373, 17 points more than Babe, and drove in 175 runs, 11 more than Ruth. In his second full year in the majors Gehrig became what he was throughout his career, one of baseball's true superstars.

To grow up in New York in the '20s was to know the special delight of rooting for the Yankees. Like youngsters the country over New York kids were, of course, Babe Ruth idolaters. The Babe was the charismatic doer of impossible deeds. He seized our imaginations, he captured the fancies of our fathers. But what is often overlooked is that the Big Fellow didn't stand alone in the esteem of New Yorkers.

For from that happy day when Lou Gehrig became a regular, and began busting fences and tiring outfielders, his name was soon linked—first tacitly, then openly—with Ruth's in game-winning exploits. Ruth and his home-run threat is the game's great, abiding legend. But Gehrig, with his power and consistency in the cleanup spot, is of almost equal stature.

Babe had an incomparable flamboyance to prompt and feed his exuberant love affair with the public; but Gehrig's contribution to his team, the game, and the fans, had its own special quality. In his quiet way, Lou, a New York boy, one of the city's own, had a calm strength to go with his enormous athletic gifts. Conservative in his private life, he was steadfast on the field, a team leader by example and prowess. It was these traits of character, these memorable gifts as a superb hitter and complete player that make his disease-afflicted career so poignant.

"Show me a hero and I will write you a tragedy," wrote F. Scott Fitzgerald in *The Crack-Up*. Our chronicler of the Jazz Age didn't have ballplayers in mind, but his aphorism surely applies to Gehrig. For the Iron Man's story has the elements of classic tragedy. It is a tale of superb gifts made palpable by uncommon deeds, the saga of a hero struck down by a cruel and skulking fate.

As early as 1935 Gehrig had nagging muscular problems that were hard to diagnose. In a game in Detroit he unaccountably doubled up while running to first, then had trouble straightening up. Yet he hit .329 that year, and continued his exceptional hitting in 1936 (.354), and 1937 (.351).

In an October 3, 1984, interview, Pete Sheehy, the veteran Yankee clubhouse man, recalled to the author:

> When we were down in spring training...and Lou was playin' first base...there were a couple of ground balls hit to Lou. And the way he went after them, I said, "You know I think there's somethin' wrong with Lou. In the movie [*The Pride of The Yankees*], in the part where he falls down and the players go over to give him a hand, I saw it happen. Only it was DiMaggio and me who went to pick him up. He wouldn't let us. "Please, I'll get up," said Gehrig, struggling to his feet without help.

In 1938 Gehrig's average skidded to .295, the first time since 1925 that he went below .300. In an athlete as well-conditioned and dedicated as Gehrig, that was odd. And he was tripping on curbstones, dropping objects for no discernible reason: his hitherto superb coordination seemed strangely flawed. The punch, the redoubtable power that had carried him to the top of the game was gone from his bat.

On March 31, 1939 the Yanks whipped the Tallahassee Capitols, a Class D minor league club, 22–3 in a spring training game. James Dawson reported the game for *The New York Times:* the following line appeared in his story. "It was ironic that in getting this plenty...Iron Man Lou Gehrig went hitless."

The world didn't yet know it, but tragedy was claiming the hero.

Lou's agony on the field didn't continue much longer. By April 30, 1939, his BA had dropped to .143; on that day he went 0 for 4. And on May 2, Gehrig, the Yankee captain, benched himself. "I haven't been a bit of good to the team since the season started," he told reporters. "It wouldn't be fair to the boys, to Joe [McCarthy], or to the baseball public for me to try going on."

He had started his streak hitting 0 for 1. He ended it 0 for 4. But for the 14 years in between, what a legacy of great ball playing he left us.

Shortly after leaving the lineup Lou's disease was diagnosed as amyotrophic lateral sclerosis, a rare illness, and was given perhaps two years to live. He had played 2,130 consecutive games since coming in as a pinch hitter in 1925: it took a killing disease to bench him.

What Lou might have accomplished had he not been struck down by what has come to be called Lou Gehrig's disease we can only conjecture. For Lou's stats are up there with the best of them. Certainly, given his commitment to staying in shape, it is likely he would have extended his string of consecutive games played beyond the remarkable mark of 2,130. Veteran Yankee play-by-play announcer Mel Allen on July 31, 1985, in an interview with the author at Yankee Stadium recalled sitting in the Yankee dugout after Lou's retirement:

> All of a sudden word came down. "Lou's here." Somebody had driven him up this particular day.
>
> You could hear Gehrig coming down the runway. The disease now had moved to an advanced stage and he would shuffle. But somebody helped him up the stairs to the dugout and everybody would holler, "Hi Lou," "Hi Captain," like he'd never been away. But all of a sudden they'd all be gone, they had to go on the field to practice. I was suddenly left alone with him.
>
> He...said, "Mel, how you doin?" And he said, "You know I have to tell you something." He lay his hand on my left thigh and gave it a little squeeze, and he said, "I never

listened to the radio, I didn't have a chance, I was always playing. But I can't play anymore, and all I do is listen. And I gotta tell you, that's the only thing that keeps me going."

I could hardly get the words out. I said, "Thanks Lou. You excuse me, I'll see you later. I've got to go upstairs and get things ready." I ran down the runway and bawled like a baby.

They gave Lou a "Day" at Yankee Stadium—the first ever for a player—on July 4, 1939. Not only were the 1939 Yankees there, led by Joe DiMaggio, but so were the 1927 Yankees, led by Babe Ruth. Lou and Babe had had their differences as Ruth's career waned and Lou asserted himself as Yankee leader and captain. But, on that day, their dispute forgotten, they embraced as the huge crowd cheered. Wally Pipp was there, as was Everett Scott who had held the consecutive game record until Gehrig surpassed it. The Baseball Writers Association came out in full force, as did politicians and dignitaries.

Most important of all, there were the 61,808 fans standing in tribute and affection for the great ballplayer who had given so much to them and to baseball. His speech to the crowd is remembered as one of those landmark statements by which we identify an era and remember a man.

"What young man wouldn't give anything to mingle with such men as I have for all these years?" said Lou to the hushed crowd. "Today I think I'm the luckiest man alive."

On June 2, 1941, Lou Gehrig died at home.

"The reward of a thing well done," wrote Emerson in "New England Reformers," "is to have done it" (166). The Iron Man did it all in his 14 years as a Yankee, and did it magnificently. Heroes and role models are in short supply these days, in baseball and everywhere else. But Lou Gehrig is one baseball immortal, an athletic hero, an American hero, who will never tarnish or disenchant. His bittersweet journey over, the tragic hero became a legend. He was one of a kind, and it's doubtful that we will ever again see another like him.

Connie Mack's A's came to New York on June 25 and won three in a row, a feat of high distinction in 1927. Then Hug's gang took the next two, a signal to the A's that life, after all, is real and earnest. Certainly the standings showed it. When the Boston Red Sox arrived at the end of June, the Yankees were 10 games in front of second place Philadelphia.

It was Yankees 8, Red Sox 2 on June 29 as Babe got three hits, and Gehrig one, a homer that tied the Bambino with 24. George Pipgras gave up a skimpy three hits and went all the way. On June 31 the Yanks closed their June schedule with a 13–6 win as Combs went 3 for 6.

Earle, dubbed "the Waiter" by Huggins for his proficiency at wangling walks, wasn't waiting much. Instead he was hitting up a storm, for him a more agreeable way to get on base. At the end of June the Hugmen were 12 games ahead of Washington, with a .710 PCT, and drawing great crowds around the league as they moved into the delights of midsummer.

Truly, in that time, it was great to be alive and a Yankee.

July 1, 1927

AMERICAN LEAGUE

STANDING OF THE CLUBS.

	Won.	Lost.	P.C.
New York	49	20	.710
Washington	37	29	.561
Chicago	40	32	.556
Philadelphia	37	32	.536
Detroit	34	30	.531
Cleveland	31	38	.449
St. Louis	27	38	.415
Boston	15	51	.227

5

July

Pennant race is a runaway, Yank batting averages bur-geon, Babe and Lou are neck-and-neck in homer derby.

July 1 arrived with a 7–4 Yankee victory over the Red Sox, their sixth straight win, and distressingly for the folks in Fenway Park, Boston's 13th straight loss. Gehrig, the ex-Babe Ruth of the high schools and colleges, hammered No. 26 to pass the authentic Babe, and Earl Combs hit 2 for 3, one of them a homer. It was 3–2 the next day as the Yanks—their streaks now a discouraging habit to the rest of the league—took their seventh in a row, with Ruether the winner.

Combs went 2 for 4 at leadoff. Earle walked when pitchers quailed at throwing near the plate, yet he found enough good pitches to send his BA well over the .300 mark. Not a nighttime bon vivant like some of his teammates, Earle was nevertheless a special Yankee.

As a ballplayer nothing about Earle Bryan Combs was commonplace except his throwing arm; that seemed ordinary only because he shared the outfield with Meusel and Ruth, both exceptional and accurate throwers. Combs was a dangerous hitter, a fleet, graceful outfielder, and the best leadoff man baseball had yet seen. In the annals of "Murderers' Row" he is celebrated as first in line of that wrecking crew.

Earle was a country boy, born May 14, 1899, on a hardscrabble hillside farm in the Cumberland Mountains of Eastern Kentucky. From the time he was a child he wanted to be a professional ballplayer, an ambition that brought him into conflict with his father, James Combs.

Farming those Kentucky hills was hard work; the living the Combs family (there were seven kids with big appetites) took from the stubborn, rock-strewn earth was marginal at best. So James Combs, seemingly an unbending father, decided that Earle would be a teacher. Teachers didn't get rich, but neither did Kentucky hill-farmers. And teachers had assured, if paltry, incomes.

Earle Bryan Combs   *Photo courtesy of the New York Yankees.*

Yet, in some obscure corner of James Combs's mind there must have lurked doubts about his decision. In a January 19, 1933, *Sporting News* interview Earle said,

> I lived on the farm until I was 17 years old, and from boyhood my brothers—Matt, Conley, and Clayton—played ball with me, and frequently Dad would join us. He made us all our balls and bats. Many a time I've watched him make a baseball. He would get some old socks which mother had knitted...an old gum shoe and an old high-topped woman's shoe for his materials. He would unravel the socks, cut a ball from the gum shoe for the center, wind the yarn about this, and then cut a cover from the shoe top. He made bats...out of hickory and poplar.

For a father who didn't want his son to be a ballplayer, James Combs had an odd way of discouraging young Earle.

A dutiful son, Earle conformed to his father's wishes by diligently preparing for teachers college. Nevertheless, in his fantasizing moments he read all he could about baseball, collected pictures of ballplayers, and daydreamed about becoming a great player like his idol, Ty Cobb. At 17 he entered Eastern Kentucky State Normal School. But, said Earle, "When I wasn't in the classrooms I was on the ball field watching games, studying players, and asking the coach questions."

Combs was 20 in 1919, desperately wanting to play professional baseball but instead teaching school in the little hill town of Ida May, Kentucky. He had 40 pupils in his one-room schoolhouse, their age span was 6 to 16.

"It wasn't much of a school," Combs recalled in the 1933 interview, "and I wasn't such a hot teacher. But we had a swell ball team and I was an excellent player/manager. Those kids played ball morning, noon, and night, whether they wanted to or not...I had the whole class, including girls, shagging baseballs."

Combs returned to Normal School in the fall of 1919 for his advanced-grade teacher's certificate, played ball on pickup teams, and taught. "I was given the Cross Roads School, and once again the whole class pitched to me and chased flies I hit." So much for education, Earle Combs style, in the Cumberland mountains.

Word got around about the baseball-crazy schoolteacher, and Combs got an offer from the Mayham Coal Company to join their company team. They would pay him $225 per month, plus room and board, a bounteous deal no hill-country school board could match. Earle joined, batted .444, and supplemented his wardrobe with a bonus of two suits from the town merchants. Inevitably, the Louisville Colonels, a AA team managed by Joe McCarthy, contacted him. Would Earle like to play with the Colonels?

Impossible, he told them; his father insisted he teach school. Fortunately, the side of James Combs that took pleasure in making balls and bats for his kids prevailed when Earle told him about the pro ball offer. "You may as well try your wings," Earle recalled his dad saying. "You'll never be satisfied until you do." Smart father: his common sense decision activated a great baseball career, one crucial to the creation of the 1927 Yanks.

Combs joined the Colonels in 1922, and began rapping the ball with the same zest he showed when he sent kids pelting after his wallops at Ida May and Cross Roads. That first pro year he got 167 hits and batted .344. In 1923 he hit .380, attracting Yankee scouts prowling the minors for a center fielder to replace Whitey Witt. The glowing report on Combs promptly loosened Colonel Ruppert's wallet: he paid the Colonels $50,000, and the erstwhile country schoolteacher came to Yankee Stadium.

Combs—six-feet, 185 pounds, batting left, throwing right—broke into the Yankee lineup on June 15, 1924, batted a lusty .400 for 24 games, then broke his ankle. That benched him for the rest of the season. It was the first of three serious injuries he would have in his career, a particularly damaging one to the Yanks that year. Ruth, who knew a great hitter when he saw one, said that Earle's injury cost the Yankees the pennant to Washington in 1924.

Back in the lineup in 1925 as the regular center fielder, Combs hit a solid .342 while fielding for a .977 PCT. In a year when the Yankees sank to an implausible seventh, the man from the Cumberland established himself as a dangerous line-drive hitter, and one of the great Yankee center fielders. Huggins knew exactly how to use his godsend from Kentucky.

Hug told him his job was to get on base and wait for Ruth, Gehrig, or some other Yankee slugger to send him home. Combs handled his assignment with a certain excess: he not only reached first by walking or singling, he hit doubles and triples with equal aplomb.

Indeed, triples were a Combs specialty: he led the league with three-baggers in 1927 (23), 1928 (21), and 1930 (22). On September 22, 1927, Earle hit three triples in one game against Detroit, a rare achievement, one that Huggins must have particularly appreciated. For back on October 8, 1904, while with Cincinnati, little Hug had flexed his muscles and smacked three triples in one game.

Opposition hurlers in 1927 were distressed because there was no slot in the Yankee lineup where a pitcher could ease off. The ordeal began at the top of the batting order when Combs stepped to the plate. A random sampling of 1927 box scores confirms his prowess at leadoff: May 31, 5 for 6 (two doubles, a triple, two singles.); June 26, 2 for 4; June 28, 4 for 5; June 30, 3 for 6; July 9, 3 for 5; and August 10, 3 for 5. And so on to the end of the season—plus 62 walks. When the bombardment ceased, Combs's 231 hits earned him a BA of .356, exactly that of Ruth in his 60-homer season.

The personality of the handsome, prematurely gray-haired Combs was in striking contrast to some of his more boisterous teammates. He didn't drink, smoke, or swear. He read his Bible, attended church, went to bed early, was conservative in habits, a complete gentleman. Huggins, who had to deal with inflated egos, wayward boozers, and insubordination of novel varieties since coming to the Yankees, was cited in the spring 1970 issue of the *Eastern Kentucky Alumnus*: "If you had nine Combses on your ball club you could go to bed every night and sleep like a baby." The high-living Ruth said of Combs, "No one ever accused him of being out on a drinking party, and you'd laugh at the words he used for cussing.... He came from a strict mountaineer family. But Earle was all man, and a great competitor" (Ruth, *The Babe Ruth Story* 129-30).

The praise for Earle's clean living might evoke snickers today, when so many athletes make the front pages and TV news with unsavory doings. But even the cynical will admit there is something gratifying about a sports hero who lives up to a commendable image. Ruth might also have acknowledged his large debt as a fielder to the Kentucky Colonel. For as Babe aged, his fielding range narrowed, and on many critical wallops into his territory the swift Combs caught fly balls that would normally have been Ruth's.

Combs spent his entire 12-year major league career with the Yankees, amassing 1,866 hits for a lifetime BA of .325, and batting .350 in 16 World Series games. If not for two serious accidents in successive years, he might well have added to those already imposing stats. By 1934, at 35, Combs was still playing a strong center field and hitting .319. On July 24, in St. Louis, he went after a long fly, struck the wall (why didn't somebody think of padding the walls in those days?), broke his shoulder and knee and fractured his skull.

Not only was he out for the rest of the season, but for part of his two-month stay in the hospital his life was in danger. Remarkably, he recovered and came back in 1935 as a player-coach for 89 games, was hitting .282 when he got hurt again, and decided it was time to hang them up. But he still had important work to do as a Yankee.

During the winter Ed Barrow wrote to him about a new prospect coming up from San Francisco whom he wanted Combs to break in—a kid named Joe DiMaggio. From the evidence Combs carried out his assignment to perfection. For center field became the turf of an outfielder the equal of Combs in speed, grace, and hitting ability. (Earle and DiMag, at .325, have exactly the same lifetime batting averages.)

Combs coached with the Yanks until 1943, then returned to his Kentucky farm for three years. But the lure of baseball was strong: he returned to coach with the Browns, Boston, and Phillies before retiring from the game permanently. A man of parts, Combs remained active. He farmed, sold insurance, served as state banking commissioner, and was on the Kentucky State Board of Regents. When elected to the Baseball Hall of Fame in 1970 he told the press, "It was the last thing I expected. I thought the Hall of Fame was for superstars, not for average players like me." Earle's self-effacement was no doubt genuine, but his notion as to what marks a player as a superstar was certainly flawed.

On July 21, 1976, Earle Bryan Combs died at the age of 77 in the Kentucky mountain country in which he was so firmly rooted. There he had learned to play ball, dreamed of becoming a big leaguer, taught school, sent his covey of pupils in frantic pursuit of fly balls. And there he had brought his father around to the wise realization that fate had destined his son to be a great ballplayer.

Earle Combs bequeathed to baseball, and to those lucky enough to see him play, the memory of outstanding exploits as a fielder, and his superb marks as leadoff in the power-packed batting order of the great 1927 club. Not least, he left us the image of a man to admire and respect.

On July 3 the Yanks lost to the Senators, in D.C., 6-5, despite Ruth's No. 26. The Babe's homer, in the first, was the longest ever hit at Griffith Field; it landed in the stands slightly to the right of dead center, 12 rows from the top. The fence was 401 feet from home plate; add what you will to that number (60? 75? feet) and you had a tremendous clout. Thirty thousand fans cheered the second place Senators as they won their tenth straight, fueling visions of a first place finish—a delusion born in a city of delusions.

Both teams traveled to Yankee Stadium for a Fourth of July doubleheader, where the Yanks let loose a bombardment appropriate to the holiday. A record-breaking 74,000 fans packed the stadium as "Murderers' Row" took aim at the fences.

Gehrig hit No. 27 and 28, and Collins, Lazzeri, and sub infielder Julian Wera also homered. It was Wera's only homer of his 43 big league career games, proving either nothing, or that hanging around with "Murderers' Row" bred contagion. And there were four triples, nine doubles, and sundry singles and walks—all of which added up to 12–1 in the first game, and 21–1 in the second. George Pipgras won the first game, justifying Hug's faith in him despite some shaky efforts on other occasions. Moore started and went the route in the second, a pleasant change from his usual rescue chores. All in all, it was a pleasant way for New York to celebrate the nation's birthday.

The Yankees made it three straight the next day with a 7–6 win, then went west where they split four with Detroit in two successive doubleheaders as Babe hit No. 28 and 29 to take the homer lead from Gehrig. Securely in first place, 11 games ahead of Washington, the Hugmen and their exuberant public were enlightened by a bashful scrivener in an unsigned column in the *New York Herald Tribune* of July 10, 1927. He pointed out what for years had been common knowledge to baseball's deep thinkers—that Miller Huggins was no ordinary manager: "The swashbuckling Yankees go on winning games...while everybody agrees that the New York American Club has a great, amazing and bewildering team," wrote the discerning reporter. Then, putting his finger on a key reason for the Yankee success, he added, "Overshadowed perhaps by his array of stars, Huggins has been in the background as far as public recognition goes, but his success in handling his temperamental stars is an achievement in itself."

So it was: that, and fearsome hitters, excellent fielders, estimable starters, and William Wilcy Moore.

At midsummer the Babe-and-Lou homer derby was what the pennant race was not in 1927, a close, exciting slugger's conflict. From the evidence, both men took the rivalry in stride, even with a touch of graciousness. Gehrig, quiet and amiable, did not sound off or make unseemly predictions. Babe, though famously extravagant in all aspects of his life on and off the field, was mannerly and generous.

Called upon to speak at a testimonial dinner to Tony Lazzeri in Boston (Lazzeri was given a diamond ring and $1,000 by admiring Italian-Americans), Babe spoke graciously about Tony's virtues then switched to his quest for a new homer record. Sure, the July 3, 1927, *New York Herald-Tribune,* reported, he wanted to beat his 1921 seasonal mark of 59 home runs. "But," said Ruth to loud applause, "if anyone is going to beat me out I hope it will be Lou Gehrig."

Gehrig took a bow, Tony slipped the sparkler onto his finger, the $1,000 into his pocket, Babe departed for further relaxation elsewhere.

Gehrig hit No. 29 to tie Ruth on July 11, in an 8–5 win over the Tigers. On the 12th Ruth slammed No. 30 as the Yanks blanked Cleveland 7–0, and Urban Shocker went the distance on a seven-hitter. They split the next two with the Indians, and on July 15 won 10–9 with an attack of their famous late-afternoon lightning to score seven runs in the final two innings.

This moved Richards Vidmer to a rapturous lead in *The New York Times* of July 16, 1927:

You may sing of the ancient Orioles. You may chant of the glory that was the Cubs a score of years ago. You may harken back to the Athletics before the wreckage. But before anyone starts making any broad statements concerning those teams of a past baseball era, let him consider the frolicking, rollicking, walloping Yanks of the present.

The perception that something extraordinary had appeared in the national pastime was taking hold as the Hugmen hit the road to St. Louis.

It was Yanks 5, St. Louis 2 on July 16, 1927, in St. Louis. Pennock was the winner on a six-hitter, as Gehrig got three hits off ex-Yankee pitcher, Sad Sam Jones. Yanks were now 61–25, sporting a .709 PCT, 14 games ahead of the Senators.

The ninth game with St. Louis, on July 17, was a 5–4 Yankee win. In the seventh the Browns knocked Shocker out of the box, scored two runs, were bedazzled by the prospect of victory as they led 4–3. In the eighth Ruth struck out to a chorus of 18,000 hecklers. Then (was it around 5 o'clock?) Gehrig parked his No. 30 in the stands to tie Ruth, Meusel followed with another homer to put the Yanks ahead, and the Browns left the field in a state of acute distress.

Game 10 with the Browns, on July 18 in St. Louis, saw a Yankee 10–6 victory before 9,006 women, admitted free, gracing the stands for Ladies Day, part of a total crowd of 18,452. Lou hit No. 31, to take the home-run lead from Babe. In the ninth, great hitter George Sisler slammed a homer with bases loaded off George Pipgras—alas, for naught. Pipgras, finally coming into his own, composed himself to finish for the win.

The July 19, 1927, Game 11 with the Browns, in St. Louis, ended with Yanks 6, St. Louis 1, as the situation degenerated into monotony. *The New York Times* waggishly reported on July 20, "The statistics show the Yankees have lost 25 games this season, but the Brownies can't understand how or why."

How or why, indeed. Lou was slugging the ball at a .393 clip, matching Babe homer for homer, and was ahead of Ruth at this date. Yet, when the Yankees left the salutary environs of St. Louis on the 19th, it was Ruth the kids encircled, clamoring for autographs or the bestowal of a smile. When Gehrig left he might as well have been a lone hot-dog vendor going home. So it also went on the trip to St. Paul, where the Yankees had an exhibition date.

When the train stopped at middle-American small towns Ruth emerged at the stations to beam at the crowds, to make a little speech, and send them home having verifiably encountered true eminence. Gehrig, too, came onto the platform—but only because Ruth took him by the hand and led him out.

On the St. Paul field Babe played first base, signed score cards and baseballs. As if drinking from a royal flagon, he quaffed a bottle of pop brought to him by an idolizing kid, and happily endured a playful pelting of leather cushions when he came out to pitch the ninth. He didn't hit a homer, but no matter. The Babe was there in the flesh, a stimulus to fond recollections for years to come.

Chicago was the final stop on the Yankees' late July western swing. On July 21 White Sox hurler George Connally held them to a single hit to the ninth, an unlikely feat unduplicated by any other pitcher that year. Then, finally getting the range, the Yanks blasted him from the mound with four runs to win, 4–1. Waite Hoyt, patiently waiting for 5 o'clock, was the starter, finisher, and winner.

The Yankees won the next two out of three from the White Sox. Cedric Durst covered center in those games, the egregiously accident-prone Combs having been whacked on the head by a ball. Durst, a grateful refugee from the Browns, was a good fielder, though an ordinary hitter. But he'd made a slugger's 1927 debut with the Yanks on April 24 by tripling with the bases loaded in a 6–2 win over Washington. With the 1927 club he played in 65 games.

Mike Gazella took over third base in Chicago, as Dugan, his sometimes ornery legs balking, had ankle trouble. "Gazook" filled in with easy competence until "Jumping Joe" returned the second week in August. On the 1927 club Mike did not have to endure the kind of nonsense that took place in 1926. That year, out of mindless greed, and/or naked stupidity, the team voted Gazella only a quarter share of the series money, perhaps because he had appeared in only 66 games.

Fuming and protesting, Gazella held out for a full share. Backed by Huggins, he took his case to Commissioner Landis who ordered the players to pay him his full share; which they did, closing the repulsive incident. All told, Gazella earned over $50,000 in series money from 1926 to 1928. Not bad for a 1920s sub who played only 160 games in his entire big league career, and spent much of the rest of his life warmed by the reflected glory of the extraordinary ball club.

The presence of Durst and Gazella was a tribute to Hug's and Barrow's trading acumen, Ruppert's confidence in their judgment, and fortune's bright, unfailing smile in 1927.

Ruth put one into the Comiskey Park stands on July 24 to tie Gehrig at 31 home runs, as Pipgras, with aid in the seventh from Hug's secret weapon, Cy Moore, won his fifth game since entering the rotation. Not that the Yank hurlers were totally dependent on relief. By July 19, of the 87 games played, the Yankee pitchers had gone the route in 45 games and won 40 of these.

Sporting a 13–5 mark for the road trip, 67–26 for a .720 PCT on the season, the Yanks were uncatchable. Said Mark Koenig in a December 16, 1984, phone interview with the author, recalling the Yankee sweep, "We were so far in the lead then, we'd have had to drop dead" to lose. And Dan Howley, speaking from disheartening, not to say numbing, experience, lamented that the Yankees should be in a league by themselves. Which, in a way, they were.

Of all the Yankees one of the most contented and effective as the season wore on was George Pipgras, for success in the majors hadn't come easily to him.

One bleak day in 1921 George William Pipgras was down on his luck, and stranded in the boondock town of Worthington, Minnesota. After a 35-cent breakfast that barely nourished his raw-boned, six-foot-two-inch frame, he was left with 15 cents and the shabby clothes on his back. George's strong right arm could whip a baseball past lustily swinging batters on those infrequent occasions when he found the plate. Now he wondered how and where he could hook up with a team, pitch often enough to gain control, and where his next meal was coming from.

Pitching for Saginaw in a recent outing, he had walked 15 men in five innings, then was promptly released by manager Red McKee. Who could fault McKee? He was, after all, the exhausted catcher lunging after George's wild heaves. But Pipgras had grit and intelligence to go with his speed; with steady work he hoped to pitch himself to the majors. Taking a chance he invested one third of his capital in a nickel phone call to a baseball-savvy pal. Was there a team in that part of the country that needed a pitcher?

"Madison, in the South Dakota League," answered his friend. "Just tell them I sent you." But the fare to Sioux City, where Madison was to open the season, was a princely 60 cents, and George had a lone dime in his pocket. So his compassionate buddy phoned the Madison manager, touted Pipgras and his fast ball, while suppressing any mention of errant control. The Madison skipper—a venturesome fellow, free with money—wired 60 cents to Worthington. George hopped the train in time to get to Sioux Falls for the opener. He stayed with Madison, found the plate more often than not, and went 12–6. Six weeks later Yankee scout Bob Connery bought him.

Pipgras spent 1922 with Charleston in the South Atlantic (Sally) League where he was an impressive 19–9, and in 1923, probably pinching himself, he became a Yankee.

George Pipgras   *Photo courtesy of the New York Yankees.*

From childhood Pipgras had wanted to pitch in the big leagues. Of Danish ancestry, he was born in Ida Grove, Iowa, on December 20, 1899. When he was a boy his family moved to a farm in Slayton, Minnesota, where George pitched for the local high school team. Of course, George's first obligation was to work on the farm, not to play ball.

In the observance of bucolic discipline—a regimen more seductive to urban romantics than to those on a farm shoveling dung piles—George's day began at 4:30 A.M. His daily chores included such earthy tasks as milking cows, feeding 150 head of sheep, and currying 15 horses. After that came breakfast, school, and—weather permitting in the often frigid north—baseball.

When America entered World War I George was only 17, an age when shooting at another person in an enemy uniform was legally impermissible, so he fibbed about his age, and the army took him. Pipgras, happy to leave all that livestock behind, served in France with the 60th Engineers, then returned home at 19 to find the horses, sheep, and cows waiting for him.

Once in awhile, in respite from animal husbandry, Pipgras pitched semipro ball. It was while hurling—and losing—for a raggle-taggle bunch of pickups at Woodstock (they had one complete uniform among them), that he got a semipro offer to pitch in Fulda, Minnesota, for the bedazzling sum of $350 per month. Pipgras grabbed it, said so long to his folks and the herds, and became a pro ballplayer, all before taking that crucial 60-cent ride to Sioux City.

Pipgras rode the bench at Yankee Stadium for most of 1923, compiling a puny won-lost of 1–3. Even more disheartening was his 0–1 mark in 1924. He was wild, and there were baseball experts who couldn't understand why Huggins kept him. But Hug saw something in Pipgras's raw talent and dedication to his craft that others did not, and in 1925 Miller sent him down to work on his control. Two years in the minor leagues would cure him, Hug believed. So it did. With Atlanta and Nashville in 1925 George's record was a healthy 19–15; with St. Paul in 1926 he was 22–19. When asked in 1985 who helped him gain good control he answered, "I worked it out myself. You see, we didn't have [pitching] coaches in those days. So I started to turn [pivot]. I kept turning a bit more, and I got my control when I was in St. Paul in '26. I was supposed to go back to St. Paul, but [the Yankees] wouldn't let me go" (interview with the author, January 28, 1985).

In July 1927, while Pipgras was again riding the bench, and the skeptics were noising their doubts, Dutch Ruether became ill or perhaps hung-over. So Hug gave Pipgras the ball, and George began winning. Now a complete pitcher, he not only had his outstanding fast ball, but also a deceptive curve, courtesy of his Yankee cohort, Herb Pennock.

In 1985, though ailing with lung cancer, Pipgras was still mentally sharp and eager to talk about his Yankee days and baseball. "Herb Pennock taught me a curve ball," he reminisced. "I had a good fast ball but my curve ball just spun up there, it didn't break much. He taught me to throw it, how to turn my wrist, and I had a good curve ball after that." Of Pennock, he said, "He was a good friend, a friend to everybody."

Pipgras spoke affectionately of his great days with the 1927 Yankees. "We had a good bunch of ballplayers on that club, a good bunch of fellows. They were all friends, there were no cliques, we all got along real good." Of Huggins, he recalled admiringly, "I remember him as a man with an iron fist, but he was a wonderful man. When he said no, he meant no; he was a little fellow, but he managed to control all the ballplayers." Which, in that club of free spirits, was a major achievement.

Pipgras was critical about many of today's pitchers not finishing. "I don't think they pace themselves. When we got a couple of runs ahead, we were pacing ourselves, you'd make them hit the ball. But they don't do that anymore. Oscar Roettger [an old Yankee then in his 80s] told me some pitchers have five inning contracts." Pipgras laughed in disbelief. "Pitch five innings! When we couldn't pitch over that we couldn't be in there very long" (personal interview, January 28, 1985).

Once he entered the starting rotation Pipgras never left it, finishing the 1927 season with a 10–3 mark. And, in control all the way, he beat the Pirates on a neat seven-hitter in the second game of the series.

Pipgras led the Yankee pitchers in 1928 with a 24–13 mark. After that he didn't have a losing season in the majors until his last, when he was 0–1 with the Red Sox in 1935. George's farewell year with the Yankees was 1932, one he fondly remembers. Not only was he 16–9 that year, but he pitched and won the famous third game of the series sweep against the Cubs—the game in which Ruth called or didn't call his homer. Others might have doubts about that exploit, but not Pipgras.

"Oh, it was just as though it happened yesterday," Pipgras recalled. "He took two strikes, then pointed to right field, and that's where he hit the ball." No *if*s, *and*s, or *but*s, Pipgras clearly saw Babe call it. He spoke fondly of Ruth's personality. "He had a heart as big as himself. He was a good fellow...a good team man. Like a lot of times when there'd be a winning run [to move over], he would bunt. Everybody looked for the home run, you know, but he was a good team man. And was well-liked by everybody." Upon quitting, Pipgras became a big league umpire for 11 years, then scouted for the Red Sox, and finally taught umpiring in the minors.

"The mass of men lead lives of quiet desperation" wrote Thoreau in a famous passage in *Walden* (8). This might be true for much of beleaguered humanity, but most ballplayers seem to have been exempt from this affliction of the soul, at least as far as their lives in baseball were concerned. Certainly this was true of George Pipgras and other old Yankees.

In answer to the question, If you had it to do all over again, would you play baseball? the answer is a unanimous yes. That's not the kind of affirmation you would get from many others past the age of, say, 50. Maybe its the adulation of the crowd, or the physical grace and team effort so notably a part of baseball, or earning good money by playing a game learned as a child. Perhaps these are what set ballplayers aside from the often humdrum existence of most people.

Whatever the reason, George Pipgras's answer to the question sums up how he, and so many other old ballplayers, felt about their profession. "I loved the game," said this fine old Yankee a year or so before he died on October 19, 1986. "I'd rather throw that ball than eat."

Upon their return to New York on July 26, the Yanks welcomed the Browns for three more days of divertissement. And for the answer to the question caustically posed around the league: When will the Browns win one from the Yanks?

Games 12 and 13 were played on July 26, 1927. Pain and travail continued for the Browns as the Yankees took both ends of the twin-bill, 15–1 and 12–3. Ruth walloped two homers; he was at No. 33. Gehrig, now affectionately called "Buster" by the press, hit No. 32. Ruether won the opener, Hoyt the second. The Yankees were 69–26 for a .726 PCT; Gehrig led the league with a .394 BA; Ruth was third with a mere .376; Meusel lagged a with piddling .368. Of such statistics are happy managers made.

On July 27, 1927, the 14th game ended with the score Yankees 4, Browns 1. Buster tied Babe with No. 33, as Lazzeri joined the carefree proceedings with No. 14, and Pennock set down the Browns in consecutive order in seven of nine innings. A paltry three balls were hit out of the infield in those first seven innings.

Yankees 9, Browns 4 was the score on July 28, as Babe passed Lou with No. 34. Urban Shocker was the winning pitcher: the win was the Yankees' 15th in a row from the Browns. But St. Louis left town on an upbeat note: upon consulting the schedule they found they did not have to meet the Yankees again for a month.

Cleveland came to town on the July 29 to win 6–4, then dropped a doubleheader on the July 30, 7–3 and 5–0. In the opener Lou busted No. 34

and 35 to go ahead of Babe. Ruether won the first, Hoyt the second. The word "bargain" doesn't adequately describe Gehrig's worth to the Yanks in 1927; he was inflicting all this mayhem on pitchers for $8,000 for the season.

At the end of July, Gehrig was hitting .389; Ruth was .377; Meusel was at .362: Combs .338; and Lazzeri .316. The team batting average was a robust .314. Hug, in a surge of untypical optimism, estimated that his men would take the pennant with 100 wins.

It was during this time of joyous excess that a kid named Michael Sheehy appeared one day at Yankee Stadium.

Stand outside the players entrance of a major league ballpark and you'll see them: the autograph hounds and idol worshipers waiting to catch a glimpse of their muscular heroes, close up and palpable, a mere arm's length away. They are there, these adulating young, even in our TV-dominated culture where cameras and commentators casually, sometimes mercilessly, strip away much of the mythic aura that once surrounded great ballplayers. At 16, Michael Joseph "Pete" Sheehy was a hero worshiper outside Yankee Stadium one summer afternoon in 1927.

"I used to come up to the ball game...and I used to stand outside the clubhouse and watch the players go in," said Pete in an October 3, 1984, interview with the author at Yankee Stadium. "One day—I must have been early—the old feller that was in charge here [Fred Logan] came out and asked if I was goin' to the game. I told him yes. So he says, 'Do you want to come in and give me a hand, and I'll save you money.'" Pete smiled at the recollection. Dear God, would he like to come in! "So I went in and gave him a hand, and he asked me, 'Will you be around tomorrow?' I said, 'Yes, I'll make it my business.'"

Pete made it his business not only the next day, but for every working day the rest of his long life. From that unexpected free admission the man and the job found each other, and another Yankee saga was born. A kid of all work Pete cleaned the clubhouse on game days, ran errands, supplied the great Ruth with bicarb, and more ordinary mortals with snacks, soft drinks, and coffee. On becoming equipment manager in 1945, he assigned uniforms and numbers to the great and the since forgotten, looked after bats and gloves that souvenir hunters would give blood and treasure for, attended to the numerous tasks that make a clubhouse habitable and a haven for players. He was part of Yankee triumphs and celebrations, privy to inner-sanctum rages and discontents.

"What you see here, what you hear here, let it stay here when you leave here" is baseball's clubhouse credo. Sheehy never violated that

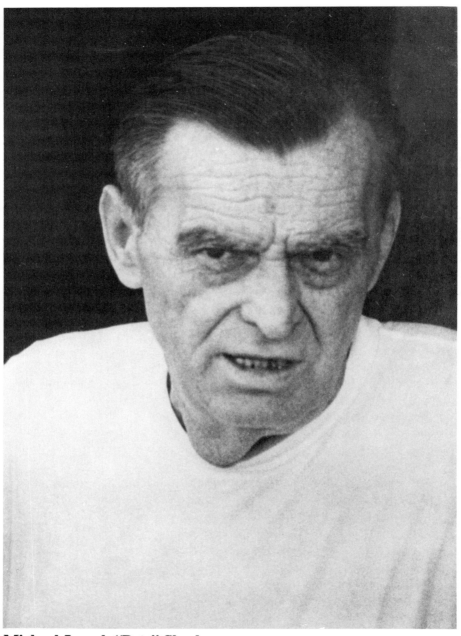

Michael Joseph "Pete" Sheehy   *Photo courtesy of the New York Yankees.*

injunction. Although christened Michael Joseph, around the clubhouse he became known as "Silent Pete"—and finally, just Pete—because of his immutable discretion. He never spoke ill of a player, including those whose characters were less than exemplary. For over half a century players confided in him, vented their frustrations to him, depended on him as a good listener. Pete was their friend for all seasons.

In the October 3, 1984, interview, he wistfully recalled the relaxed pace of baseball in the 1920s. "In those days they played only day ball. [The players] were home every night at 6 o'clock for supper. They spent all night with their wives." (Pete could be forgiven this generalization. He was only 16 when he came to the Yankees, and 16 then wasn't what 16 is now.) "They lived up the street. They'd have eight or ten hours of sleep, get up the next morning and have a big breakfast, and come to the ballpark." Expanded leagues and coast-to-coast air trips have changed the way players live. "Today," Pete sighed, "everything is a rat race."

There were convivial exceptions to the relaxed, domestic scene Pete described. He grinned impishly at one bygone social arrangement of the Prohibition '20s. After a game, "Most of the players, they all went in different directions. Unless somebody made a fresh batch of home brew. We used to have a trainer, I think he used to make some home brew in those days, and he'd invite the players over." More than 50 years later, Pete, ever the prudent one, wouldn't reveal the name of the benevolent braumeister. But the imagination spins blithe fantasies of several Yankee notables of the pre-repeal days hoisting steins of homemade suds in defiance of the Prohibition laws.

Of some of the 1927 team Pete recalled, "Huggins never said much.... He was such a lovable little person. Everybody loved him." Pete smiled, "He used to tickle me—actually."

The Bible-reading Earle Combs was "one of those fellows who stayed home every night, went to bed early." But Jumping Joe Dugan was an arch reveler. "Dugan was like New York, Joe was great. After he quit Joe opened up a bar. He didn't study for the priesthood, Joe."

Tony Lazzeri was "mischievous, pulling gags on players, a prankster." Then, as an aside, "Of course, when they went on the road you never knew what the hell they did at night."

Of one of the '27 season's memorable events he related, "In those days it was a 3 o'clock game; they never opened the top deck [in the middle of the week]. It was the Wall Street crowd that came up." On September 30, 1927, there were a mere 10,000 fans in the cavernous Stadium when young Pete, sensing that history was about to be made, left the clubhouse for the dugout. Sure enough, the Babe slammed a pitch off the Senators' Tom Zachary into the right field stands.

"I was sitting there in the dugout when he hit his 60th," Pete recalled. "It was no big deal. Next year he might hit 62. Of course, there was a lot of hand shaking." Then he added wryly, images of TV cameras whirring and nationwide hoopla stirring his imagination, "Today it would be a madhouse."

Pete had a wife, two daughters, seven grandchildren, and a house in suburbia, but his true home was Yankee Stadium. In 1977, when they named the Yankee clubhouse "The Pete Sheehy Clubhouse," it was an appropriate tribute to this oldest and most abiding of Yankees. It wasn't happenstance that every year on Old Timers Day the first thing most old Yanks did was to seek out Pete. For Yankees, past and present, were Pete's extended family.

On February 12, 1981, Pete told writer Craig Barnes of the *Williamson Sun-Sentinel*, "I'll retire when they take me out of here." He meant it.

On the evening of July 8, 1985, Pete sat slumped in a chair outside the Yankee clubhouse as the Stadium filled and the teams went through pregame practice. Slight, craggy, he was a tenacious presence even as it was plain that his time was running out. Yet there he sat as pregame commotions swirled around him, as they had since that day in 1927 when, at 16, he first became a Yankee.

Half dozing, barely able to answer a salutation of "Hiya, Pete," he was reluctant to leave his domain. It was here he had found his true metier, the tasks and disciplines that had given joy and meaning to his life. And for all we knew, the psyche of the ballplayer-worshiping kid who stood at the players entrance in 1927 still inhabited the body of the failing 75-year-old man.

Five weeks later, on August 13, 1985, "Silent Pete" Sheehy died, taking with him a treasure trove of baseball history going back to 1927. A history that will never be told.

August 1, 1927

AMERICAN LEAGUE

STANDING OF THE CLUBS.

	Won.	Lost.	P.C.
New York	73	27	.730
Washington	59	39	.602
Detroit	52	44	.542
Philadelphia	51	47	.520
Chicago	50	51	.495
Cleveland	41	59	.410
St. Louis	39	58	.402
Boston	29	69	.296

6

August

Yanks on a roll towards pennant, 17 games ahead of second place A's. Browns have yet to beat them in 1927.

Cleveland defeated the Yankees, 2–1, on August 1, in a rain-shortened game, giving the Indians a split on the four-game series—an admirable, if infrequent accomplishment. Flexing their muscles as they left town, the elated Indians shouted encouragement to the arriving Detroit Tigers. So inspiriting was the sight of a team playing .500 ball against New York that Manush, Heilmann, Gehringer and Co.—future Hall of Fame Tigers all—took heart.

In the four-game split with Detroit, Gehrig hit two into the stands, giving him a total of 37. Though Babe hit No. 35, here it was August, the season more than half gone, and he was runner-up to Lou, a status uncongenial to the King of Swat. Something had to be done about Buster, the question was when. And how many.

As Chicago arrived at the Stadium on August 6, the Yankees were 13 ahead in the won column. But ace pitcher Ted Lyons, unintimidated by the standings, beat the Hugmen 6–3. The loss, the fifth out of the last nine, activated singular anxieties in Jake Ruppert's nervous system and alarm among Yankee rooters. But apprehension eased when the Yankees beat Chicago 4–3, and headed for a one-game stand in Philadelphia.

Alas, on August 9 they were bashed by the A's, 8–1; the sole Yank tally was Lou's No. 38. As for Babe, he was hitless for the third game in a row, an implausible and uncommon state of affairs. The next day, August 10, in D.C., in what was, by Senator boosters, talked up as the first of four crucial games, Babe took charge. In the top of the first he drove in Combs with a single; in the third he hit No. 36 to drive in three more, sufficient for a 4–3 win for New York and Waite Hoyt, with help from the ever-willing Moore in the the sixth.

So aggravated by Babe's rude assault on their optimism were Senators fans, that they relieved their animosities by castigating umpire Clarence Rowland for irksome calls on two borderline pitches. Threats and imprecations assailed the beleaguered Rowland, and he had to be escorted from the ballpark by the cops. Even in 1927 the rule of law had its limits in the nation's capital.

August 11 saw Washington win in the eleventh inning, 3–2, when Mark Koenig took a relay from Ruth, revved up his robust arm, and threw the ball to a startled fan in a seat behind third base. A run was scored, earning the Senators the game, and Mark some pungent observations from both dugouts. But the Yankees won the next two, 6–3 and 6–2, making it three out of four for the "crucial" series, and cooling unbridled expectations in the American League.

During the White Sox games Joe Dugan returned to play third, territory he owned since becoming a Yankee in midseason of 1922. Despite a trick knee that sometimes locked and sent him despondently limping to the bench, and a recently sprained ankle, he was still a famously gifted third baseman.

Joseph Anthony Dugan was born in the coal-country town of Mahonoy City, Pennsylvania, on May 12, 1897, five years before there was an American League or the Yankees. When he was 15 months old the Dugans moved to Winstead, Connecticut, and it was in New England that Joe grew up and played ball. By the time he was a high school junior, in nearby New Haven, word spread beyond the Nutmeg State that this kid had good hands and could hit. One person who got the message was Connie Mack.

Dinner at the Dugan household must have resembled a communal clambake, what with Joe, his parents, and seven brothers and two sisters at the table. One evening the doorbell rang. Mrs. Dugan opened the door and saw a tall, lean, kindly looking stranger. Was Joseph home? the man asked. In a February 12, 1970, interview with John Buckley of the *Worcester Evening Gazette,* Dugan recalled, "I got up from the table and almost fainted. It was Connie Mack."

Cornelius McGillicuddy didn't mince words: he wanted Joe to play for the A's. To encourage the young man he did what has been customary and pertinent in baseball negotiations—although today in much larger denominations. "Mack reached into his pocket and put five $100 bills on the table in front of my father, a poor workingman who had never seen a sawbuck in his life." There was no contract, all Connie wanted was the promise that when Joe came of age he would join the A's.

"My father looked at the money," said Joe. "He couldn't contain himself. He said, 'For $500 you can take the whole family!'"

After high school Dugan spent a year at the College of the Holy Cross, played semipro ball, and in 1917, at age 20, joined the A's as a shortstop. For a guy who became a good hitter (.280 is his lifetime BA), Dugan's debut was distressing. He broke in against the Red Sox in a Fenway Park

Joseph Anthony Dugan   *Photo courtesy of New York Yankees.*

doubleheader, faced Carl Mays and Ernie Shore—both tough pitchers—and went 0–8. The next day, against Dutch Leonard, he was 0–4. And in the final, facing Ruth (yes, the same Ruth, in his pitching days), he was 0–4 again. "Mr. Mack," Joe asked plaintively, "are they all like this?"

Connie reassured his bewildered rookie: "Don't worry, they'll get easier as you go along." There was more big league wisdom for Joe to learn when the A's went to Chicago. There, Joe was confronted by top spitballer and future Hall of Famer Urban "Red" Faber. "Here am I," Joe told Jack McCarthy, writing in the *Boston Herald-American,* February 4, 1977, "a little innocent guy from Holy Cross, and the first pitch comes up and hits me in the cap. He turned my cap around!" As Joe walked to first he wrathfully shouted at Faber, "What's that for?"

"Respect," snapped Faber.

Learning deference to pitchers didn't help Joe's batting average, though in later years he became a formidable auxiliary to "Murderers' Row." For his first two seasons with the A's he hit a paltry .195. Respect, however, should be mutual, among ballplayers no less than the rest of us, and Dugan soon earned it with his bat. In 1919 he hit .271; in 1920 he reached a .322 career high; in 1921 his mark was .295. Dugan's batting average as a Yankee was .286. And pitchers, Faber included, thought twice about revolving Joe's cap with a knockdown pitch.

Some fans, and even a few sports writers, assumed Dugan got his nickname of "Jumping Joe" because of infield acrobatics. Not so. Although Joe liked Connie Mack ("He was a wonderful gentleman. I always thought Connie Mack should have been a parish priest" [Buckley interview]). During Joe's five years with the A's the team—which Dugan tagged "Connie's Bloomer Girls"—was an habitual cellar-dweller. In perversely un-Quakerlike behavior, the Philadelphia fans took out their frustrations on the players by booing and catcalling them mercilessly.

To escape the harassment and soothe his frazzled ego, Dugan, when the spirit moved him, "jumped" the team, taking off for parts unknown and private capers. Upon his return Connie always took him back with fatherly admonitions to behave, stay put, and play ball. But the fans kept booing, Dugan kept jumping, and the nickname stuck. For the rest of his life Joseph Anthony was known as "Jumping Joe." In 1922, in a slickly maneuvered deal, Dugan was sold to the Boston Red Sox, who promptly and obligingly dealt him to the Yankees. It was a match made in heaven—with an assist from that shrewdest of deal makers, Ed Barrow.

According to John Kieran, writing in the *New York Tribune* of June 17, 1923, Joe announced breezily on joining the Yankees. "I'm here to stay. The only way they'll get me off this team is to throw me off," which the Yankees weren't about to do. For Dugan arrived in time to plug a large gap at third, and hit .286 in the final 60 games of the season. That year he was the deciding factor in New York's pennant victory by one game over the Browns. During Joe's tenure at third the Yankees won four more pennants and three World Series. His often spectacular playing was a key reason for those victories.

In his seven outstanding Yankee years Joe leaped, dove, scrambled, and threw as if born and raised at the hot corner. The Yanks would have some fine third basemen in later years—Rolfe, Boyer, Nettles—but none was better than "Jumping Joe." In his day it was commonly agreed he was the best third-sacker the Yanks had had since their start in 1903.

Huggins said of him, "In the list of present day players Joe Dugan is first, second, and third. He can run, catch, hit, and throw." Then Hug added, "Outside of that he is practically useless on my ball club." The *New York World* of June 24, 1923, reinforced Hug's assessment with a snappy ditty.

> Where Haney misses, Dugan spears 'em,
> Where Lutzke fumbles, Dugan smears 'em.
> Where Kamm falls down and lets them go,
> They're in the mitt of Jumping Joe.

In 1925 Dugan wrenched his knee when sliding into third. After surgery (chancier in the '20s than it is today), and six weeks on his back, he was told he could play again. But he now had a trick knee that could shorten his career—and Dugan knew it. Interviewed by John Ward in *Baseball Magazine,* November 1927, he said, "Baseball has been good to me, but you can't bank too much on good fortune. That bum knee...taught me the uncertainties of the game. Some little slip and you're liable to be out of it for good. So I try to make hay while the sun shines."

Fortunately the sun shone on him long enough so he could play a vital role on the 1927 team, and the almost-as-good 1928 club. But by 1929 it was plain that Joe Dugan was about finished. When he was released to the Boston Braves, it was a sad move: in a few months he went from the greatest of ball clubs to what was then the worst.

He appeared in only 60 games for the last place Braves, didn't play at all in 1930, played a final eight games with Detroit in 1931 as his knee popped in and out of place, and at the age of only 33 he hung up his spikes.

For awhile Dugan ran a bar and grill in New York, a misguided enterprise for a man with a penchant for drinkable alcohol. After failing as a saloon keeper he did some scouting for the Boston Red Sox, but never settled into a sound and lasting post-baseball career. However, he seemed to get along comfortably. Dugan showed up at Old Timers games, there to extol to receptive reporters the outstanding Yankee teams he played on, and the great players of his era. Not least, he praised his close friend and associate in extracurricular activities, Babe Ruth.

The Babe, Joe always insisted, was No. 1. Better than Cobb, who, Dugan pointed out, wasn't a good fielder (which Ruth in his prime was), and couldn't throw well (which Ruth could). And—as a clincher—Babe had been a first-rate pitcher before shifting to the outfield. Furthermore, since Ruth could down and hold large quantities of beer, to Dugan that put Babe in a special category of humankind.

At 84 Joe was a frail old man, "waiting for the man upstairs," he said, to call him to his eternal reward in some baseball Valhalla. His reflexes were faded. He couldn't hear well. His once agile legs, those supple underpinnings that had enabled him to play so spectacularly, were weary and tottering. When the spirit moved him (which was often) "Jumping Joe" would spend a few hours at Irish Heaven, a cozy pub near his Norwood, Massachusetts, home.

There he warmed his frail body with a spot or two, and told tales of his Yank days among fabled players. And if one or two of his stories were outsized and burnished with blarney, that was forgivable. For this old man was talking of the greatest of clubs, in a great season. And he had been part of it. In his prime it was written of Joe Dugan in the *New York World* of June 24, 1923, "He can throw out of a cellar. He can throw from a running high jump seven feet in the air. He can fling 'em side arm from one-hand bunt pickups, or he can wing 'em overhand when the situation demands blazing speed. And they're on the pin."

And were beautiful to see. Joe Dugan passed away at 85 on July 7, 1982.

Comiskey Park, home of the Chicago White Sox, was built as a model of symmetry in compliance with owner Charley Comiskey's equipoised state of mind. This is in marked contrast to many old ballparks. In 1927 Comiskey Park measured 365 feet to the right field stands, 375 feet in the power alleys, 455 feet to center, 365 feet to left. On August 16, 1927, Ruth walloped an Alphonse Thomas fast ball over the double-decked right field stands, out of the park, out of sight, out of the realm of the impossible. Where the ball landed on its spectacular journey for Babe's No. 37 nobody ever knew. But it was the first time anybody ever drove one out of that harmoniously proportioned ballpark. The Yankees won, 8–1, as Babe, a versatile fellow, also doubled, walked twice, and threw a perfect strike from far left field to nail a venturesome fellow named Flaskamper at home.

The next day Babe struck out twice to the raucous taunts of Chicago fans seeking consolation in small events. But on the August 17 he broke a 2–2 impasse with No. 38, tying Gehrig and sending the fans and athletes to the exits. The Yankees won 5–4 on August 18, putting them 16 games ahead of second place Washington, with Detroit and Philadelphia 18 games behind and jostling for third.

The sad truth that nobody would catch the Yanks was sinking in around the league: even overindulgent optimists knew it. Now it was a matter of transitory distinction to beat them once in a while. Chicago finally won a game, 3–2, and bid the Hugmen good riddance. Ruth tied Gehrig with No. 39 on August 20 as the Yanks were shellacked 14–8 by Cleveland. Ruether, Shawkey, Thomas, and Giard were the Yank pitchers in the trouncing, as Hug mused on life's uncertainties and the vagaries of pitchers. Giard, obtained from the Browns at the end of 1926, was no prize. In 16 games in 1927 he would be 0–0, with an 8.00 ERA. His brief moment of glory came on August 26 in Detroit. With nobody out and the bases loaded, Giard arrived from the bullpen, got two men out on a double play (one pitch), and a third out when Fothergill was caught stealing (second pitch). Then he started a four-run Yank rally with a single. At which point—not a man to push his luck—Huggins removed the euphoric Giard. Alas, after the 1927 season Giard was permanently gone from the majors. But for the rest of his life he comforted himself that he had been part of a baseball epic.

To joy unrestrained in six other cities around the American League, New York lost two more to Cleveland, making it the first time in 1927 that the Yankees dropped four straight, and the first time any team swept them. But, despite the exhilaration among Yankee loathers, those who bothered to read the standings noted that Hug's club was still first by a healthy 14 games.

Meanwhile Detroit was riding a streak of its own, 13 wins in a row, the longest in Tiger history to that time, putting them in second, a game ahead of the A's. On August 24 the Yanks made short shrift of Detroit's 13 straight, and stopped their own run of four losses. With the score 5–5 in the ninth, and two out, Combs walked and waited, Koenig sacrificed him to second, and Ruth's fly to deep center moved Earle to third. Tiger hurler Ownie Carroll, ensnared in a dilemma common to pitchers of the time, walked Gehrig and Meusel to load the bases. Up came Tony Lazzeri, the day's personification of "Five O'Clock Lightning," who slammed the ball over the fence. Final score, 9–5 Yanks. Winning pitcher, Wilcy Moore.

The Yankees won two more from Detroit as Lou, on August 25, hit his 40th to tie the Babe. The best Ruth could accomplish in Detroit was a triple with the bases loaded on August 26, a stimulating event but not what the customers paid to see him do. Pennock and Hoyt were the winning pitchers as statisticians noted that the Yanks were yet to be shut out. If they could avoid this indignity for the remaining 33 games, it would be a first since Abner Doubleday didn't invent baseball.

St. Louis, home of the hospitable Browns, was next on the Yankee westward swing.

The score was Yanks 14, Browns 4, on August 27, 1927, in their 16th encounter of the season. Ruth hit No. 41 over the right field stands, out of the park. He also tripled, Meusel and Combs homered, as Hoyt won his 18th. St. Louis tried to curtail their agony by offering to move a game up, by one day, and play a doubleheader. Huggins politely refused, saying, "They can't get rid of us so easily."

On August 28, 1927, the Yankees beat the Browns 10–6. Ruth hit his No. 42 to move two ahead of Gehrig. Shocker took over from Ruether, and was credited with the win. Shocker would beat the Browns four times in 1927, a year of triumph, but a prelude to tragedy for Urban Shocker.

On August 29, 1927, in their eighteenth meeting, the score was Yanks 8, Browns 3, as Lou walloped No. 41. Pennock was the winner. Babe was large, round, and had skinny legs, but he could go get 'em: he made six great catches in left field.

Urban James Shocker began his baseball career as a catcher with semipro teams in Michigan and Canada, which was a waste of a great arm and a brain finely attuned to the strategies of pitching. Windsor, of the long defunct Border League, was his first stop with a pro team: there, while catching, a ball broke the third finger of his right hand. When the finger healed, Shocker found he had a hook at the last joint, a not uncommon result from a catching injury and a boon to the righty Urban.

"That broken finger may not be pretty to look at but has been very useful to me," Shocker told F.C. Lane in a lengthy interview published in *Baseball Magazine*, January 1921. Describing his hooked finger as "useful" was an understatement. For when he switched from catching to pitching, it enabled him to add another baffling pitch to his inventory of deliveries. This included a spitter, for Urban was a spitball pitcher when the spitter was legal, when a moistened ball didn't have to be thrown by a hurler acting like a thief in the night. To have heard Shocker tell it, more pitchers should have broken, badly healed fingers on their pitching hands to succeed in the majors. "It hooks over a baseball just right so that I can get a fine break on my slow ball, and that's one of the best balls I throw," he said, speaking fondly of the irregular digit. "I can get a slow ball to drop just like a spitter, and as I occasionally use a true spitter you will find

Urban James Shocker   Photo courtesy of the New York Yankees.

players all over the league talking about my slow spitter, which isn't a spitter at all, but a slow ball with a freak break."

Then Shocker, an amusing fellow, added in the F.C. Lane interview, "Perhaps if I broke some of my other fingers I could get the ball to roll over sideways or maybe jump up in the air." Such drastic measures weren't necessary. Shocker's record in only 12 full years in the American League was 187–117, for a .615 PCT and a 3.17 ERA, percentages better than some Hall of Famers sport. He would probably have entered the Pantheon but for his lamentably shortened career.

For most of his time in the majors Shocker played for American League teams who had no shot at a pennant—the pre-Huggins Yanks and, except for 1922 when the Browns were contenders down to the last day, St. Louis. Indeed, Shocker never had a losing season. Until the sudden and tragic end of his life he was an outstanding pitcher, a bane to batters, esteemed by his manager and teammates.

Shocker came to the majors in 1916 as a Yankee, and had a 4–3 mark as the team finished fourth. In 1917 he went 8–5 with a sixth-place Yankee club. Then he became the centerpiece of one of Miller Huggins's few trading goofs, one that gave Hug periodic headaches for the next seven years.

The club Miller took over in 1918 had, among other shortcomings, an infield that leaked baseballs through the right side. Hug knew that the Yanks wouldn't get to first place without a good second baseman. He also knew where to obtain one; over in St. Louis Del Pratt was available.

Pratt covered the territory expertly, was a solid hitter (lifetime .292), and did not like the town, the team, or the owner. So Hug made his first big trade, sending four players of minimal talents, plus Urban Shocker, for Pratt and pitcher Eddie Plank. Plank, a great pitcher with a dead arm (327–193, Hall of Fame in 1946), promptly retired; Pratt plugged the leak at second; Shocker became one of baseball's best hurlers, and a plague to the Yanks.

With his crooked-finger curves, his spitter, and a good fast ball, Urban was 6–5 in 1918, his first Brown season, and 13–11 in 1919. Not that it did the Browns much good: both years they ended in fifth place. Then, in 1920, despite a Browns' fourth place finish, Shocker reached his more normal level with a 20–10 mark. In compiling those numbers he took pleasure in beating the Hugmen; in particular, he enjoyed regularly striking out Ruth.

In a 1920 game at the Polo Grounds (then the Yanks' home park), before 40,000 fans, he whiffed Babe three times as Hug wondered what had possessed him to give up this skilled hurler. Still, experience taught Shocker never to take the Bambino for granted.

"I was pitching against Babe Ruth in St. Louis," Urban remembered in the *Baseball Magazine* story, "and I had him puffing and blowing and swinging in wide circles. Twice I had his number on a little teasing slow ball that came floating up to him, grinned in his face, and then dove head first under his bat." But the next time up, Babe "got that slow ball...and somehow drove it on a line to the far bleachers and right through a wire screen without stopping."

There were no computers in Shocker's day. Players and managers had to do without all those stats flooding from electronic number-crunchers, so Shocker relied on intense and constant study of batters to keep him in the win column. "You can tell very often what is in a batter's mind by the way he shifts his feet or hitches his belt or wiggles his bat," said Shocker. And there were the box scores to give him an idea of what strategies other teams were following.

How much were they sacrificing? Were they trying to steal? Who was blasting the ball? Who was striking out, or grounding out, or hitting long fly balls that usually ended up in the outfielder's glove as he backed against the fence? For players like Shocker, pitching was serious business; studying box scores was part of his pitcher's survival plan.

In 1921 Shocker led the American League with a 27–12 record. In 1922, the year the Browns fought the Yanks for the pennant down to the last day, he was 24–17; in 1923, 20–12; in 1924, 16–13. And though the Yanks were flag-winners from 1921 to 1923, Huggins made no secret of the fact that he wanted Shocker in New York. If for no other reason than to spare Hug the indignity of being often beaten by Urban, no matter what kind of club St. Louis had.

Finally, in 1925 Hug got his nemesis back in the Yank dugout. It cost him three pitchers (Joe Bush, Milt Gaston, and Joe Giard) to make the deal, but it was a sweet one for the Yanks, even though the pitcher they were getting was seriously ill with heart trouble.

We think of Hoyt and Pennock as the hurling mainstays of the 1927 Yanks, of Wilcy Moore as their great reliever. But Urban Shocker was worthy company for them. In 1925, toiling with a collapsing Yank team, Shocker was 12–12 with a 3.65 ERA, the only time he came near to a losing season. In 1926, with the Yankees the flag-winner, he was an impressive 19–11 with a 3.38 ERA. And with the 1927 club—his condition deteriorating, his days numbered—Shocker's record was an outstanding 18–6, his ERA was 2.84, his PCT 750. It was his farewell to baseball, a remarkable achievement considering his condition, for he would die the next year.

Shocker contracted heart disease, probably sometime around 1925, but only close friends knew it. By Christmas of 1927, his impressive season behind him, Urban was a very sick man. Weighing only 115 pounds, he was fighting for his life. He knew he'd never again take a regular turn on the mound. But he had unfinished business to take care of, and how he did it says a great deal about the man's grit. Urban held a legitimate, long-standing grievance against the Yankees, and he wanted it righted. So he returned his unsigned 1928 contract to the team, and waited.

Nobody contacted him. When he skipped 1928 spring training he was automatically suspended. Neither Huggins nor Ed Barrow seemed upset. In May Shocker rejoined the team saying he had signed, would work into shape and get ready to pitch. Then, while pitching batting practice at Comiskey Park, he collapsed. At his and the club's request, the reporters who saw him pass out did not write about it. After that he took the mound just once, pitched two scoreless innings of relief against the Senators, and never pitched again.

According to a February 15, 1957, *New York Journal-American* story by Bill Corum, around July 4, 1928, Shocker received a slip of paper from the Yankees on which was written, "You are hereby notified as follows. That you are unconditionally released."

"I've had a bum heart for some time," he told Corum. "You've seen me sitting up late at night in my Pullman berth. I couldn't lie down. Choked when I did." Shocker then revealed that he had visited Huggins about two months before.

Did Hug know about his bad heart? he was asked.

"Oh sure."

"And he signed you. Why?"

"When Hug got me from the Browns a few years ago he promised to pay me fifteen hundred for moving expenses. But he couldn't get it from the front office." It seemed that Barrow wouldn't authorize the payment. When Hug offered to pay the money out of his own pocket, Shocker refused to take it.

"I wanted it from the club," he said smiling. "It took me nearly four years, but I got it. My July 1 check squares the promise." Then he added, tapping his chest, "I'm going to Denver to fight this thing."

He had little left to fight with. On September 9, 1928, Urban Shocker died of heart disease complicated by pneumonia. He was 38.

They did an autopsy on him and found that his heart was half again as large as a normal one, which should have been no surprise to anyone. For what Urban Shocker accomplished in his last Yankee years—with the knowledge of his mortality hanging over him—took not only his superb skills, but lots of heart to go with them.

For the last game in August the Yanks met their chums from Fenway Park, and blasted them and future Yankee great Charley Ruffing, 10–3. Lazzeri socked two homers with strict impartiality as to location: the first went into the left-field bleachers, the second among the right-field customers. Babe weighed in with No. 43, and Pipgras, pitching to Benny Bengough, his preferred catcher, went the distance for the win.

It was Bengough who helped cure Pipgras of his wildness. "He was like a box back there," said Pipgras of Bengough, in a 1985 interview with the author. "He couldn't throw very good after he hurt his arm, but he was a great receiver." Benny, a Yank since 1923, became first string receiver in 1925, taking over the job the same day Gehrig replaced Pipp. After his arm went dead in the spring of 1926, Bengough rode the bench into July. Hot weather revived the arm: he caught until one deplorable day in late September when pitcher George Uhle of Cleveland threw at his head.

September 1, 1927

AMERICAN LEAGUE

STANDING OF THE CLUBS.

	Won.	Lost.	P.C.
New York	89	37	.706
Philadelphia	72	54	.571
Detroit	68	56	.548
Washington	67	57	.540
Chicago	59	64	.430
Cleveland	55	70	.440
St. Louis	49	75	.395
Boston	39	85	.315

"I put my arm up to protect myself," he told baseball historian Larry Ritter in an unpublished interview. "It [the ball] hit my arm and poked the bone right through and hit my forehead." Every year thereafter Bengough was able to catch and throw only when hot weather arrived, but he never again was the exceptional first-string receiver of 1925. Third string in 1927, he was a smart, dependable alternate for Collins and Grabowski.

As the days shortened towards autumn, New York was in first place by 17 games over Philadelphia. Eleven more and they would clinch their fifth flag in seven years. "Life," the celebrated Justice Oliver Wendell Holmes said an 1884 Memorial Day address, "is action and passion." For Yankees and Yankee fans, basking in the late summer euphoria of a remarkable season, it was also delightful.

7

September

Babe wallops his way to a record 60, but Lou outranks him with .373 BA and 175 RBIs, Yanks finish with record 110–44 won-lost, 19 games ahead of second place Philadelphia.

With the American League race nonexistent, and prospects bleak for clubs north and west of the Hudson, a lament arose in certain provinces where big league baseball was played. It would be heard many times in future years as the Yankee dynasty flourished into the mid-1960s. In particular the wail emanated from Phil Ball, tightwad owner of the seventh place Browns, and Bill Carrigan, tormented manager of the cellar-dwelling Red Sox.

"Break up the Yankees!" was the substance of that cry, one of those shrill demands for leveling and equality-by-dictate that has been the bane of excellence since the human race came down from the trees. Though the plaint awakened sympathy in Jake Ruppert's heart, and Ed Barrow concentrated on counting gate receipts and questing for ballplayers, neither of them made the slightest gesture towards parceling out men named Ruth or Lazzeri or Gehrig to rival teams. How much more diverting it was for the Colonel and his associates to see the Hugmen on a juggernaut roll through the league.

The Athletics returned from a trip westward where they won 12 out of 14 games, thus stimulating visions of whittling down the overachieving Yankee lead to a more tolerable number, understandable for a team that had been the cynosure of the press back in April. But this was September 2, a day of truth in the Quaker City, as the Yanks bashed the A's 12–2. Ruth smacked No. 44; Gehrig hit No. 42 and 43, Combs went 4 for 6, including his specialty, a triple.

Hoyt was the winner, with Tharon Leslie Collins—dependable receiver, O.K. hitter, sometime roomie of the Babe—catching.

Tharon Leslie Collins   *Photo courtesy of the New York Yankees.*

Collins was the No. 1 Yankee catcher in 1927, though he needed plenty of help because of a strained righty throwing arm. Yet he played in 92 games (Grabowski appeared in 70 games, Bengough in 31), and threw out his share of impetuous base runners. Pat came up to the majors from the Browns, where he played from 1919 to 1926.

It was with St. Louis that he made the *Official Baseball Record Book* with a bizarre entry. On June 8, 1923, playing against the A's, Pat pinch-hit and pinch-ran in the same game, a neat trick and a challenge to future generations of trivia buffs. It happened this way.

Homer Ezzell of the Browns got on first safely in the second inning, and was shaken up. Whereupon the Browns asked Connie Mack for permission to use a "courtesy runner," allowed in those days. Since the runner was to be the sloth-footed Collins, O.K. said the obliging Connie. When the inning ended Ezzell felt better, and he went back to his position on third base. But Collins, the "courtesy runner" (what an odd designation for a ballplayer), was still eligible to play. In the ninth Collins pinch-hit for hurler Ray Kolp, drew a walk, and was replaced by Cedric Durst. This multiple subbing in one game never happened before, it hasn't happened since, and it isn't likely to happen again. You can look it up.

Collins caught for the three Yankee pennant winners, 1926–28, but never for a complete season. When the exceptional Bill Dickey came up for his first full season in 1929, Collins was sold to the Red Sox, where he played only seven games before dropping from the majors to play with several minor league clubs. He retired from baseball in 1932.

On May 20, 1960, Collins died in his sleep, at age 63, in his Kansas City home.

Overexertion from swinging bats and running the base paths temporarily enervated the Yankees. On September 3 the masterful Lefty Grove pacified Hug's marauders with a 1–0 four-hitter beautiful to behold. The first and only time the Yanks were shut out that season, it was appropriate that a great pitcher brought off the small miracle. At the end of the game 25,000 Philadelphians so shook the heavens with their cheering, one would have thought Mack's club has just won the pennant instead of being mired in second place by 17 games. But it was understandable: under the circumstances who would deny the A's fans their small pleasures?

The Boston Red Sox were firmly implanted in eighth place as the Yanks arrived in Fenway Park for a September 5 doubleheader, brandishing their averages and eyeing the bleachers in that gem of an old ballpark, long may it stand. Word had reached the cradle of American culture that two fellows named Ruth and Gehrig were locked in a fierce competition to see who could hit the most baseballs into the seats. On that steamy day all roads led to Fenway.

Some 36,000 Bostonians jammed the park, and spilled onto the playing area, as the cops were called to clear the field before game time. Another 15,000 packed the streets of America's Athens, hammered at the locked Fenway gates, denied and frustrated. What the unfortunates missed was an afternoon of unforeseen events.

With a fury born of season-long affliction the heretofore supine Sox beat up on Pipgras, Giard, and Shawkey to lead 8–6 going into the ninth. In the top of the ninth the Yankees tied the score, Moore came in for New York, the struggle went into extra innings. The Yanks pushed across three runs in the top of the 17th, but the tenacious Sox were undaunted. In the home half they tied the game with three, knocked out Wilcy, and chastised Hoyt. The crowd wilted in the heat, ice cream melted to sugary goo, peanuts and crackerjacks were in short supply, as the Red Sox ended the marathon with a run in the bottom of the 18th to win 12–11.

So did the doormat club of the league take vengeance on the team ahead of them by a full 50 games in the standings. Gehrig hit 4 for 6 in the endurance contest, one of them his No. 44 to tie the Babe who got a lone double in seven at-bats. Mercifully for the athletes, and those baseball-addicted still in the park, darkness descended after five innings of the second game, and the umps sent everybody home, giving the Yanks a 5–0 triumph. Shocker got the win; Ruth flexed his muscles.

September 6 was breakaway day for Babe. Being locked in a tie with Lou for smiting homers was all very well for the diversion of those who savored innocent competition, but it did nothing for Babe's ego, a component of his character that matched his earthy appetites. On that day, in another doubleheader, the Bambino sent three baseballs into the stands of his old playground.

After Gehrig passed Ruth in the homer race by socking No. 45 in the first game, Babe also slammed one over the centerfield wall. The wall stood 488 feet from home in 1927, so the ball must have gone at least 500 feet. A thing of wonder and beauty, that shot was by common agreement the longest home run ever hit in Fenway Park. Babe followed with another into the right field bleachers in the first game, and in the second game still another into the right field stands. That the Yanks won the first game 14–2, and lost the second 5–2, was secondary to Babe's exploits. The question now confronting America's citizenry was, How many will the Big Fellow hit by season's end?

Part of the answer came on September 7, when Ruth hit No. 48 and 49 in a 12–10 slugfest win over the Red Sox. Babe was now ahead of Lou by four home runs, and aiming at who knew what number in the vicinity of 59, the record he set in 1921. So ended the final Yankee road game of the season, and the club headed for a New York social engagement in the grand ballroom of the Hotel Commodore that evening.

The big feed at the Commodore was in honor of Tony Lazzeri, now the pride of New York's large Italian community. There were speeches by Ruth, Gehrig, Huggins, and Colonel Ruppert; Tony was presented with a $1,000 silver service, a striking contrast to the cascade of offerings bequeathed by commercial sponsors and pressed on today's baseball eminences. Lazzeri accepted the gift graciously and prepared to maybe "poosh up" a few the next day.

He didn't, probably out of perplexity and embarrassment, because before the game he was favored with a floral horseshoe wreathe, a gift more appropriate to a horse than a ballplayer. Against the accommodating Browns, Lazzeri struck out twice, (once with the bases loaded), and failed to reach first in five times at bat. Not that it mattered against the athletes from St. Louis, who were on hand at Yankee Stadium, spooked and dazed.

On September 8, 1927, in Yankee Stadium, the Yanks beat the Browns 2–1 for their 19th straight win over their fellow athletes from the Midwest. Ex-Yankee "Sad Sam" Jones held New York to a picayune four hits, but Waite Hoyt, a perverse fellow, upstaged Sad Sam with only three, as the Yanks won again. Hoyt, the perennial "Schoolboy," was at the top of his game.

Game 20 of the season's matchup ended Yankees 9, Browns 3, as Shocker spun a three-hitter. The Yankees needed only two more wins to set a record as the first major league team to win an entire season's series from another club.

Game 21, on September 10, 1927, ended Yanks 1, Browns 0. The valiant loser for St. Louis was Walter Stewart, a good pitcher. Moore was the winner; the Yankees got their lone run in the eighth. Each team got seven hits, Babe and Lou were hitless. Whatever else they were— embarrassed, bedeviled, snake-bit—the Brownies weren't quitters.

With pluck born of desperation and affliction, the St. Louis Browns won the final game of their season's matchup with New York, 6–2, on September 11, 1927. In the fourth inning they rose up and whacked Herb Pennock for four runs, knocked him out of the box and went on to triumph. Milt Gaston, the resplendent winning pitcher, held the Yankees to five hits.

The Browns belonged in the American League after all.

On September 13 the Yankees won both games of a doubleheader from Cleveland as Ruth hit No. 51 and 52. Pipgras won the first, Hoyt the second. How appropriate that Waite Hoyt took that second game. For this was the pennant clincher, the fifth in Yankee history, and Hoyt—along with Ruth, Meusel, Shawkey, and Huggins—had been on all five flag winners, and contributed substantially to each of them.

He was called the Schoolboy, and the name fit. Endowed with an enduring arm, a lively fastball, and a youthful, spirited disposition, he was one of Brooklyn's illustrious gifts to baseball.

Waite Charles Hoyt was born in the Flatbush section of Brooklyn on September 9, 1899, into a show-business family. Ad Hoyt, his father, was a headliner in Hoyt's Minstrels, and like many show-business people a rabid baseball fan. Ad had an accomplished eye for a buck-and-wing, a well-attuned ear for a tender ballad, and the conviction that his son had the makings of a ballplayer. So he became Waite's chief rooter and critic.

Young Hoyt played second base at P.S. 92. When the family moved, he played third base for P.S. 89, chief rival of his former school. Here was the Schoolboy telling J. Taylor Spink of the *Sporting News,* in November 2, 1939, about his comportment in a momentous game between the two Flatbush adversaries. "I was disdainful of my former teammates. I appeared without a uniform, and in an Eton collar. I made four errors. I failed to run out a long fly that dropped. I ruined the game.... Dad booted me home just like Sande booted home Man o' War." (For those unfamiliar with the Sport of Kings in the 1920s, Man o' War was a great horse, Earle Sande the premiere jockey of the time.)

Waite's aching rump, and those four bobbles, made him rethink his relationship with our national pastime. When a friend invited him to join a local sandlot club, Waite asked what position was open. Pitcher, he was told. "I'm just your man," answered the audacious Waite, and from then on he was a pitcher.

As a teenager Hoyt was the star hurler for the sandlot Wyandottes, and, auspiciously, for Erasmus Hall H.S. At Erasmus he pitched three no-hitters in one season, and struck out 24 in one game—all before he was 16. Being a Brooklyn kid, he tried to break into pro ball with the Dodgers, but was cold-shouldered. Fortunately, Giants coach Red Dooin saw Waite pitch, and asked him to report to the Polo Grounds.

Waite did. In fact he reported for days on end, traveling back and forth from Flatbush without getting a tryout from the dictatorial John McGraw. Finally, the hotheaded Waite had enough of the McGraw runaround. "I was a fresh kid," he recalled in the interview with Spink. "I crashed into his office and said, 'I'm tired of working this way. To hell with it.'"

McGraw, startled yet admiring the feisty kid, took an option on Waite's services, with Ad Hoyt signing for his underage son. Waite returned to Erasmus High, his ego appeased, his pro career imminent. In 1916 Ad Hoyt signed a Giants contract for his still underage son for $90 per month, and a $5 bonus. (That's not a typo: an extra $5 is what the 16-year-old Brooklyn phenom got for signing.) He would be known as the Schoolboy for the rest of his career.

Waite Charles Hoyt   *Photo courtesy of the New York Yankees.*

Hoyt bounced around the minors for the next two years, his fastball taking on velocity, his curve becoming sharper. Finally, in 1918, he broke into the majors in the ninth inning of a game between the Giants and Cards, and struck out the Cardinal side. For his sterling performance Waite was promptly shipped to Newark to finish the season. Hoyt went, fuming at John McGraw his bête noire. Soon after, he got into an explosive argument with McGraw, and found out why his skipper was called the Little Napoleon. McGraw, who wouldn't take lip from anyone, sold him to New Orleans.

The incensed Hoyt refused to go. Instead, he quit the majors to pitch for the semipro Baltimore Dry Docks. It was a bitter comedown for the kid the who had signed with a big-league club at the age of 16, had tasted life in organized ball, and knew he had the stuff to be a big league hurler.

He was not a Dry Dock for long. Ed Barrow, then the Boston Red Sox manager, in 1919 gave Waite a tryout and offered him a contract as $600 per month. Hoyt, his recent wandering in the bushes a depressing memory, accepted on condition that Barrow start him within four days. And he wanted the promise in writing, "Barrow got sore at this," Hoyt later remembered, "but he admired my stand. That promise was put into the agreement; on the fourth day I started against the Tigers." He won 2–1 in 13 innings.

It was in that first game, Hoyt told Spink, that "Ty Cobb tried to make a sap out of me by turning his back...at the plate for five minutes. Then he faced me, and I said, 'No you don't.' I walked off the mound and turned my back on the great Cobb. For five minutes. He was fit to be tied. What he called me! But I only grinned and made him wilder." Cobb holds the big league all-time career batting average record of .367; but he was held to a measly career .167 by the nervy Schoolboy. And he never again turned his back on Waite.

Hoyt was a commonplace 4–6 in his first big league season, but one of his losses was a memorable 12-inning game against his future Yankee teammates. On September 24, 1919, he hurled a perfect game from the second through the eleventh inning. Then Wally Pipp tripled, scored on a sacrifice fly by Del Pratt, and that was the game. Unfortunately, Waite's exceptional performance was upstaged by a score-tying Ruth homer, his 29th of the season, topping Ed Williamson's record, set in 1884.

When Ed Barrow became Yankee business manager at the end of the 1920 season, he wasted no time in founding the Yankee dynasty. That year he brought Hoyt and catcher Wally Schang to New York where they joined Ruth, who had arrived the year before. It was a crucial deal for the Yankees.

In addition to Ruth they now had a first-class young righty in Hoyt, an excellent hard-hitting catcher in Schang, as well as Carl Mays, an enormously talented pitcher of unbecoming disposition, who was not above throwing in the vicinity of a batter's head. The result was the first Yankee pennant. Hoyt was 19–13 for the season: in the series he was superb.

He pitched three full games against the Giants and his old adversary, McGraw, in those 27 innings giving up only two runs—both unearned. Matched against Art Nehf in each game, Hoyt and the Yanks won 3–0 and 3–1. But he lost the final of the series, 1–0, when Yank shortstop Roger Peckinpaugh fumbled a grounder in the eighth, allowing Dave Bancroft to score. Hoyt's series ERA was a remarkable 0.00, tying a record set by Christy Mathewson in 1905, and giving McGraw an instructive look at the kid he had scorned, and who was now a great pitcher. Hoyt always considered those three games his greatest pitching achievement.

According to Tom Meany, writing in the *Baseball Digest* of January 1952, Yankee scout Paul Krichell said of the Schoolboy, "Hoyt has all the qualifications to be a good pitcher.... He has a good arm meaning stuff and speed, a smart head which means control, and pitching know-how. And he has guts." When Hoyt heard of Krichell's analysis he smiled and said, "The secret was to get a job with the Yankees and joy-ride on their home runs." Hoyt, in his flip way, was too modest. He was a great clutch hurler who won the big ones and close ones when they counted, which didn't always please his boss, Jake Ruppert, who did not like close games.

The New York Times columnist Arthur Daley reported in an August 23, 1965, story that during a salary squabble with Hoyt, Ruppert berated his star righty. "What's the matter with you Hoyts?" snapped the irate Colonel, characteristically garbling Waite's name. "You win your games 1–0 and 2–1. But my other pitchers win 9–2 and 10–3. Why don't you win games like that?" In the face of the Colonel's bizarre logic even the sassy Hoyt was speechless.

Hoyt was part of the frolicsome crew of Yanks that brought excitement to days at the Stadium, and zest to night life along Broadway. Reminiscing about those days, Hoyt told James Enright in a *Sporting News* article of August 7, 1965, "When the Yanks first became a dynasty it was the middle of the Roaring Twenties...everybody wanted to meet ball players. It was fashionable to say, 'I met so and so last night at such and such night club....' Another thing that is forgotten: then we played strictly day baseball and we had ample time at night to go here and there." So the handsome, elegantly dressed Waite, went "here and there" with Ruth, Meusel, Dugan and Co., often disquieting Miller Huggins.

Yet, there was in Hoyt's life a special influence that surfaced in the spring of 1927. In his unpublished autobiography now in the archives of the Cincinnati Historical Society, Hoyt writes,

> Huggins took an interest in me, and helped me to the best season I ever recorded. In 1927 at St. Petersburg he gave me a long fatherly lecture on concentration. I could, he told me, lead the league in pitching year after year if I would devote myself more seriously to the job.... I knew that Hug was not merely trying to con me into winning a few more ball games.... And for the first time in my life the words began to sink in.
>
> That night, in answer to some mysterious urge I walked far out on the pier at St. Petersburg.... I was conscious suddenly that there was some Power somewhere that had lit the lights of these countless stars and kept them spinning through their appointed orbits, that this same Power had ordered my life too, and that it was meant to be more than baseball, more than today—that I could become something more important than just a ballplayer bent on having fun.... It impelled me to take my job far more seriously.

Whatever the catalyst—Hug's counsel, a mystical revelation—it was probably the beginning of a crucial shift in Hoyt's life. He led the league in 1927 with his 22–7, eventually he would quit drinking, and the hell-raising would diminish. In his tenth season in the majors the Schoolboy became an adult.

Hoyt's won-lost of 23–7 in 1928 surpassed his 1927 mark, but in 1929 he was 10–9, and in 1930 his numbers were 2–2 before being dealt to Detroit. That was a Yankee front-office blunder; if the Yanks believed Hoyt was finished, they were mistaken. He pitched in the majors until 1938, chalking up 70 more wins. His longest stretch, from 1932 to 1937, was with Pittsburgh. But though he gave the best of himself to the Pirates, Waite always thought of himself as a Yankee.

One day in 1933 he was hurling against the Cubs, who the year before had been shellacked four straight in the series by the Yanks. Now the intemperate Cubs bench-jockeys were ferociously riding Hoyt. Finally, Waite had enough. He called time, approached the Chicago dugout, and said contemptuously, "If you guys don't shut up, I'll put on my old Yankee uniform and scare you to death." The Cubbies shut up.

In 1934, though his playing days were running out, Hoyt was still good enough to post a 15–6 mark with the Pirates. Then he began losing his stuff. While with the Dodgers, in 1938, he entered the clubhouse on May 8 and found a telegram on his chair stating that he was released. It took some time before the meaning of the telegram sank in. The underage Schoolboy, whose father had to sign for him with the Giants in 1915, was through.

"Then is when I realized this was the end of a very vital part of my life," he told writer James Enright. "I'd seemingly lost my reason for living the full life I'd enjoyed so much.... It just didn't seem possible that this could happen to me at the age of 38." Fortunately, a new life close to baseball awaited him.

A year before he quit playing Hoyt began doing radio interviews and baseball commentary. His stories and reminiscences of great games and colorful players, particularly his old Yankee teammates, intrigued listeners. In January 1942 Waite was hired to do play-by-play for the Cincinnati Reds and became one of the most popular public personalities in Cincinnati. During rain delays few listeners turned off their radios or, in later years, the TV channel. Instead, they settled back to enjoy Hoyt's beguiling tales of baseball's past, of great games and players and, not least, of the 1920s Yankees.

Hoyt was elected to the Baseball Hall of Fame in 1969, an honor he well deserved. When he died on August 25, 1984, at the age of 84, the old Schoolboy took with him a fund of baseball memories that were irreplaceable. A witty and engaging man, Waite Hoyt was a link with the days when the Yankees moved into the modern era and began their extraordinary string of pennants and World Championships. A premier pitcher, a survivor of a lively, optimistic time in American history, Waite Hoyt was special as a player, and as a pioneering baseball broadcaster.

––––––––––

There was no Yankee letdown after winning the flag. They beat the Indians on September 14 for their 99th victory of the season, lost to them the next day. Chicago arrived, to be trounced 7–2 on September 16 for the 100th Yankee win. Though Ruth hit No. 53 that day, it was Wilcy Moore who set the fans to cheering. Hug's Okie ace started, finished, won a neat seven hitter, and added to his season's legacy by singling in the second inning for his first Stadium hit of the year. Then, for emphasis, Wilcy slugged one into the right field stands for the first and only big-league homer of his career. As for Babe, he was three home runs behind his 1921 record. With 12 games left, six homers would tie the mark, seven would break it. A tough chance: the odds were long, but Ruth's pace was torrid. On September 17 the Yanks won two more from Chicago. Between games, the bleacher customers—who knew class when they saw it—presented Earle Combs with an engraved gold watch and chain, a gift bought with loose-change donations by the fans.

The Yank win total stood at 102, Babe's home run total was 53, and demand for series tickets inundated the Yankee office. The Pirates were in first place in the National League by two games, with the Giants in hot pursuit.

Ruth socked No. 54 on September 18 as the Yankees won two more from the White Sox, making it five straight from Chicago. Bloody and bowed, the Sox left Yankee Stadium looking forward to the tranquillities of winter. Detroit came to town on September 21. They won the first of four games, 6–1, as the Yankees made six errors, the Tigers four, and Ruth hit No. 55. The next day Babe socked No. 56 in the home half of the ninth to drive in Koenig for an 8–7, 105th-game victory. As Ruth, carrying his bat, rounded the bases, a kid leaped from the bleachers, dashed across the field and grabbed one end of the bat. Clutching the talisman the elated youth accompanied the Grand Sorcerer across home plate and into the dugout, as a gaggle of other kids spilled onto the field to join in the uproar.

With six games left to play Ruth needed three homers to tie his record, four to surpass. The Yankee victory equaled the American League season mark set by the Red Sox in 1912. Gehrig, outdistanced in the homer derby, his modest personality submerged in Ruthmania, would not be deprived of his own laurels. Lou drove in two runs to break Babe's 1921 mark of 170 RBIs. It was Yankees 6–0 over Tigers the next day, setting a new American League record for season's wins at 106. Babe didn't homer; he was a game behind his 1921 pace.

Nor did Babe homer on September 25 as Detroit won 6–1. He needed a homer a day to top his 1921 mark.

The Yankees won their 107th on September 27; Philadelphia was the victim. But the big news of the day was Ruth's No. 57, a mighty wallop off Lefty Grove with the bases full. Lou got No. 46, his first since September 7, the day Babe began his September assault on pitchers. The Senators arrived in the Stadium on the 29th, Babe welcomed them with No. 58 and 59, both into the right field bleachers, an area in Yankee Stadium forever to be known as Ruthville. The record-tying shot was off Paul Hopkins with the bases loaded in the 15–4 Yank win.

The victory was their 108th; Shocker was the winner. There were two games left to play.

On September 30, 1927, in the bottom of the eighth, with the score tied 2–2, Babe Ruth, international celebrity with many cognomens, lashed into a pitch thrown by Washington Senators hurler Tom Zachary, and sent it into the right field bleachers where it was caught by one Joe Forner. (Where is that ball today? There was no mention in news stories of its ultimate disposal.)

It was Babe's No. 60, breaking his own record of 59, scoring himself and Koenig to win the game 4–2, for the 109th Yankee victory. A paltry 10,000 fans were on hand, yelling like ten times that number as Babe circled the bases, shook hands with Gehrig at home plate, and entered the dugout to the plaudits of his Yankee cohorts. When Babe went out to right field for the top half of the ninth, he acknowledged the applause of the crowd and their waving handkerchiefs with a series of salutes, military style.

That was Ruth in his public demeanor of polite appreciation. In the clubhouse he was his normal self as he bellowed to his teammates, to the world in general, "Sixty, count 'em, sixty! Let's see some other son of a bitch match that!" Nobody, son of a bitch or otherwise, did for another 34 years. And though Babe would hit more homers and add to his records, that shot into the stands was the pinnacle of his career.

The season ended on October 1, 1927. Gehrig hit No. 47; his finishing BA was .373, his slugging average (SA) .765. Ruth didn't hit: he struck out his last time at bat as the Yankees beat the Senators 4–3 to finish with a 110–44 won-lost and a .714 PCT.

That percentage stands as the highest ever for a pennant winner, as does the Yank .307 team BA. Philadelphia finished second with an estimable 91–63, yet trailed the Yankees by a woeful 19 games. Fate had her own design in 1927: to finish first you had to be a New York Yankee.

Over in the National League a very good Pittsburgh Pirates club won the flag, and awaited the Hugmen and their formidable bats and stats. As for the once and future Babe, he was what he was when he first came on the baseball scene—indisputably human, yet somehow larger than life.

In 1946 I was in an Upper West Side New York movie theatre; when the film ended, I headed for the exits and saw him for the last time. Unmistakable: it was Ruth, Babe himself, standing only a few feet away. A big man, he seemed larger than he had on the field where, from the upper reaches of the Stadium, the players seem diminished in height though not in deeds.

His face was broad, beefy, the nose spread and flattened slightly around the nostrils. Predictably, he wore a camel's hair, belted overcoat, and a brown cap. He seemed to hulk forward, a man at odds with the space he filled, looking towards the aisles, the exits, as if seeking, waiting. For

George Herman "Babe" Ruth   *Photo courtesy of the New York Yankees.*

what?, I later wondered. A sweet pitch, waist high? An elusive memory? A job in baseball?

For a moment I thought of approaching him to say hello, to tell him, in what would surely have been a stumble of words, how great it was to see him play. I didn't. Somehow it seemed better to just watch—as I had watched him years before—at a distance. Soon he was joined by a woman, Claire Ruth I presumed, and they disappeared through the front doors.

He was to die two years later. But the mythic figure that was Babe Ruth would remain and grow, not only in my mind, but in the consciousness of people wherever baseball is played, and indeed, in places where it is not. And, like so many others fortunate to see him play, I'll never forget Ruth's grand, accommodating gesture, that recurrent deed that made him an unforgettable hero for millions of small boys and their fathers. How, on one fat pitch he would swing with an awesome, prodigious motion, and the ball would take off as the adoring crowd rose and roared, thunderous in acclaim, as it did up to that last 714th shot in Forbes Field in 1935.

There was the 60th of the glorious 1927 season. And the called homer, the controversial Roshomon of homers—a marvel of excessive chutzpah—in Wrigley Field in the 1932 series. And the three with the Braves in his last season, the final one a clout that exited the park. That last homer was also his last major league hit, a farewell beautifully in character for an authentic folk hero who began his big league career in 1914.

He did not descend from Olympus, lusty, full grown, carrying a bat. Like the rest of us he was born of mortals, and not exceedingly blessed ones at that. His father a saloon keeper, his mother a woman weary from too many pregnancies and life's slings and arrows, named him George Herman when he came into the world on February 6, 1895, in Baltimore. From the time little George could walk he seems to have been what today's social workers call "a problem child," what the rest of us tag as a rotten kid.

George hated school. He played the hook, drank booze at an early age, roamed the streets, got into trouble. By Babe's own admission, Robert Creamer states in *Babe: The Legend Comes To Life,* Ruth later admitted, "I was a bum." Self-control and civilizing restraints were foreign to this delinquent kid: indeed, those marks of maturity were never to be sufficiently a part of his character.

No doubt it was with relief that his distressed parents, on June 4, 1904, placed him at the age of eight under the strict control of the Catholic Brothers at St. Mary's Industrial Home for Boys. Organized baseball might well commemorate that date as a momentous one in its history. For it was at St. Mary's—an orphanage and reform school—that Ruth found the game of baseball, the one thing that would give meaning to his life.

Babe was a catcher when he first began playing ball at St. Mary's. A lefty using a righty catcher's mitt, young George would catch the pitch in his left, mitted hand, quickly place the mitt under his right arm, the ball to his left hand, and throw. From all reports Babe cut down plenty of challenging base runners with this unorthodox technique. But he wasn't fated to be a catcher.

When Babe was 17, Brother Mathias, his mentor at St. Mary's, a man he respected for the rest of his life, gave him a shot at pitching. That was Babe's first step to the majors.

Babe pitched for St. Mary's, and on weekends was permitted to pitch for other teams outside the Home. Soon word filtered out into the Baltimore area about the young lefty who struck out batters in double numbers, once in a while caught, and—intriguingly—sent baseballs flying over the heads of outfielders. One man who heard about the St. Mary's phenom was Jack Dunn, who managed and owned the Baltimore Orioles, then of the International League.

The baseball-wise Dunn watched Ruth strike out 14 in an interschool game, and at once signed him to a contract. Jack Dunn had a long and productive career in organized baseball, but nothing he ever did would have the impact on the game as the signing of the big kid from St. Mary's.

On April 22, 1914, Ruth pitched and won his first game in the pros, a six-hit, 6–0 shutout of the Buffalo Bisons. In late May he started the second game of a doubleheader against Newark, was ahead 8–1, but was taken out when touched for three runs. Nevertheless, Baltimore won and Ruth was credited with the win. Then he started the second game, and in a performance inimitably Ruthian, went the distance for an 11-inning shutout.

By midseason Ruth was 14–6 when Dunn, who earned much of his living by developing young ballplayers and peddling them to the majors, sold Ruth to the Boston Red Sox. Pitcher Ernie Shore (a Yankee in 1919 and 1920), and Ben Egan, a catcher, were part of the deal. The price for this package, containing the most celebrated, and arguably the greatest ballplayer who ever lived, was $25,000 to $30,000.

Ruth didn't set the American League on fire in his short 1914 season. He won a game for Boston, lost one, then was sent to Providence of the International League—a Boston farm team—to help them win the pennant. He did, winning nine games for Providence. All told, in 1914 his major league mark was an unimpressive 2–1, but his minor league record was a spectacular 23–9.

In 1915, Ruth at 21 came into his own as a big-league pitcher. Under manager Bill Carrigan that was a pennant-winning year for the Red Sox, and Ruth's hurling was one reason the Sox took the flag. It was that year, too, that marked the beginning of Babe's long line of shots into the seats.

In May 1915, pitching in New York against the Yankees at the Polo Grounds, Ruth slammed his first big-league homer into the upper right-field stands, off Jack Warhop. Going all the way he lost the 13 inning game, 4-3. That bothered him.

For although Ruth loved to swing a bat, in those early pro days he thought of himself as a pitcher. But that shot into the Polo Grounds seats, and his .315 BA in 1915, gave other hurlers around the league something to worry about. The next year, 1916, Ruth had a 23–12 mark and an eye-opening 1.75 ERA as Boston again won the American League pennant.

"One of the greatest natural pitchers who ever broke into the major circuits," *Baseball Magazine* headlined in a July 1916 story. And, writer John J. Ward noted, "Babe was dreaded for his tremendous wallops almost as much as for his pitching skill." Actually, Ruth hit only three homers in 136 at-bats, but with typical flair he hit them in three successive games in which he appeared.

In the 1916 World Series against Brooklyn, which Boston won 4 games to 1, Babe hurled the second game, going 14 innings while giving up only six hits, to win 2–1. Many considered him the best pitcher in baseball that year. And that was the heyday of the great Walter Johnson, who went 25–20 with a 1.89 ERA in 1916. Not only was Ruth's pitching record better than Johnson's, but The Big Train (Johnson's nickname), couldn't rattle the fences like the kid from Baltimore.

Boston did not win the pennant in 1917, but Babe continued his superb pitching with a 24–13 mark and a 2.01 ERA. Not as good as Eddie Cicotte of the pennant-winning Chicago White Sox (28–12 and 1.53 ERA), but good enough to lead the Red Sox staff in wins. And significantly for Ruth and baseball, he compiled a healthy BA of .325.

The next year, under new manager Ed Barrow, Babe moved into the role he was fated to play since he first walked onto a ball field. Years later, in his autobiography, Barrow wrote about Ruth, "He loved to play ball. When he pitched...I frequently used him in the cleanup spot. He played in 95 games as an outfielder [in 1918], hitting an even .300, and getting 26 two-baggers, 11 triples, and 11 home runs! And as a pitcher in 20 games he still came up with 13 victories!" (94-95).

The Ruth we would come to know and remember best—the consummate slugger, the home run hitter—was taking shape.

The 1918 World Series between the Red Sox and the Chicago Cubs went to Boston 4 games to 3, with Ruth pitching two of those wins. In doing so he set a record for pitching 29 consecutive scoreless World Series innings, (13 innings in 1916, 16 innings in 1918.) According to Barrow, Ruth was as proud of that record as he was of the 60 homers he slammed into the stands in 1927. That mark was a farewell to his regular pitching days.

"I like to pitch but my main objection has always been that pitching keeps you out of so many games," said Ruth in an October 1918 story by F.C. Lane in *Baseball Magazine.* Earlier in that year he (or some writing wraith) wrote in the same magazine, "I used to hit .450 or .500 [at St. Mary's]. I kept track one season and found that I made over 60 home runs.... I never lost my taste for hitting and don't ever expect to." The whiff of malarkey aside—perish the thought.

In 1919 Ruth pitched less and hit more. His hurling mark was 9–5 as he upped his hitting numbers to 29 homers and a .322 BA. In 1920 he came to the Yanks; that year his pitching record totaled a perfect 3–0. Not that anyone noticed or cared. The Ruthian personality, grounded on a remarkable flair for slugging a baseball and dominating the game, had come swaggering upon the American scene. Waite Hoyt caught something of the Ruthian phenomenon in a radio broadcast he did when the Babe was dying. The text is in the Hoyt Papers archived in the Cincinnati Historical Society.

"Ruth was the pioneer of this age of slugging," Hoyt pointed out. "Today we're rather used to the home run. But in the early twenties fans sat with their mouths wide open when Ruth came to bat. Popularity to the extent of the most intense hero worship was showered on the Big Babe.... The Babe's is an extravagant nature. The powerful swish of his big bat was practically the symbol of his life. Everything done with the big flourish."

We are told that Babe Ruth was something of a boozer, often obscene, an all-night carouser, an overgrown kid who gave Miller Huggins an ongoing heartache. To his regret he defied Baseball Commissioner Landis; he gorged himself into a hospital in 1925; he womanized with an almost frantic excess. A Freudian psychoanalyst would have had a field day exploring the Ruthian psyche.

Yet he was also, as the current vernacular has it, something else: a larger-than-life legend in his own time. The great home-run hitters who came later—Aaron, Mays, Mantle, Williams, all the rest—their talents were surely formidable. But none had the singular, mythic touch that Ruth brought to the game.

That mythic quality has become rare, perhaps extinct in this time of electronic marvels. When every move of our gifted athletes is analyzed in instant and endless slo-mo replay; when their personal lives, union negotiations, trivial opinions, neuroticisms, are transmitted relentlessly into our living rooms; when we see them nightly as pitchmen in the commonplace business of huckstering—how can they evolve into heroes?

Their voices, their personalities, every mark and blemish on their faces and characters, are too available, too close to us in our living rooms. Whatever fabled qualities they might have are inevitably devalued and dissipated through electronic proximity and incessant exposure. We have celebrities aplenty, but no transcendent folk heroes.

On May 10, 1935, Babe Ruth struck out in the top of the first while playing for the Boston Braves against the Phillies. Then, in the bottom of the inning—fat, hurting, his reflexes no longer responsive to his enormous wants—he walked off the field for the last time as a major league ball player. And when he quit, the center of his life gave way.

For the 13 years that were left to him he waited and hoped for a job that would return him to baseball. It never came. With the exception of a few months coaching for the Dodgers, more of a public relations stunt than a serious use of Babe's baseball knowledge, he never again was part of the game he had played so marvelously.

Pro baseball, it has been said, is a kid's game played by grownups for money. True, but only partially so. For along with his desire for big money your dedicated professional has a passion for the game itself. Ask any great, or just good ballplayer and he will tell you that—the money aside—most of all he just likes to play ball. This transcending hunger to perform supremely well before the huge, and often severely critical, crowd is what fuels the competitiveness of athletes. Ruth was a prize example of this kind of player.

"Although Ruth was our highest paid ball player, money to Ruth was nothing," said Waite Hoyt in his 1948 memorial broadcast about Babe. "We, and all the fellows who ever knew him, were sure in a pinch the Babe would have played ball for a room and three meals a day, he loved the game that much." The Schoolboy was no doubt exaggerating to make his point, but only slightly.

Ruth was, of course, in a class by himself as a unique, charismatic attraction for the fans. But what is often overlooked is that he played ball with an artful, instinctive intelligence.

Joe Glenn, the old Yankee backup catcher of the '30s, said in a 1985 phone interview with the author that Paul Krichell told him, "You know, nobody realizes it, but the Babe is a smart ballplayer. All the years he played the outfield he never threw to the wrong base. A lot of people don't realize that because of his home run hitting" (Glenn interview with author, 1984, no record of day or month).

Others have attested to the Babe's acute instinct for playing baseball: that shouldn't surprise us. He was, after all, the archetype natural, a stunning performer whose exploits in the varied aspects of the game are on a par with the two or three best of all time. Given this innate talent, the question often arises, Why didn't Ruth manage or coach after he quit playing?

Mark Koenig touched upon the answer in an interview with the author, December 26, 1984. Chuckling, he said of the Babe, "As far as I was concerned he was just a big overgrown kid." Others who knew Ruth well concur with Koenig's affectionate but accurate appraisal. Kids, overgrown or not, though they play the game skillfully, do not make good managers, coaches, or baseball executives. The trading and finances, the contract negotiations, the handling of men on the field or in the front office—those jobs are reserved for grownups. And Ruth never quite grew up.

This was made clear in Ruth's explosive 1925 confrontation with Miller Huggins. When Babe, like a delinquent kid, misbehaved by flouting club rules and defying Hug, with a consequent effect on the morale of the team, Miller, a man of emotional and cerebral maturity, suspended his star and hung a heavy fine on him. And when Huggins, backed by Ruppert and Barrow, prevailed, Ruth's demeanor was strikingly like that of a chastened and contrite child who had (thank heaven!) been allowed back on the ball field.

It is a psychological truth that each of us must find something to shield us from the chaos, and even misery, that life can be without a central purpose to it. George Herman Ruth found that purpose in playing baseball. If he had not, the odds were that, considering his unstable and ungoverned childhood, he might well have come to a bad end. So it was all the more poignant that he couldn't spend at least some of his final years in the game he loved.

But if the defining center of his existence vanished that day in 1935, when he removed himself from the lineup, the Bunyanesque sports hero remains. The Ruthian legend grows, even as new athletes arrive to assault his records and trigger the cheers of the crowd. Because on the diamond he was, somehow, larger than life and one of a kind.

They gave Babe a "Day" at Yankee Stadium on April 27, 1947. He was ill with throat cancer; it was obvious that his time was running out. On June 13, 1948, he appeared at a Yankee Old Timers game where his illustrious number 3 was retired. Babe was too ill to take part in the ceremonies. On August 16, 1948, he died. His passing and funeral were front-page news the country over. Which was only appropriate; for the Babe had been front page as a premier sports celebrity for most of his adult life.

I'm glad now I did not approach the Babe that day at Loew's 83rd Street Theatre. Better to remember him as he was on that first, shining summer afternoon many years ago in 1927. A magnetic, powerful man, who, in his 22 years in the big leagues grew to the stature of a folk myth. The kid from the orphanage, the sandlot natural, the ace pitcher, the nonpareil slugger. A superb athlete of redoubtable qualities who performed the archetypical, ritual feat of this sports-mad century: hitting a small white spheroid past the despairing grasp of outfielders, into a section of Yankee Stadium where, to this day, he is an enduring presence in the expanse of seats we call "Ruthville."

October 3, 1927

AMERICAN LEAGUE

FINAL STANDING OF CLUBS.

	Won.	Lost.	P.C.
New York	110	44	.714
Philadelphia	91	63	.591
Washington	85	69	.552
Detroit	82	71	.536
Chicago	70	83	.458
Cleveland	66	87	.431
St. Louis	59	94	.386
Boston	51	103	.331

8

The 1927 World Series

The established lore has it that the Yankees won the 1927 World Series before a ball was pitched or a bat swung. That they appeared like titans in Pittsburgh's Forbes Field, slammed a succession of deliberately grooved pitches by Waite Hoyt into the stands during batting practice, inducing dread among the Pirates and undermining their will to win. And that this was the result of a premeditated strategy, plotted with cunning intent by Miller Huggins.

It's an amusing tale stemming, as far as I can tell, from a May 1951 article written by Paul Gallico in *Sport Magazine* and accepted by many as gospel. Including once (I repent) by me. On examination the story is unconvincing, a fable spun out by an overheated fancy.

Yes, the Yankees took batting practice first on October 4, but according to *The New York Times* of October 5 Hoyt didn't even work out because Huggins was resting him for the opening game. And yes, Ruth hit five batting practice shots into the stands as the Pirates watched. And, reported Richards Vidmer describing the Ruthian practice assault on the fences, he "left the interested onlookers, including the Pirates, open-mouthed in wonder." But nowhere in the New York press is there the slightest indication that the Pirates were unmanned and ready to fold after seeing the Yankee sluggers in action.

The fact is, the Pittsburgh team was the best of a strong National League that year, an outstanding ball club recognized as such by sportswriters and baseball men. Indeed, three of them were future Hall of Famers: Paul "Big Poison" Waner, his brother Lloyd "Little Poison" Waner, and the illustrious Pie Traynor. Pittsburgh had played a grueling season, winning the pennant over the hard-driving St. Louis Cardinals, and the New York Giants, only in the last week of the campaign. While perhaps not as relaxed as the Yankees, who had breezed through their schedule without so much as a significant slump, the Pirates were by no means rated a pushover.

In a September 29, 1927, *Sporting News* poll of 32 prominent sportswriters covering major league teams, New York was chosen to win by 17 reporters, Pittsburgh by 13, with 2 irresolute types straddling. Few predicted a bashing by the Yankees, several believed the Pirates would win

117

handily, almost all forecast a hard-fought series. A close look at the Pirates lineup lent credence to that view.

First baseman Joe Harris at 36 was no Gehrig, but he played the bag adequately and hit a solid .326 in 1927. At second base George Grantham could not cover ground quite like the younger Lazzeri, but his .305 BA was up there with Tony's .309 for the season. Shortstop Glenn Wright led the National League with put-outs at 296, was a fine glove man, had a .281 BA in '27, and was rated a steadier shortstop than Koenig. At third it was no contest. Despite Joe Dugan's agility when his legs were not giving him miseries, he was no longer on the level of Pie Traynor, one of the game's all-time great third baseman. And Traynor hit the ball at an intimidating .342 clip that year. The Pirate outfield was outstanding.

Paul Waner in right field led the National League in hitting with a smashing .380 BA, fielded and threw with the best, was acknowledged to be the top all-around player in the league. To say he wasn't a Ruth took nothing away from him: neither was any other ball player. His brother Lloyd was an excellent center fielder, had a better arm than Earle Combs, and hit a lusty .355. Left fielder Clyde Barnhart fielded well, hit .319, but didn't have an arm like Meusel's. But he always hustled, unlike the occasionally diffident Meusel.

That outfield couldn't hit the long ball with Yankee power, but they were of champion class, and had proven themselves in a tough race. As for catchers Smith, Gooch, and Spencer, they were considered the equal of the Yankee receivers.

The Pirates' first-line pitchers, Kremer, Hill, Aldridge, and Meadows were not of quite the same quality as Hoyt, Pennock, and Co. But they had been good enough to win 75 games between them, while losing only 39. Kremer, in particular, had an outstanding rising fast ball, a pitch that had given the Yanks occasional difficulty during the season, notably by Hod Lisenbee of Washington. If anything caused anxiety about that staff among Pirates rooters it was that every one was a righty. And much of the Yank power—for example, Ruth, Combs, Gehrig—erupted from lefty batters.

Pitchers and substitutes aside, and assuming Johnny Gooch as the Pirates principal catcher at .258, and Collins as the main Yankee catcher at .275, the Pittsburgh regular team BA of .320 surprisingly equals that of the Yank regulars. They lacked the Yankee home-run punch, as did every other club in the majors, but the 1927 Pittsburgh Pirates were a first-rate club.

Donie Bush, the Pirates manager, had been a good big-league shortstop, in 1923 a manager of the Senators (they finished fourth), and had brought the Pirates to the top in his first year with them. Like Huggins, he was a small, intense man, prey to nervous tensions. There the comparison ended: though Bush handled his team expertly in 1927, he was no Huggins. In his career he would manage for seven years with four different clubs; only in 1927 would he skipper a pennant winner.

A thousand raucous fans, 700 of them boys, thronged the gate to the train called the Yankee Special at the old Pennsylvania Station (a noble architectural gem since demolished by cultural vandals), on the evening of October 2, 1927, to see the Yankees off for the Smokey City. A large detail of cops kept the crowd from overwhelming their heroes. We have no immortal or historic quotes from any Yankee, except the always amenable Babe.

Above the uproar, the great man said that he "felt in his bones" he was going to crash a few in the World Series, so gladdening well-wishers, and eliciting cheers from America's youth. Then the Yankee Special pulled out for Pittsburgh.

The weather was balmy as 41,467 people packed the stands, and $182,477 filled the till, an unimpressive, even picayune sum by today's standards, but a bonanza in 1927. The odds were 7–5 Yankees, with lots of New York money on the line in Pittsburgh.

A brass band marched to the outfield, the flag was raised. There were no player intros as in our day. And no TV, so no TV interviews by sports-anchor types asking redundant questions of carefully equivocal athletes. Hoyt took the mound for the Yankees; Remy Kremer, Pirate ace (explosive fastball, good curve and change of pace, 19–8 on season) pitched for the Pirates.

The Yankees scored in the first inning when Ruth singled and Gehrig drove him in with a triple. Pittsburgh tied the score in the home half of the first when Lloyd "Little Poison" Waner went to first base after being nicked by a pitch. Paul "Big Poison" Waner then doubled, sending his kid brother to third, from where Lloyd scored on Wright's sac fly.

The Yankees broke it open in the third on only one hit—a single by Ruth—two walks, and two Pittsburgh errors. When the inning ended, the score stood 4–2, an object lesson in the danger of errant fielding and the prevalence of Yankee good fortune.

In the fifth the Yankees scored another run, the Pirates scored one in the fifth, another in the ninth. Kremer had left the premises in the sixth; Moore relieved a tiring Hoyt in the eighth. Babe showed he had his eye on the ball when, in the seventh, he socked his third single. To no avail did the Pirates outhit the Yankees 9 hits to 6: the Yanks won the humdrum game 5–4.

Pittsburgh owner Barney Dreyfuss was dejected by the outcome; Jake Ruppert was pleased but emotionally frazzled by the close score. If the series went beyond four games Ruppert's already sizable fortune would increase; but the Colonel preferred to win the series four-straight—by big scores. "We have the jump on them now," declared Huggins, belaboring the obvious.

"Well, it won't be long now, boys, it won't be long now," enthused Ruth, the day's pre-eminent singles hitter.

It was George Pipgras's day, as the big Yank from the farm country mowed down the Pirates in the second game, holding them to seven trifling hits for the full nine innings. The Yankees won 6–2 as George's fast ball, a thing of beauty and unfailing vitality whooshed into Bengough's mitt, evoking a gladsome smile on Hug's pinched countenance. And why not? After all, it was Hug who ignored the men of little faith, and stuck with the big Minnesota Dane until he became a winning pitcher.

Pittsburgh had picked up a run in the first on Lloyd Waner's triple and Barnhart's sac fly. After that it was no-contest as the Yankees scored three in the third, and three more in the eighth to send hurler Aldridge to the showers. Pittsburgh tallied one in the eighth when Big Poison scored Little Poison from third with a sac fly, after which Pipgras shut them down.

There were no Yankee homers, but they collected 11 hits with Koenig getting three of them. Ruth didn't get a hit, struck out in the first to the huzzahs of the crowd, which, the way things were going for the Pirates, took comfort from small events.

Said Huggins to Pipgras after the game, before the assembled emissaries of the fourth estate, as he gripped George's right hand, "You pitched a great game. A wonderful game, and I'm proud of you."

Answered George, "I'm the happiest guy in the world. Winning was all right, but I'm happier to have Hug say he's proud of me."

In the gloomy Pittsburgh clubhouse Donie Bush averred to the sportswriters, "The series isn't over yet. Not by a long shot. The Yankees have two games now, but this is a seven game series. We're not licked yet." Many years later the great Yogi, the people's philosopher, in one of his timeless sagacities echoed Bush's brave assertion when he said, "It ain't over till it's over." But except for a few details, it was beginning to look like, indeed, it was over as the Yanks and Pirates headed for New York.

Which wasn't too soon for Messrs. Hoyt and Dugan who had $300 and $80, respectively, swiped from their wallets while in Pittsburgh. Surely the more virtuous ambiance of New York would be more to their liking.

Dietary note. On October 7 an ad appeared in the New York papers extolling the virtues of consuming a portion of Fleischmann's Yeast in the daily diet. A goodly part of the Yankee roster, it seemed, savored the stuff as they would a choice cut of broiled sirloin accompanied by peas and mashed potatoes. Hoyt, Lazzeri, Bengough, Koenig, and a clutch of other Yanks endorsed the efficacies of the self-replicating fungus for keeping them fit, clearing the skin, and—the secret was out—helping them win the pennant by 19 games.

Cultural note and social notes. Mr. John Green of Washington, D.C., was in line early at the bleachers gate at Yankee Stadium for the third game. He carried a rabbit's foot which he promised to rub when Ruth came to bat.

Also early in line were Mr. Samuel Rauszer of 180th Street; Frank Higgins, a one-legged newsboy from Troy, New York, who had hitchhiked his way to town; Mr. Tom Barry, a Bronx native; and three anonymous railroad workers from Virginia. Before Ted Turner and the Atlanta Braves saw the light of day, the New York Yankees was America's team.

New York's boulevardier Mayor "Gentleman Jimmy" Walker, arrived too late to throw out the first pitch. His place was taken by Admiral Plunkett, boss of the Brooklyn Navy Yard, who wound up at the behest of photographers and heaved the ball in the general direction of the mound. Unfortunately the media event was private, taking place about three minutes after the third game started. When the baseball materialized from the stands, this startled Herb Pennock as he concentrated on the Pirate batters.

Cool, canny, controlled, Herb Pennock's assortment of elusive pitches bewildered the Pirate batters. A snapping curve here, a corner-clipping fastball there, a floater tempting then befuddling the hitter, Pennock set down in succession the first 22 Pirates. Nobody hit, nobody walked; first base was foreign territory to the perplexed Pittsburghers as they popped up, dribbled out, flailed the air. While this masterful exhibition enthralled the jam-packed Stadium, Yankee bats were busy.

The Yankees got only nine hits, not exactly aggravated assault for "Murderers' Row," but enough to garner them eight runs. They scored twice in the first when Gehrig slammed his second triple of the series to drive in Combs and Koenig, then held off until the seventh when, following the counsel of the immortal Willie Keeler to "Hit 'em where they ain't," they scored six runs to knock out Pirates hurler Lee Meadows. Babe drove in three of the six with a mighty wallop to his bleacher pals glutting the right-field stands, prompting a tumult that must have been heard beyond the confines of the great city, perhaps even in Pittsburgh.

Not until the eighth did a Pirate get to first, when Pie Traynor singled cleanly to left, spoiling Herb's perfect game. Perhaps a bit wearied, or just easing up, Pennock yielded a run when Barnhart scored Traynor with a double. In the ninth Lloyd Waner singled, and that ended the Pittsburgh hitting.

The Yanks won 8–1 for their third straight. It was Pennock's fifth series win: he had never lost a series game, and never would. Herb finished his career with a 5–0 series record.

"Of course the Pirates are down in spirits now," said a sympathetic Hug to the press after the game. "But I want to dispel the idea that the Pirates are not a good ball club. They are a great ball club. We're just better, that's all."

"When I've got control I can come pretty near making that ball do anything I want," said Pennock, a candid and analytical fellow. "My idea is to mix them up, and that's what I did this afternoon."

Now given to meditative silence in their clubhouse, there were no quotes from the Pirates.

Social note. Some heartless, ill-bred fellow sitting near the press box yelled at the Pirates, "Take off those Pittsburgh uniforms. We know you. You're the St. Louis Browns."

John Kenneth Miljus went 8–3 for the flag-winning Pirates in 1927, but the pennant, and the plaudits that go with it, were forgotten after the ninth inning of the final game of the 1927 World Series. On October 8, 1927, "Big Serb" Miljus, six feet one, Pittsburgh born and bred, became a dolorous footnote in the splendid history of the '27 Yankees.

Game 4, hard-fought, close, a thriller to the last fateful pitch, was played on a cloudy, damp day. Wilcy Moore hurled for the Yanks, Carmen Hill, a 22–11 winner that year, pitched for Pittsburgh.

The Pirates scored a run in the first inning, the Yankees tied it in their half when Combs singled, advanced to second on Koenig's single, and came home on a single by Ruth. Koenig, the billy goat of the 1926 series, was hitting up a storm in this one to compile a rousing series .500 BA, play a perfect short, and confound the naysayers who accused him of choking under pressure.

Neither team scored again until the fifth when Combs singled, then took his ease on first base until Ruth homered to drive in two more runs. In the top of the seventh the spunky Pirates—cheered on by the Yankee multitude that welcomed the close battle!—tied it with one hit and two Yankee errors, one by Wilcy Moore, who dropped a ball tossed to him at first base, the other a bobble by Lazzeri.

Miljus and Gooch, the new battery in the Yankee half of the seventh, now arrived on the scene. Big Serb held the Yankees runless going into the bottom of the ninth, a fateful half-inning, an incredible mix of triumph and calamity that must have haunted Miljus's dreams for the rest of his days.

The inning began with a crucial lapse, when Miljus committed a primal transgression of pitching: he walked leadoff man Combs on four straight balls. Koenig bunted, safely sending Earle to second. Now—the moving finger wrote large and ominously—Miljus wild-pitched, and Combs went to third, Koenig to second. Ruth stood by, stalled, galled, his muscles vainly flexing, mouthing imprecations as he was deliberately walked. The bases were loaded when Gehrig, sporting a .373 BA for the year, came to bat. The crowd waited for an inevitable that didn't happen: Lou struck out.

Meusel came up to face the now enheartened, but still beleaguered, Miljus. Meusel struck out. As Tony Lazzeri came to bat, the crowd, in an uproar, was on its feet as it recalled Tony's strikeout with the bases loaded in the seventh game of the 1926 series. And the home crowd, the Yankee crowd, savoring the drama in what had so far been a tame series, cheered the embattled Miljus!

Tony sent Miljus's first pitch screaming into foul territory in the left-field stands. Strike one.

Miljus got the sign from Gooch, wound, delivered.

The ball, an inanimate object, yet seemingly with a perverse mind of its own, sped towards the plate. It veered, went high and wide as Gooch desperately lunged for it, stuck his mitt out only to have the ball glance off and roll towards the stands. Combs, Hug's "waiter," didn't wait: he took off, hell-bent for the plate before Gooch could retrieve the errant ball.

Combs touched home, the Yankees won 4–3.

The game, the series, the great season for the greatest of ball clubs was over. The Yankees were World Champions for the second time in their history.

In the visitors clubhouse owner Barney Dreyfuss consoled his manager. "It's a tough way to lose a ball game," said Barney. "Any other way but that way. I'd rather lose by a base hit." Miljus, a man fingered by an implacable fate, was stunned, relied for solace on expiatory incantation. "Any other way but that, any way at all but that way," he pitifully intoned to the press. "A drive over the fence, a hit of any kind, anything at all but that way." Explained a mournful Johnny Gooch, "It wasn't a wild pitch. It wasn't the fault of Miljus. It was my fault for letting that ball get away." On reflection others agreed with Gooch, but the score was 5-4 Yankees, and *mea culpa*s wouldn't alter the record books.

To the reporters in the Yankee clubhouse, Miller Huggins, a man who had had his share of adversity, made a chivalrous request. "I want you to say something nice about the Pittsburgh team. They've had a lot of tough luck in this series." Then, so nobody would think him unduly self-effacing, Miller added, "I'm happy beyond words that we took this series in four games. I've known all along that we had a great ball club. Now I guess everybody will admit we have."

Everybody did.

Epilogue

Towards the end of his life Waite Hoyt was asked by Jim Ogle, director of the Yankee Alumni Association, if he believed the 1927 Yankees were the best team of all time. Hoyt responded in a letter to Ogle headlined ATTENTION PINSTRIPERS, "I do not believe myself qualified to render such an estimate." He didn't want to slight other great teams, said Hoyt, pointing out that the 1929–31 Philadelphia Athletics, the Yankees of the '30s, '40s, and '50s, the Big Red Machine of the '70s, and some of "the Cards, Giants, and others who can legitimately boast of deserved greatness," were all superlative ball clubs.

But, stressed Hoyt, he was "very, very proud of having played for that club.... The Baseball Writers' Association voted them the honor [of being the best of all time] so I'll be selfish enough to revel in the collective decision of that group of experts." Fair enough. A modest and reasonable answer from the old Schoolboy. Then he astutely pointed out a quality of the 1927 Yankees that helps explain their extraordinary dominance:

The one intangible factor was their utter belief in their invincibility. It transcended that worthwhile but rather overworked term, "spirit"—it wasn't the dash, the verve, the hip-hip, let's go get 'em stuff.... You had to experience the year to believe what you saw. There was the positive confidence that no team could beat them—freakish in its nature, abetted by the super-super performances of Ruth, Gehrig, Lazzeri, Dugan, Combs, Meusel and the others.

Why that confidence was there, what were its obscure springs, its hidden origins, is in the final analysis unknowable. But, as it is with persons who think of themselves as somehow "chosen" to lead and achieve beyond the commonplace, that confidence was a powerful motivator. When combined with the "super-super performances" that Hoyt notes, it resulted in a ball club that was, quite simply, irresistible. The record of the season bears it out. Their performance against a strong league, their statistics, their overpowering, buoyant presence on the diamond gives to the 1927 Yankees an aura of unmatched achievement.

The determined, remarkably cooperative triumvirate of Ruppert, Barrow, and Huggins had moved in signal, effectual ways to assemble a team that would win a pennant and World Championship. That the 1927 club fulfilled their wishes is understandable; that it surpassed their expectations and reached a pinnacle to become a legend was surely unforeseen. In one of those enigmatic resolutions of history, the year 1927—the culminating year of a fabled decade—produced a fabled ball club.

There were no superheroes in the 1927 series, just a superteam that carried its record-breaking performance into the October Classic to confirm its phenomenal skills. They had opened the season with four straight over the favored A's, they closed with four straight over the Pirates in the series, and divided a record-breaking $399,440.67, which came to $5,592.17 apiece for the winners. Chicken feed by today's bloated standards, but real money over 60 years ago. For Ruth and Gehrig the extra money was welcome; the season having been so pleasant, they decided to play more baseball.

As the Yanks disbanded the day after the series, Babe and Lou, and some other big leaguers began a barnstorming tour to bring baseball to outlying provinces between New York and the West Coast. The rest of the Yankees scattered to their homes around the U.S.A. They would reunite in the spring of 1928 to train for a season that would bring them another pennant and World Championship, this time by three games over the much improved A's.

But Dugan would lose a step, Meusel would be a couple of seasons from the end, Ruether was finished in the majors, Shocker near to death and possibly knowing it. As for the Babe, though he would continue to hammer the ball and hit 54 homers in 1928, he would be a shade heavier, a bit slower in the field. While the best of 1928, the team would lack the uncommon brilliance of the 1927 club. And at the end of the 1929 season, Miller Huggins, the manager who had taken them through the often turbulent '20s to the eminence of the 1927 team, would die suddenly and tragically of blood poisoning.

Will we ever see another ball club as overwhelming as the 1927 Yankees? Perhaps. But it will take more than pouring money into the free-agent market for stars, more than brilliant trading, or exceptional management, or a talent-heavy farm system—all of which occur in baseball today. It will require that these elements come together at the right time, under the right leadership, with a measure of good luck thrown in. And that won't be easy to come by.

For greatness is an accident of history: it can't be predicted, it can't be planned. Appearing unexpectedly, it makes its mark on our lives and departs. So it has been with the small number of genuine superplayers who have come through baseball, so it was with the 1927 Yankees. A storied legacy from a time of carefree respite in a hard century, they were distinctive in personality, unequaled in comparison, supreme in achievement.

Peerless, they stand on a baseball peak: they endure as a timeless American sports legend.

Team Totals

		W	AB	H	2B	3B	HR	R	RBI	BA	BB	SO	ERA
NY	A	4	136	38	6	2	2	23	20	.279	13	25	2.00
PIT	N	0	130	29	6	1	0	10	10	.223	4	7	5.19

Individual Pitching

NEW YORK (A.L.)

	W	L	ERA	IP	H	BB	SO	SV
W. Moore	1	0	0.84	10.3	11	2	2	1
H. Pennock	1	0	1.00	9	3	0	1	0
G. Pipgras	1	0	2.00	9	7	1	2	0
W. Hoyt	1	0	4.91	7.1	8	1	2	0

PITTSBURGH (N.L.)

	W	L	ERA	IP	H	BB	SO	SV
V. Aldridge	0	1	7.36	7.1	10	4	4	0
C. Hill	0	0	4.50	6	9	1	6	0
L. Meadows	0	1	9.95	6.1	7	1	6	0
J. Miljus	0	1	1.35	6.2	4	4	6	0
R. Kremer	0	1	3.60	5	5	3	1	0
M. Cvengros	0	0	3.86	2.1	3	0	2	0
J. Dawson	0	0	0.00	1	0	0	0	0

Individual Batting

NEW YORK (A.L.)

	AB	H	2B	3B	HR	R	RBI	BA
M. Koenig, ss	18	9	2	0	0	5	2	.500
B. Meusel, of	17	2	0	0	0	1	1	.118
E. Combs, of	16	5	0	0	0	6	2	.313
J. Dugan, 3b	15	3	0	0	0	2	0	.200
T. Lazzeri, 2b	15	4	1	0	0	1	2	.267
B. Ruth, of	15	6	0	0	2	4	7	.400
L. Gehrig, 1b	13	4	2	2	0	2	5	.308
P. Collins, c	5	3	1	0	0	0	0	.600
W. Moore, p	5	1	0	0	0	0	0	.200
B. Bengough, c	4	0	0	0	0	1	0	.000
H. Pennock, p	4	0	0	0	0	1	1	.000
W. Hoyt, p	3	0	0	0	0	0	0	.000
G. Pipgras, p	3	1	0	0	0	0	0	.333
J. Grabowski, c	2	0	0	0	0	0	0	.000
C. Durst	1	0	0	0	0	0	0	.000

Errors: T. Lazzeri, B. Meusel, W. Moore

Stolen bases: B. Meusel, B. Ruth

PITTSBURGH (N.L.)

	AB	H	2B	3B	HR	R	RBI	BA
C. Barnhart, of	16	5	1	0	0	0	4	.313
J. Harris, 1b	15	3	0	0	0	0	1	.200
P. Traynor, 3b	15	3	1	0	0	1	0	.200
L. Waner, of	15	6	1	1	0	5	0	.400
P. Waner, of	15	5	1	0	0	0	3	.333
G. Wright ss	13	2	0	0	0	1	2	.154
G. Grantham, 2b	11	4	1	0	0	0	0	.364
E. Smith, c	8	0	0	0	0	0	0	.000
J. Gooch, c	5	0	0	0	0	0	0	.000
H. Rhyne, 2b	4	0	0	0	0	0	0	.000
V. Aldridge, p	2	0	0	0	0	0	0	.000
F. Brickell	2	0	0	0	0	1	0	.000
R. Kremer, p	2	1	1	0	0	1	0	.500
L. Meadows, p	2	0	0	0	0	0	0	.000
J. Miljus, p	2	0	0	0	0	0	0	.000
H. Groh	1	0	0	0	0	0	0	.000
C. Hill, p	1	0	0	0	0	0	0	.000
R. Spencer, c	1	0	0	0	0	0	0	.000
E. Yde	0	0	0	0	0	1	0	-

Errors: L. Waner (2), G. Grantham, E. Smith, P. Traynor, G. Wright

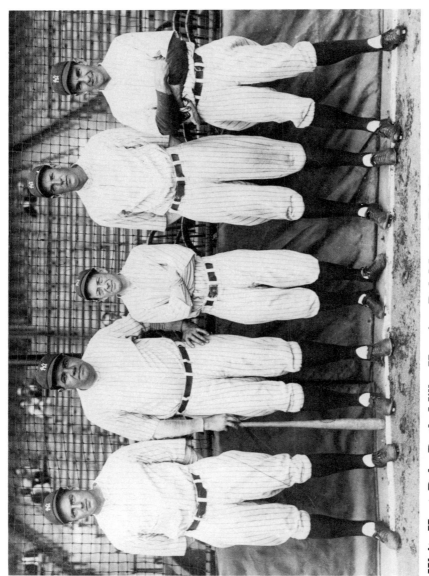

Waite Hoyt, Babe Ruth, Miller Huggins, Bob Meusel, Bob Shawkey

Photo courtesy of the New York Yankees.

Biographies

1927 New York Yankees Management

Ruppert, Colonel Jacob   **"Jake"**   **Owner**
Born: August 5, 1867, New York, New York
Died: January 13, 1939

Colonel Jacob Ruppert was a portly, dignified man with a pleasant, cherubic smile, an astute mind, and a ready bankroll. He also liked to win. Of course, all ball club owners like to win, but in some the passion for pennants burns brighter than in others; it is central to their lives, the defining key to their characters. Jake Ruppert was that kind of owner.

The Colonel hated close games. The 2–1 squeakers that captivate so many fans were an abomination to him: what made Colonel Jake's day was an 11–2 score with the Yanks on top. Close games racked his nerves. "Boys, win. Win one for the Colonel.... If you win I'll give you the brewery," Waite Hoyt quoted Ruppert as saying (Hoyt Papers, Memorial Broadcast to Ruppert, January 13, 1939).

To spare himself this kind of draining agony Ruppert liked to win pennants early and often. It is in no small measure a tribute to the Colonel's unflagging desire to finish first that the Yankees became the greatest of all baseball dynasties.

When excited or agitated Colonel Ruppert sometimes lapsed into an ancestral German accent, a linguistic quirk that was deceptive. For he was an American, a New Yorker born in the Ruppert family home on Lexington Avenue and 93rd Street. His father was the owner of one of New York's great breweries, a business founded by the Colonel's grandfather who had arrived from Germany in the early nineteenth century.

Young Jacob attended Columbia Grammar School, and played the primitive baseball of the time on a local kids' team. Indeed, all his life this man, who owned the baseball club with the most famous collection of ballplayers extant, was fond of showing an old photo of himself as a child playing on a Yorkville team. But if young Jake, in a boyhood fantasy, ever thought of himself as a future ballplayer he had to put that fancy aside. For his father had other plans for him.

Miller Huggins and Colonel Ruppert   *Photo courtesy of the New York Yankees.*

At 19 Jacob bypassed college and went to work in the family brewery. There he washed and loaded beer kegs, was a gofer for his superiors and—not incidentally—became a master brewer. When his father retired, Jacob became president of the brewery, brewed good beer, and cultivated other, wide-ranging, tastes and interests. In 1898 Ruppert, a Democrat, was elected to Congress, an office he held for several terms. He became a colonel in the Seventh Regiment of the National Guard, collected fine paintings, books, and Chinese porcelain. And, of significance for future Yankee fans, developed a taste for the sporting life.

Ruppert bred and raced some of the premier horses of his time, was a noted breeder of show dogs, and with his father as partner ran the largest and most profitable trotting horse farm in the Eastern United States. He was the president of the Astoria Silk Works, a director of the Yorkville Bank, of the German Hospital, and also a canny investor in real estate.

The Colonel was quite a joiner: he was a member of the Catholic, Lambs, Larchmont Yacht, Jockey, New York Yacht, Sleepy Hollow, New York Athletic, Lotus, and Manhattan Clubs. And—just to fill in some open time—the Liederkrantz Society, the Arion Society, and a few more lost in the rummage of New York history. Yet somewhere in the energetic persona of the conservative brewer, public figure, and sportsman there lurked the unappeased desires of the boy who had played neighborhood baseball.

Around 1900 the New York Giants, a team at that time first in the Colonel's heart and favor and last in the National League, was up for sale. Ruppert offered Giants' owner Andrew Freedman (a perverse and quarrelsome man easy to dislike) $150,000 for the team. Freedman refused the bid. Then, in a move which reflected his deviant personality, Freedman sold the club to John T. Brush for exactly the sum Ruppert had offered—a rebuff the Colonel did not relish. When, in 1912, the Colonel had a chance to buy the Chicago Cubs he decided not to do so. New York was his city; in New York he would remain. Ruppert's decision was a wise one, for a new opportunity to buy a New York ball club arose in late 1914.

Frank Farrell and Big Bill Devery, Yankee owners since the franchise was organized in 1903, were short of good players, short of cash, and short of pennants. In the long, barren years the team had never won a flag nor built a following of loyal fans. So Farrell and Devery put their troubled franchise on the block, attracting the attention of Colonel Jacob Ruppert and Captain (later Colonel) T.L. Huston.

Tillinghast L'Hommedieu Huston was an engineer who made his considerable fortune in Cuba after serving with the army during the Spanish-American War. A baseball fan, Huston was introduced to Ruppert by a mutual friend: with the negotiating help of John McGraw, and Ban Johnson, president of the American League, the two men bought the floundering Yankees.

For $450,000, "we got an orphan ball club, without a home of its own, without players of outstanding ability, without prestige," Ruppert was quoted in his obituary in *The New York Times*, January 14, 1939. This state of affairs did not last. With the advent of Colonel Ruppert the orphan team gained a strong-willed, caring father who would provide it with an imposing home in the Bronx. A home that would house some of the most illustrious of players, men who brought prestige to the franchise, added wealth to the colonels, and made the name New York Yankees synonymous with superlative, winning baseball.

From the beginning of their partnership the colonels were at odds; they agreed on very little and everyone around them knew it. Ruppert was patrician in bearing, fastidious in dress, a patron of art and culture, conservative in every aspect of his life. His discretion was so ingrained that when, after his death, it was revealed that the bachelor colonel had left a large sum to a woman, probably an ex-chorus girl, even many close to him, and the nosier members of the press, were surprised.

Huston was the antithesis of Colonel Jake. Bluff, rough-and-ready, unlike the more formal Ruppert, he called everyone by his first name, and was a drinking buddy of Dodger manager Wilbert Robinson and others in the sporting crowd. When the Yanks, from 1915 to 1917, finished fifth, fourth, and sixth to the acute distress of the colonels, Ruppert asked Ban Johnson for advice.

"Get Miller Huggins," urged Johnson.

"I want Wilbert Robinson," was the gist of Huston's cable from wartime France, where he was serving with the Engineers. Obviously, not even 3,000 miles of ocean could calm the temperaments of the clashing colonels.

Uncle Robbie, as Wilbert Robinson was known from Flatbush to Broadway and points west, was without doubt a genial fellow. But the record shows he was less than formidable as a manager. In 19 years of piloting, all but one of them with Brooklyn, he brought in a pennant just twice. When Ruppert ignored Huston and hired Huggins the decision heated up the vendetta between the discordant owners, a rancorous ruckus that ended only when Ruppert bought out Huston in 1923.

Now sole owner, with Barrow and Huggins trading and buying shrewdly, with Hug managing masterfully, Colonel Jake finally got his heart's desire, a consistent winner. In the 24 years that Ruppert owned his beloved Yankees, a period terminated only by his death, the club presented him and its legion of fans with 10 pennants and 7 world championships. Ruppert not only bought the best players available, but he backed Ed Barrow in building a first-class farm system. And he helped endow his Yankees with an aura of class.

"It was at the Colonel's insistence that every Yankee was provided with four complete uniforms," Waite Hoyt wrote in his unpublished autobiography, now in the Cincinnati Historical Society. "As the Colonel himself always dressed with the utmost dignity, so he wanted his team to be dressed, off the field as well as on. There were no flea-bag hotels for Yankee teams and no day coach travel" (164).

Ruppert and Huston financed and built Yankee Stadium, but to the vast baseball public it was "The House That Ruth Built." For it was the Babe who put his inimitable mark on the great structure, slamming homers into the right-field stands, dominating the team and the game with his unique personality. It was Ruth's magnetic presence that was so often linked with Ruppert's reserved demeanor for many unforgettable Yankee years. Their salary duels made headlines during otherwise dull late winters; once the race began it was Ruth who gratified Colonel Jake with his prodigious contributions to great teams and victorious seasons. And it was the often unruly Babe who gave the Colonel a surfeit of headaches and heartaches.

Yet, through all the turmoil and tribulation there was a fundamental mutual regard between the two men. From 1920, the year Ruth came to the Yanks, until 1934, the Babe's last Yankee year, the conservative Colonel and the idolized, one-of-a-kind, rambunctious Babe were linked in a common destiny. It was a relationship that endured for most of Ruppert's years of ownership, and beyond Ruth's playing days.

On January 13, 1939, when the 71-year-old Colonel lay dying in Lenox Hill Hospital in New York, *The New York Times* reported that Ruth came to see him. The nurses removed the oxygen tent from Ruppert's bed for a few moments and the old man said, "I want to see the Babe."

"Here he is, right beside you," the nurse answered. Ruppert put out his hand to the Babe, but he was too weak to speak.

"Colonel," said Ruth, "you are going to snap out of this, and you and I are going to the opening game of the season." Ruppert smiled. Ruth, in tears, turned to go, but the Colonel mustered enough strength to call to him, "Babe, come back."

Ruth returned to the bedside. Colonel Jake put out his hand. "Babe," he whispered. Then he closed his eyes. Ruth left the room. He told reporters, "It was the only time in his life he ever called me 'Babe' to my face. I couldn't help crying when I went out." Aside from the Colonel's family, Ruth was the last man to see him alive. Later that day Colonel Jacob Ruppert—patrician New Yorker, master brewer, great Yankee owner—passed away.

Waite Hoyt, in a radio broadcast said of the Colonel, "I know his team won ten pennants for him. But don't ever make this mistake. The players didn't do it alone. Ruppert was as much a part of that team as Ruth, Gehrig, DiMaggio, Ruffing, or Dickey.... In saying goodbye, I speak for every

Yankee. There'll never be in their careers a man to whom they could be so earnestly and sincerely attached. I know it was that way with me and it shall ever be."

In the fall of that year, 1939, the Yankees won another pennant and World Championship. It was only fitting that they did so, for, after all, the Colonel always wanted a winner.

In the memorial section of Yankee Stadium is a plaque dedicated to Ruppert's memory. It is inscribed:

> To The Memory Of
> JACOB RUPPERT
> 1867–1939
> GENTLEMAN–AMERICAN–SPORTSMAN
> THROUGH WHOSE VISION AND
> COURAGE THIS IMPOSING EDIFICE,
> DESTINED TO BECOME THE HOME
> OF CHAMPIONS, WAS ERECTED AND
> DEDICATED TO THE AMERICAN GAME OF BASEBALL

Barrow, Edward Grant   **"Cousin Ed"**   **Business Manager**
Born: May 10, 1868, Springfield, Illinois
Died: December 15, 1953

When Ed Barrow passed away in 1953 *The New York Times* eulogized in an editorial, "his greatest tribute is the cry that has been echoing around the leagues for years: 'Break Up The Yankees.'" It was an astute comment on a brilliant baseball executive, for though Jake Ruppert provided the money, and Miller Huggins (and later, Joe McCarthy) the field savvy, it was "Cousin Ed" Barrow who gave masterful guidance to the New York Yankees.

His father, John Barrow, a Civil War veteran, was "powerful and full of guts," Barrow recalled in his autobiography, *My Fifty Years in Baseball*. Without doubt, much of John's character was passed on to his son, for that description fitted the formidable Ed Barrow throughout his long life and baseball career.

The conventional tale has it that Ed was born in a covered wagon going west, but that is not quite true. His father had been granted 160 acres of Nebraska farmland by the U.S. government, so he bundled his wife, Effie, his mother, four children, and the family's possessions into a wagon train and, their cattle plodding along, set out for the Midwest. It was during a stopover at a relative's farm in Springfield, Illinois, that Ed was born. They christened the future baseball great Edward Grant Barrow, the middle name bestowed in honor of the great Civil War general and President.

Edward Grant Barrow   *Photo courtesy of the New York Yankees.*

Farming their desolate acreage proved to be no bucolic paradise for John Barrow and his family, what with prairie fires, clouds of crop-devouring grasshoppers, and unfriendly Indians to contend with. But it was a valuable preparation for Ed's later experiences in the often precarious environment of early pro baseball. After six years the Barrows family had had its fill of pioneering: they sold their farm and moved to the more hospitable surroundings of Des Moines, Iowa.

At 16 Ed quit school to work as a mail clerk for the *Des Moines Daily Register,* which was probably just as well. For Barrow was one of those restless people never at home with formal education: he preferred, and thrived in, the often turbulent world of business and enterprise—in particular sports promotion.

Ed moved to Pittsburgh at 19, clerked in a hotel, and became a familiar figure at sports events: prizefights, horse racing, and not least, ball games. Quickly he developed two prime attributes for success in the flourishing business atmosphere of late nineteenth-century America—an aptitude for meeting influential people, and a nose for the sweet smell of opportunity.

In 1893 Harry Stevens ("Score Card Harry"), founder of the Stevens concession and catering empire, asked Barrow to run the concessions at the Pittsburgh ballpark, and Ed accepted. It was his first foot in the door of a pro-ball enterprise; from that day until he retired he was never away from some aspect of organized baseball. "I was lost in baseball," he wrote. "It had got into my blood" (138).

The next year, 1894, with an investment of $100 he became part owner of the Wheeling, West Virginia, franchise of the newly formed Inter-State League. When the manager quit in mid-season Ed took over and managed the team into first place—after which, typically, the league folded. For in those formative years professional baseball was still a chancy enterprise; players jumped teams, owners raided rival clubs and leagues for good ballplayers, finances were shaky. Leagues and teams sprouted like weeds in a late summer garden, and died just as quickly. But the public demanded baseball, so there was no dearth of promoters and investors to form teams and leagues.

Barrow never played ball, but over the years he worked in every management phase of baseball and acquired a profound knowledge of the game and its business structure. No other baseball executive, past or present, would know as much about every aspect of pro ball as did the shrewd, tough-minded, usually unsmiling Barrow. In his minor league days he was associated with the Paterson Club of the Atlantic League, the Iron and Oil League, and Montreal and Toronto of the Eastern League. He served in various capacities: owner, sometimes field manager, league president. Not always liked, often feared for his explosive temper, he was nevertheless respected for his baseball knowledge and business acumen. And—in one celebrated case—for discovering an all-time baseball great.

According to Barrow, one day he walked to the railroad tracks in Mansfield, Pennsylvania, where he was told a kid named Wagner was hanging out. "I asked him if he wanted to play ball for me in Paterson," wrote Barrow. "He didn't know whether he wanted to play ball at all. As we talked he would stoop over every once in awhile and pick up a lump of coal or a stone and heave it up the railroad tracks.... As I watched the rocks sail a couple of hundred feet up the track I knew I had to have this fellow on my ball club" (31).

Although the salary limit in the league was $100 per month, Barrow offered him $125. The kid—his name was Honus Wagner—signed, and "The Flying Dutchman," who Barrow always insisted was the greatest of all players, greater than Ruth and Cobb, became his discovery and property. Later, mostly with the Pittsburgh Pirates, Wagner had a distinguished 21-year career, and in 1936 was one of the first five men inducted into the Baseball Hall of Fame (the others are Ty Cobb, Babe Ruth, Walter Johnson, Christy Mathewson).

Though a baseball conservative in his big league days, early in his career Barrow was not above gimmickry to bring in the customers. On the Fourth of July 1896, in Wilmington, Delaware, his Paterson team played Wilmington in the first night game on record. (Barrow would oppose night baseball in the majors.) The contest ended in the sixth when the prankish Wilmington pitcher, Doc Amole, threw a large white torpedo instead of a ball to Honus Wagner. In the primitive lighting conditions Wagner didn't know it was a hunk of fireworks coming at the plate. He smacked the torpedo, causing pandemonium on the field, hilarity among the spectators, and an abrupt end to the game.

Ed used a woman pitcher, Lizzie Arlington (real name, Stroud), in a series of games. John L. Sullivan, last of the bare-knuckle heavyweight champions, umpired for Barrow, and another heavyweight champ, James Corbett, played first base—and played well—for him. Even the late Bill Veeck, promoter extraordinary, could have learned a thing or two from Barrow about filling a ballpark.

After 14 years in the minors, and a stint managing Detroit in the newly formed American League in 1903 and 1904, Barrow in 1918 became manager of the Boston Red Sox—a propitious day for him, and ultimately the Yankees. For it was in Boston that he got to manage the young lefty pitcher, Babe Ruth. When Ruth began to sock the ball into the stands, it was Barrow who moved him to the outfield so that Babe could play—and bat—every day.

In the 1918 pennant-winning year for Boston, Ruth played the outfield in 95 games and hit .300 and 11 homers, while winning 13 games as a pitcher. When Barrow shifted Ruth to the outfield full time, Babe responded by batting .322 and walloping 29 home runs, a record for the time. Then, at the end of that season, Red Sox owner Harry Frazee, a man who seemed perpetually in debt, sold Ruth to the Yanks. And on October 29, 1920, Barrow, sensing that the Red Sox were fated to spend years deep in the American League cellar, quit the Sox to become business manager of the Yankees. What he had accomplished to that time was only prelude: his great years and true destiny was to be as a Yankee.

Aside from his own considerable gifts, Barrow was endowed with three other major assets when he took over the Yankee front office: Miller Huggins, Jacob Ruppert, and Babe Ruth. One of his first moves was to tell Huggins, "You're the manager.... Your job is to win...my job is to see that you have the players to win with" (126). Both men kept their part of the bargain.

With Ruppert—and until he sold out in 1923, Til Huston—supplying the cash, Barrow got Waite Hoyt, Wally Schang, Harry Harper, and Mike McNally from the dollar-hungry Frazee. Bob Meusel and his strong hitting had come up from the minors in 1920, and in 1921 the greatly improved Yankees won their first pennant. During Barrow's stay with the Yankees the club would win 14 pennants and 10 World Championships,

In his unpublished autobiography (178-79), Waite Hoyt has left us vivid recollections of Barrow, a man he knew well during his years with the Yankees. "He was quiet. He never seemed to act on impulse. He would listen and consider and make his decisions slowly.... Cousin Ed was a baseball man. But there were few men in the game who could match him in business acumen. He knew where to look for leaks in the cash box, could estimate costs within a few dollars, and knew exactly what he could afford to spend on salaries. He was a sharp trader, and, as every good trader has to be, a gambler." But beneath the chilly, businesslike exterior there was an unbanked fire that could flare up at any time.

Nobody messed with Ed Barrow. To meet him in a salary negotiation was like walking through a minefield. To cross him, insult him, to demean him in any way, was to risk his terrible wrath. When Barrow took exception to one of umpire George Moriarty's calls he told everyone within earshot, according to Hoyt, "that he had once set big George across his knee and walloped him as if he were a small boy. 'And I can do it again,' he promised."

The story that he had whipped ballplayers in bare-knuckled fights while managing Detroit is probably true; it fits the personality. And Hoyt wrote that he saw Barrow slug sportswriter Bill Corum with a roundhouse punch and knock Corum over a desk. "What the fight was about I'll never know," wrote Hoyt. Considering Barrow's hair-trigger response to insults, real or imagined, perhaps Corum didn't know either.

Hoyt credits Barrow with making the Yankees conduct themselves as if they could beat any team, any place, any time. "He did not want men to drag themselves around the diamond as if every step cost them blood. He did not even want a man to wipe sweat or rub an injury. You were to be spruce, alert, and operating in high gear at every turn. If a man in the bullpen or on the bench decided to slump down or doze in the sun, he would be there but a few seconds when the phone would ring and word would come from Cousin Ed: 'Tell so and so to straighten up on the bench'" (179).

Joe McCarthy came to the Yankees in 1931, beginning another great Barrow-administered era. McCarthy, in Barrow's opinion, was the greatest of all managers, and he might well have been right. For during McCarthy's almost 15-year tenure the Yankees won eight pennants and seven World Series. Four of these championships were successive (1936–39): the Yanks were the first to accomplish this feat. It was during this period that Barrow brought up such excellent players as Gomez, Rolfe, Crosetti, Gordon, and Rizzuto. And, of course, the peerless Joe DiMaggio.

DiMaggio cost the Yankees $25,000, not a large sum even in the depression-plagued '30s. Looking back on Joe D's superlative career it is hard to believe that some clubs that might have bought him were leery about the Clipper. Joe had injured his knee (not playing, but in getting out of a car), and it took a meeting of the whole Yankee clan, from Ruppert and Barrow down, to decide to buy him. "I think he's worth a chance," said Barrow in a memorable understatement (Hoyt autobiography 178). Some chance.

After Jake Ruppert died Barrow was elected president of the Yankees. It was a fitting culmination to his outstanding service to the team, to a baseball journey that began in the nineteenth century overseeing the sale of scorecards and candy in the Pittsburgh ballpark. The McPhail-Webb-Topping group bought the Yanks from the Ruppert family in 1945; the next year, at 79, Barrow retired.

No doubt this hard-nosed baseball man was weary after 51 years in the game, 25 of them glorious ones with the Yankees. He had bought and sold players shrewdly, and supported the masterful field leadership of two great managers. He had built a farm system second to none. In a game in which the amalgam of brains, talent, and guts is the only sure recipe for success—all of which Barrow was plentifully endowed with—he had established a tradition of ongoing Yankee triumphs unsurpassed to this day.

Barrow received many awards and honors through the years, but none must have pleased him as much as his election to the Baseball Hall of Fame in 1953. That same year, on December 15, Edward Grant Barrow died in New York at 85. General manager, field manager, owner, promoter, league president, he was a consummate baseball man, a unique and key figure in the history of the national pastime. And though he never fielded a grounder, or hit a curve, or wore the pinstripes, nevertheless he was a great Yankee.

Ed Barrow's plaque in the Yankees Monument Park reads as follows:

EDWARD GRANT BARROW
1868–1953
Moulder of a Tradition of Victory
Under Whose Guidance The Yankees Won
Fourteen American League Pennants and
Ten World Championships and Brought
to This Field Some of the Greatest
Baseball Stars of All Time.
This Memorial Is a Tribute From Those
Who Seek to Carry On His Great Works
Erected April 15, 1954

Huggins, Miller James   **"The Mighty Mite"**   **Manager**
Born: March 27, 1879, Cincinnati, Ohio
Died: September 25, 1929

In 1898 Miller James Huggins enrolled at the University of Cincinnati to study law, a profession he had no intention of pursuing. Miller had been an excellent shortstop at Walnut Hills High School in his hometown of Cincinnati. Now, while boning up on torts and contracts, he also studied box scores, played semipro ball and cast a wishful eye at the majors. Unfortunately his father, James Huggins, a man of conventional rectitude, did not care for professional baseball and he let Miller know it. From what we know of the elder Huggins his aversion is understandable.

When James Huggins came to the United States from England, his birthplace, he took a job with Peeples and Co., a large wholesale and retail grocery business in Cincinnati. There he would remain for 43 years, his entire working life. There was no taking of perilous vocational risk for James Huggins. Small wonder that the chancy and peripatetic life of a ballplayer was not what he wanted for his son, Miller. Something solid and indisputably respectable, a step upward in society—like the law—was preferable. Considering the pervasive public image of ballplayers in James Huggins's time, we can appreciate his feelings.

In those still primordial days of our national pastime ballplayers ranked on the social scale somewhere between circus roustabouts and scruffy vaudevillians in the eyes of conservative citizenry. They traveled around like Gypsies, were prey to "loose women" and attendant perils (they still are), and did not get rich (times have changed). "The respectable middle classes" (of which James Huggins was an example in the lower echelons), "frowned upon earning a living from sport," writes Stephan Riess in *Touching Base,* his examination of pro ball during the latter part of the nineteenth century. He notes that "the main reason for their low prestige was the ballplayers' poor moral conduct and their ill-mannered behavior on and off the field" (155).

In his seminal work *Baseball: The Early Years,* Harold Seymour states that in the 1890s (when Miller was still in school), "Hoodlumism and dirty playing...were worse than ever. There was scarcely an issue of the *Sporting News* that didn't tell of kicking and wrangling with umpires, fights among players, indecent language, and incidents of rowdyism in general" (289). Worst of all to the churchgoing James Huggins, when games were played on Sunday—as the semipros often were—they diverted the minds of young men from sermons and the contemplation of eternity. Miller met his father's objections with a simple solution.

A September 9, 1899, box score of an Inter-State League game between Mansfield and Dayton lists one "Proctor" playing third base, with one at-bat, for Mansfield. "Proctor" was Miller Huggins playing under a pseudonym (one half of Procter and Gamble, the Cincinnati soap tycoons) to avoid conflict with his father. This is the first time the name pops up in a professional league box score. It was probably Miller's first pro game, although he had used the assumed name in the semipros.

Who can fault Hug for his small deception? Playing ball was his meat and drink, a vocation more agreeable than defending miscreants or plowing through legal papers. It was a choice he never regretted, even when the burdens of managing the often turbulent Yankees of the 1920s were taking a heavy toll on him.

Huggins graduated from law school in 1902 and was admitted to the Ohio bar, but except for six desultory months in a law office he never practiced. By this time his father had accommodated himself to his son's playing ball for a living. After all, Miller did earn his law degree; he could always fall back on being a lawyer if he failed as a ballplayer. Besides, baseball was becoming more reputable by the turn of the century. Indeed, the pioneering player and owner/manager of the Chicago White Stockings, A.G. Spalding, had taken steps to clean up the behavior of players as early as the 1880s.

"Spalding enthusiastically endorsed the National League's pitch to make professional baseball respectable for America's middle class," writes

Peter Levine in *A.G. Spalding and the Rise of Baseball.* "Central here was
the public image of ballplayers...wherever the White Stockings stepped out
of line, Spalding was there to enforce discipline, morality, and good
behavior, whether they liked it or not" (41-42). But Miller had his own
reasons for playing ball; though a principled man, virtuous conduct wasn't
one of those reasons.

"I gave up the law for baseball," he told *Sporting News* in 1914,
"because...it is more than a game, for the real ball player employs his brains
as much as the shrewdest business man." He was perhaps overstating the
case for superior intellect on the diamond. Most ballplayers are bright
enough, but an IQ of 100 will enable one to learn the cutoff throw and the
belly slide. And some players with porridge between their ears have hung
around the majors for 10 or more years. But Hug's respect for brains to go
with brawn was genuine, a mark of his character and achievements in the
game that challenged and gratified him as nothing else did.

Miller was a small man and the world never let him forget it.
Depending on the source you consult he stood five feet three inches and
weighed 130 pounds, or was perhaps as tall as five feet six and one-half
inches and weighed 140 pounds. In any case, his unusually small stature
invited comments ranging from affectionate to derisive. When he broke
into the majors in 1904 as a hustling second baseman with Cincinnati he
was dubbed "Little Mr. Everywhere" and "The Rabbit" by the press and
fans. Throughout his career friendly writers called him "Little Hug," the
"Midget Manager, and the nickname that has come down to us, "The
Mighty Mite."

But in his early Yankee days a contemptuous Babe Ruth referred to
Miller as "The Flea," and fans in rival cities shouted "Here comes the
mouse!" when Hug emerged from the dugout. Once umpire Bill Guthrie
called him "the batboy" when he tossed Hug out of a game. Ridicule by
bench jockeys and fans has been part of professional baseball since its
beginnings. Hug took them as inevitable, and never let on publicly how he
felt about these insults. But being targeted for what was perceived as a
comic abnormality might have motivated him to compensate for his small
stature.

Given his natural talent for playing ball there is evidence that he
pushed himself to excel over those around him. By the time he graduated
from Walnut Hills High his athletic prowess stood out despite—or perhaps
because of—his small size. A series of entries in his school magazine, *The
Gleam,* in 1897, strongly suggest this. In the Field Day competition Miller
took first place in "Throwing a Baseball" with a 255-feet 3-inch heave. He
won the "Hop, Skip and Jump" with a 39-feet 10-1/2-inch mark, and placed
second in the "Broad Jump" with 18 feet 4 inches. And, as an indication of

things to come, Miller was captain of the baseball team in his graduating year of 1897.

Huggins was a busy young man after his high school graduation. Aside from attending law school and playing in the local semipros and with Mansfield, he also toured with the independent Fleischman Catskill Mountain team, owned by Julius Fleischman, a sometime mayor of Cincinnati and part owner of the Cincinnati Reds. That law degree, so prized by James Huggins, was put away when Miller signed with St. Paul of the American Association. He played with St. Paul for the 1903 season, then was bought by his hometown Reds.

From the day he broke into the majors, in 1904, as the Reds' regular second baseman, until he quit playing in 1916, Miller was a sure-handed, agile fielder, a smart base runner and stealer, an excellent leadoff man and bunter. Because he was short, with a pronounced crouch at the plate, he had an unusually narrow strike zone, and thus wangled many walks. He wasn't a slugger; nevertheless, his lifetime batting average was a respectable .265.

After six seasons with the Reds as one of the best second baseman in the game, Hug was traded to the St. Louis Cardinals in February 1910. He remained there for eight years; three as a player, four as a player/manager, and in 1917, as manager.

As Cardinal pilot Huggins never had players who were better than mediocre, and some were downright awful. (The great Rogers Hornsby excepted. He came to the Cards as a rookie toward the end of the 1915 season: it was Hug who broke him in at second.) Yet, after finishing last in 1913, his first year as player/manager, Miller brought the Cards to third in 1914, and again in 1917. *Sporting News,* on July 12, 1917, hailed him as "The Little Miracle Worker of the West." Those third place finishes were the highest in Cardinal history up to that time; owners of teams stuck in the second division wondered what Miller might accomplish for them. They did not have long to wonder.

In early 1917 a St. Louis group (with Branch Rickey as team president), bought the Cardinals, and Rickey, a man uncongenial to Hug's personality and managing style, sacked Miller at season's end. This baseball limbo was new and strange to the recently acclaimed Miracle Worker. He was too old to play, did not own a team (he had tried to get financing to buy the Cards and failed), and did not manage one. What he did have was the esteem of his baseball peers.

On October 25, 1917, *Sporting News* put it this way. "There is no doubt that Huggins is one of the smartest managers in baseball.... He has never had a first class club to operate.... He has worked without pitchers of class.... He has had no $50 gold pieces to hand to pitchers who win games. [But] he wins his men by his squareness." Unfortunately, you cannot put esteem in the bank, and Hug's outlook—as on that famous day in Mudville—was not brilliant. Then destiny beckoned in the persons of two colonels.

How the sad sack Yankees of 1915—perennial losers since their founding in 1903—were bought by Colonel Jacob Ruppert and Colonel Tillinghast L'Hommedieu Huston is a tale more than twice told. Let it suffice that after their Yankees spent three years in the second division Colonel Ruppert wanted Hug as manager, that Huston preferred his jolly drinking buddy, Dodger manager Wilbert Robinson, and that Ruppert prevailed. This embittered Huston: from the day Hug came to the Yanks, Huston was gunning for him and Hug knew it.

Ed Barrow began his long and distinguished career as Yankee business manager in 1920, and knew the colonels well. In his autobiography, *My Fifty Years in Baseball,* he writes, "The Yankee Colonels were the strangest pair of men I have ever known in baseball.... When [they] agreed to buy the Yankees...it must have been the only time they ever did agree" (123). Into this festering relationship stepped the reserved, contemplative Miller Huggins, baseball-wise, something of a loner, a bachelor, a man married to a game.

The pre-Huggins Yank infield had leaked up the middle like a cracked dike, so Hug sent five players of disparate talents, plus a bundle of the colonels' plentiful cash, to the St. Louis Browns for slick-fielding second baseman Del Pratt. Eyebrows were raised at Miller's generosity, but fewer baseballs slipped through the Yank infield in 1918 as the team acquired an aura of first division excellence rarely evident in its previous 15 years of existence. On June 6, 1918, an out-of-control headline in *Sporting News* clamored, "Miller Huggins' Name on All Lips. Little Manager of Ruppert's Team Has Replaced McGraw As Idol of Fans of New York Town."

That burst of journalistic moonshine must surely have activated Miller's chronic dyspepsia, for up in Boston Ed Barrow, then Red Sox manager, led a first-class club which included a pitcher named Ruth. And Hug had no illusions about the kind of players he needed to win pennants or to match the Little Napoleon, McGraw, in adulation along Broadway. By late August reality set in: the Red Sox were on their way to a flag as the Yanks slid to their final 1918 standing of fourth.

Though this was two slots above their 1917 finish, some writers and fans carped about Hug's managing. "Gotham Knockers Turn on Yanks," ran a *Sporting News* headline on August 29, 1918, as reporter Joe Vila took the "knockers" to task, writing, "In no other major league town is such merciless hammering permitted in the daily newspapers."

The year 1919 wasn't much better as the Yankees finished third behind Cleveland and the pennant-winning, soon-to-be infamous Chicago White Sox. By now Til Huston, a perpetual affliction, was home from wartime

France nursing his disaffections, jousting with Ruppert, and feeding disruptive tidbits about Huggins to his sportswriting chums. We can guess Hug's feelings when he saw the *Sporting News* of September 26, 1919, with its picture of a smiling Wilbert Robinson under a headline that read "Picked to Lead Yankees."

Miller, it seemed, "displayed poor judgment in handling pitchers, in directing plays and in selecting material...the dope seems to be straight that he is doomed." But if Miller was doomed the crepe hangers didn't tell Ruppert about it. In October 1919 the beer-brewing colonel re-signed the beleaguered Huggins to a one-year contract, and Miller and the Yanks headed into the new decade. Then followed the fateful move for the Yanks and baseball, one that even both colonels agreed on.

The arrival of George Herman Ruth to the Yankees on January 3, 1920, was an appropriate introduction to the Prohibition-nurtured hijinks of the '20s. For the Babe swaggered onto the New York scene at a time when the public was particularly receptive to his outsize personality, his flamboyance, his prodigious talents. A raffish phenomenon, Ruth was consummately in sync with a decade we have come to think of as "roaring." And when he came to New York the press was ready for him.

As never before, adulation for well-publicized, transcending achievers was a mark of the '20s: Ruth is right up there in newspaper headlines with Lucky Lindy, Jack Dempsey, and Man o' War. With his unmatched flair for baseball's grand dramatic gesture—the high, soaring shot into the stands—he was surely in a class by himself. The adored of the crowds, a boon to the press, he was the Bambino, Paul Bunyan with a bat, the Big Fellow. And his manager was "little Miller Huggins."

"I think you and me ought to get along all right together," the *New York Times* of January 16, 1920, quoted Ruth as saying to Huggins as "Ruth looked down on the diminutive New York manager." Whatever "get along" meant to George Herman, it didn't include unfailingly adult behavior, a quality he never quite mastered. Robert Creamer's excellent biography of Ruth, *Babe: The Legend Comes To Life,* pulls into focus the image of a perpetual adolescent who has discovered, but never learned to moderate, the sybaritic delights of drinking, gourmandising, and philandering.

Ruth hit an astonishing 54 homers in 1920 and batted .376, but New York finished third again, which was raw meat for the Huston-led pack yelping for Miller's hide. Arthur Mann was a respected writer who covered the Yankees for the *New York Evening World* in the 1920s, and also wrote for other New York papers. In 1945 he became assistant to Branch Rickey with whom he worked closely in signing Jackie Robinson. Mann wrote of Huggins, in the November 2, 1939, *Sporting News,* "I knew him intimately only a few years, but during that period I was a bold and presumptuous young baseball writer...and because he tolerated my constant inquisition, I was privileged...to hear him reveal much."

According to Mann, a Ruth-for-manager campaign surfaced around the end of the 1920 season, a gross mischief in which Huston probably had a hand. And while one would think that a Yankee pennant win in 1920—their first ever—would silence the anti-Huggins cabal, that didn't happen. Reporter Frank Graham traveled with the Yankees in the 1920s for the *New York Sun*. Reminiscing about the 1921 pennant victory Graham wrote, in a February 5, 1964, column for the *New York Journal-American,* "Ruth and the other players received all the credit. Save almost in Ruppert's estimation alone, he [Huggins] was just a scrawny little man who happened to be around as the Yankees advanced to a peak."

As for the Ruth-for-manager movement, Mann states that it accelerated when the Yankees lost the 1921 series to McGraw's Giants. But though Miller was disquieted by the attempt to unseat him, he also held it in contempt. "You will find that ball players who get too ambitious are always dumb," said Huggins to Mann in *Sporting News*, November 2, 1939. "They are easy to outsmart.... Those fellows after my job hitched their wagon to the wrong star." The campaign ultimately collapsed under the weight of its own idiocy. The undisciplined Babe could no more command a ball club than he could the Salvation Army. But there was worse in the offing as turmoil engulfed the club in 1922.

Trouble began during spring training and continued into the season as a number of Hug's gifted players lapsed into unruliness and license. They caroused all night, flouted curfews, ignored team discipline. Meusel and Schang fought on the bench; Ruth was fined for going into the stands after a heckler; Ruth and Wally Pipp came to blows. What should have been a runaway for a powerful club became a cliffhanger.

Huggins suffered through it all, sorrowed by the wasting of abundant gifts, his always precarious health undermined, his authority flouted. In *Baseball As I Have Known It,* veteran sportswriter Fred Lieb, a man who knew the Yanks well in the '20s, states that Ruth "never could accept managerial discipline. He gave Miller Huggins...a miserable time" (154). The turmoil in the club was no secret. Wrote Joe Vila in *Sporting News* of October 5, 1922, "Huggins hasn't chucked up the sponge yet and is working diligently to inspire his fading champions.... If he succeeds he will prove indeed that he is among the best of managers; if he fails his friends will be convinced that he is the victim of a dastardly conspiracy."

Conspiracy or not, Hug demanded that Ruppert uphold him as manager of the team or the Colonel could have Hug's job. Ruppert, as he would throughout his long association with Huggins, supported Miller. The Yankees got their act together and nosed out the St. Louis Browns by one game for their second pennant in a row. But in the World Series they came apart: the Giants decimated them 4 games to none.

After the debacle Huston raged that Huggins had managed his last Yankee game. But Ruppert (and Ed Barrow, signed as business manager in 1921) stood firm for Hug and signed him again. This prompted a biting editorial in the *Sporting News* of October 5, 1922. Huggins, it said, "has won pennants, or the tribe of Bolsheviks he manages has, but no one gives him credit...we can't help recalling the reported suggestion of [a] friend of the little fellow—that if he had a 'spark of manhood' he would tell them to take their job.... Perhaps never in the history of the game has a manager been so flouted, reviled, and ridiculed." If any man was due for a break, it was Miller Huggins. He soon got it.

At the end of 1922 Til Huston sold out to Ruppert. Ed Barrow writes in his autobiography, "Huston was bought out for $1,500,000 and when the deal was completed I made Ruppert send the following telegram to the Yankees in Chicago: I AM NOW SOLE OWNER OF THE YANKEES. MILLER HUGGINS IS MY MANAGER. Hug said to me in later years, 'I wouldn't go through the years from 1919 to 1923 again for all the money in the world'" (140).

In 1923 the Yanks won their third straight pennant, and beat the Giants in the series for their first world championship. Huggins was unanimously praised by the press and fans. No doubt he savored the accolades, but it's unlikely he had illusions about the fickleness of crowds or the behavior of wayward athletes. When the Yankees finished second behind Washington in 1924, and began collapsing towards seventh in 1925, Miller resolved not only to rebuild his club but to once and for all assert authority over his star player.

For Miller had had it with Ruth: the contemptuous ignoring of signs, the after-hours hell-raising, the refusal to stay in shape. According to Waite Hoyt, "Hug's greatest problem was Babe Ruth, who for a time seemed to believe that his mere presence in the lineup was all he owed to the club. The Babe paid no attention to curfew, never took the room assigned to him, and often trotted into the clubhouse just barely in time to make the game" (Hoyt autobiography 191-92).

Robert Creamer, in his biography of Ruth, wrote that on August 29, 1925, Huggins accosted Ruth in the visitors clubhouse in St. Louis. "Don't bother getting dressed, Babe," said Huggins, so triggering what became baseball's most famous confrontation (292).

"I had envied big fellows all my life," Hug told Arthur Mann, "and nursed my strength like a miser, and here was a hitting marvel...throwing youth and strength in all directions." Before suspending him Huggins had summoned Babe to his hotel room. "I talked to him as a father would to make him realize that he was still young with a life before him," Miller related to Mann in *Sporting News*, November 2, 1939. "I wound up with a plea for him to settle down and make something of his life as a ball player, but more important, as a man."

Mann doesn't tell us Ruth's response but, he writes, it "left Miller Huggins chalk-white and ashamed...of human nature." In fining Ruth $5,000 and suspending him, Huggins—backed by Ruppert and Barrow— was laying it on the line not only to the Babe but to his entire team.

The test of wills ended with Ruth humbled. After spending nine miserable days out of the lineup, with Ruppert and Barrow standing fast for Hug, Ruth apologized to Miller before the team and paid the $5,000 (a considerable sum in 1927). The message was plain: Miller Huggins was the boss—this, eight often stormy years after his arrival in New York. And so he would remain until his time ran out four years later.

"Eventually," claims Waite Hoyt, "a very deep affection grew up between Babe and Huggins. One of my fondest memories is a picture of Babe spouting threats at an umpire and marching towards his victim, while little Hug stood between Babe and the umpire, shoving hard at Babe's chest, and giving ground with each of Babe's charges."

And, adds Hoyt, "The knowledge that Hug had full control and that even a man with a solid playing record could be traded off the team did much to pull the Yanks together" (Hoyt autobiography 199).

In 1926 the powerful Yankee team of the second half of the decade was in place, the team that took three straight pennants (1926–28), and two world championships (1927–28). And in those championship days of the late '20s, what about Hug?

"I remember him as a man with an iron fist," recalled George Pipgras in a December 1984 interview with the author. "When he said No, he meant No. He was a little fellow, but he managed to control all the ballplayers." Ken Smith covered the Yankees for the *New York Daily Mirror* and the *New York Evening Graphic* for part of the late '20s; later he worked for the Hall of Fame. Of Hug, he remembered in a phone interview with the author on March 26, 1987, "The first thing that strikes on your mind was that everybody trusted him, and...admired him. He was no phony. He was a complete baseball man, highly respected." And, Smith emphasized, "He was a teacher. He knew how to instruct, he had that knack."

Ed Wells pitched for the Yankees in 1929, Miller's last season. Speaking of Hug in a 1985 phone interview with the author, Wells recalled, "He was a very good man, he had a quiet compassion for ballplayers...He was a man of very few words, strictly business.... Hug was very much respected by all the ballplayers; in the American League, too, not only the Yankees.... I thought a lot of Hug, and always have and always will." Yet, by Miller's own admission, something vital was missing from his life.

Huggins led a lonely bachelor's existence, with very few close friends to talk with about troubles. In his reminiscence of Huggins, Arthur Mann relates that one night in Cleveland Hug told Mann how he envied him for having a wife and kids. "Take care of it all," he said. "You don't realize what you have." This frustrated longing for a family perhaps explains Miller's special concern for his ballplayers, and his success in bringing along young players.

The *1929 Spalding Official Base Ball Guide* noted in its obituary of him, "Huggins was a student of Base Ball possibilities that might lurk in the bodies and minds of younger players...he made ball players of young men who were criticized by others as lacking in mental and physical qualities."

Tony Lazzeri told *Literary Digest,* on October 12, 1929, "I don't think anybody could bring along a kid player like Huggins could."

Leo Durocher, a Yankee in 1928 and 1929, writes in *Nice Guys Finish Last,* his autobiography, "I was Miller Huggins' boy.... He loved me like a father and I loved him like a son. I couldn't hit worth a damn...but Mr. Huggins kept telling me I'd stick around for a long time if I kept my cockiness and scrappiness. 'Little guys like us can win games,' he would say, tapping his head...up here'" (45-46). (It is striking to note that the three greatest Yankee managers—Huggins, McCarthy, Stengel—were all childless.)

By the end of the decade the stresses of managing, of turbulent days on the field and in the clubhouse, were all too evident in Hug. "He was an ill man in St. Petersburg in the Spring of 1929," wrote Frank Graham in the *New York Journal-American* on October 7, 1964, "but he hung on as he would." In late September, with the Yankees slipping behind a powerful Philadelphia A's club into second place where they would finish, Mann saw Huggins sitting in front of his locker at Yankee Stadium.

"He was smaller, thinner, and wearier: he was picking at an ugly infection on his cheekbone. I slapped the hand away.... He sighed and leaned against the locker. 'I'm so tired, kid,' he murmured. 'I could sit here until tomorrow's game.'" A day later Miller told head coach Art Fletcher to take the club, that he would return the next day. He never came back.

Three days later, on September 29, 1929, Miller Huggins died of erysipelas (blood poisoning) at St. Vincent's Hospital. He was 50 years old. At his bedside were his sister Myrtle, his brother Arthur, his old friend, baseball executive Bob Connery, and Charles McManus the Stadium superintendent. The Yankees heard about it in the middle of a game at Fenway Park.

Earle Combs broke down and wept. The Babe, "silent and distraught," said, "He was a great little guy.... I'm sorry he couldn't win the last pennant he tried for." Gehrig, shaken and despondent, said he felt like the bottom had dropped out of his life. "Next to my father and mother he was the best friend a boy could have. He told me I was the rawest, most awkward rookie that ever came into baseball. He taught me everything I know.... There never was a more patient or more pleasant man to work for. I can't realize that he won't join us again."

They took Hug home to Cincinnati: on the day of his funeral every game in the American League was canceled, all ballpark flags flew at half mast. For all of baseball, and much of the nation, knew that a great manager was gone. Brainy, gritty, principled, in Mark Koenig's words, "a baseball scholar," he was equaled by few and excelled by none in the long history of the game that was central to his life. Hug was an original, a true baseball immortal, and what he left us has become a timeless American sports legend: the tempestuous, troublesome, but finally magnificent New York Yankees of the 1920s.

The plaque and monument in the Yankees Memorial Park dedicated to Huggins reads:

MILLER JAMES HUGGINS
Manager of New York Yankees 1918–1929
Pennant Winners, 1921–22–23...1926–27–28
World Champions, 1923, 1927 and 1928
As a Tribute to a Splendid Character
Who Made Priceless Contributions to Baseball
And on This Field Brought Glory to the
New York Club of the American League
This Memorial Is Erected By
COLONEL JACOB RUPPERT
And
BASEBALL WRITERS OF NEW YORK
May 30, 1932

1927 New York Yankees Players

Beall, Walter Esau   **Pitcher**
Born: July 29, 1899, Washington, D.C.
BR, TR, 178 lbs.
Died: January 28, 1959

	W	L	PCT	ERA	G	GS	CG	IP	H	BB	SO	ShO	Relief Pitching W	L	SV	BA
1927	0	0	-	9.00	1	0	0	1	1	0	0	0	0	0	0	-

Walter Beall is the least known of the '27 Yanks. Though he appears on the team photograph, his name is not on the listing under the photo. At the spot where his name should be is the word "unknown." Which about sums up the importance of Beall's contribution to the Yankee record. He pitched in only one inning, had a 0-0 record, gave up one hit, and had a 9.00 ERA. These numbers are hardly an indication of the high hopes held for Walter Beall when he first came into the majors.

In 1924 he won 25 and lost 8 with Rochester of the International League, the best record in the circuit, prompting the Yanks to pay $50,000 for him. With the Yanks he was 2–0 in '24, 0–1 in '25, 2–4 in '26. Though Beall had a wicked curve he could not control it—at least, not in the majors—and spent much of his time shuttling to and from the minors. After a 1–0 stint with the Senators in 1929, he was through in the big leagues.

The information on Beall's post-majors career is sparse. He died at 59 in Suitland, Maryland.

Bengough, Bernard Oliver   **"Benny"**   **Catcher**
Born: July 27, 1898, Niagara Falls, New York
BR, TR, 5' 7-1/2", 168 lbs.
Died: December 22, 1968

	G	AB	H	2B	3B	HR	HR %	R	RBI	BB	SO	SB	BA	SA	Pinch Hit AB	H	G by POS
1927	31	85	21	3	3	0	0.0	6	10	4	4	0	.247	.353	1	0	C-30

Bengough was of Irish-Scotch-French-German ancestry. Raised and educated in Niagara Falls, New York, he attended Niagara University and starred as catcher on the school team. For awhile Benny thought seriously of becoming a priest, but "My dad and mother always wanted me to play ball. They always followed me around to see me play," said Bengough in an interview around 1961. So, play ball he did.

During his 1917 summer vacation he was bullpen catcher for the Buffalo Bisons for $5 per day. His mother one day called Bisons manager Patsy Donovan. Why wasn't her boy Benny getting more work with the team? she demanded. Donovan, taken aback by the insurgent Mrs. Bengough, put Benny into an exhibition game against the St. Louis Browns. When Benny threw out the speedy Burt Shotten (years later a Dodger manager) three times in that game, he was given a contract at $150 per month.

After six seasons with the Bisons Benny came to the Yanks in 1923 after being rejected by John McGraw for the New York Giants. He was third-string backup with the Yankees for two seasons, first-string in 1925. After he hurt his arm in 1926 spring training, he became backup for the rest of his career. When his arm was sound (in hot weather and after sufficient rest), his catching was faultless. Base runners took few liberties with Bengough. A great friend of Ruth, he was also a favorite of Huggins, who respected him as a hustling player and smart catcher. Benny considered Huggins as the greatest manager of all time, particularly since Hug had some difficult players to handle.

Bengough appeared in the 1927 and 1928 World Series. He caught all four games of the 1928 Yank sweep. As a hitter he was ordinary; his lifetime BA is .255.

He was released by the Yanks to Milwaukee at end of 1930 season, he was traded by Milwaukee to the Browns where he played two seasons as backup, was sent back to Milwaukee where he played in 1933. Benny ended his playing career in the minors in 1937 after appearing with Little Rock, Washington of the Penn State League (player/manager), and Joplin (player/manager).

Then he coached for Newark, the Browns, the Senators, the Boston Braves, and the Phillies. After retiring from coaching in 1959, he made public-relations appearances on the banquet circuit for the Phillies. Benny was a popular speaker. When asked why he was successful at public speaking, the facetious Benny explained that he told lies to keep his listeners entertained.

After a few years on the banquet circuit Bengough's weight went to a roly-poly 200 pounds. He suffered a heart attack in 1959, but kept on with public appearances. Benny Bengough collapsed and died at 70 after coming out of church after Mass.

Collins, Tharon Leslie   "Pat"   Catcher
Born: September 13, 1896, Sweet Springs, Missouri
BR, TR, 5' 11-1/2", 178 lbs.
Died: May 20, 1960

	G	AB	H	2B	3B	HR	HR %	R	RBI	BB	SO	SB	BA	SA	Pinch Hit AB	Pinch Hit H	G by POS
1927	92	251	69	9	3	7	2.8	38	36	54	24	0	.275	.418	1	1	C-89

Collins was brought up and educated in Sweet Springs, Missouri. He played sandlot ball in Kansas City, Kansas, then broke into organized baseball in 1917 with Joplin of the Western League. After three years with Joplin, Pat was sold to the St. Louis Browns in 1919.

He was with the Browns as a backup catcher through 1924, then played for St. Paul of the American Association in 1925. At the close of the 1925 season the Yankees bought him.

A Yankee from 1926 to 1928, Collins was a first-string catcher but never played an entire season. When Bill Dickey, arguably the greatest of all catchers, came to the Yanks in 1929, Collins was sold to the Boston Braves of the National League.

After playing seven games with the Braves, he was released to Buffalo. Pat then played for Kansas City of the American Association, Seattle of the Pacific Coast League, and Omaha of the Western League. He retired from playing in 1932.

Pat Collins, who had a heart ailment, died in his sleep at 63 in his home in Kansas City, Missouri.

Combs, Earle Bryan   "The Kentucky Colonel"   Outfielder
Born: May 4, 1899, Pebworth, Kentucky
BL, TR, 6', 185 lbs.
Died: July 21, 1976   1927 salary: $10,000

	G	AB	H	2B	3B	HR	HR %	R	RBI	BB	SO	SB	BA	SA	Pinch Hit AB	Pinch Hit H	G by POS
1927	152	648	231	36	23	6	0.9	137	64	62	31	15	.356	.511	0	0	OF-152

Earle Combs was born on a farm, educated in the Kentucky public schools, and became a schoolteacher. Combs played ball as a child; as a young adult he played with semipros while teaching school. His first pro year was with the Louisville Colonels in AAA ball, where in 1992 he batted .344, followed with .380 in 1923. In 1924 he went to the Yankees, thus beginning a career as a great hitter and center fielder.

A 12-year career Yankee through 1935, Earle was a great leadoff man for the "Murderers' Row" 1920s clubs. In 1927 he led Yanks with 231 hits, 161 singles, 23 triples. He amassed 331 total bases in 1927, third in AL behind Ruth and Gehrig. On September 22, 1927, he hit three triples in row.

Earle hit 154 lifetime triples; his lifetime BA is .325; his lifetime series BA is .350; his slugging average (SA) is .462.

As either player or coach Earle was a Yankee from 1924 to 1944. He played on 11 American League flag winners and nine world championships. In 1947 he coached for the Browns, for the Red Sox from 1948 to 1952, and the Phillies in 1954.

Combs led an active post-baseball life in Kentucky as a farmer and businessman. He was elected to the Baseball Hall of Fame in 1970.

Earle Combs died at 77 in Kentucky.

Dugan, Joseph Anthony   **"Jumping Joe"**   **Third Base**
Born: May 12, 1897, Mahanoy City, Pennsylvania
BR, TR, 5' 11", 160 lbs.
Died: July 7, 1982   1927 salary: $12,000

	G	AB	H	2B	3B	HR	HR %	R	RBI	BB	SO	SB	BA	SA	Pinch Hit AB	Pinch Hit H	G by POS
1927	112	387	104	24	3	2	0.5	44	43	27	37	1	.269	.362	1	1	3B-111

Dugan was of Irish descent. His family moved to Winstead, Connecticut, when Joe was 15 months old. He attended elementary and high school in New Haven, then spent one year at the College of the Holy Cross. Dugan played ball in high school and college, and with semipros. He was never in the minors. At 20, in 1917, he became a shortstop with the Philadelphia Athletics.

Dugan played short and second base through 1919. In 1920 he played third, short, and second, in 1921 only third base. Traded to the Boston Red Sox in 1922, he then immediately went to the New York Yankees where he became the regular third baseman. An outstanding fielder with a strong, accurate arm, Joe was also great at handling bunts. He led the league in third base fielding in 1923 and 1925, and set a major league record for third basemen in 1924 with four unassisted double plays. Dugan played in five World Series, all with the Yankees. His World Series lifetime BA is .267.

Dugan remained a Yankee until the end of the 1928 season, was waived in December 1928 to the Boston Braves where he played 60 games that year. He did not play at all in 1930, went to Detroit in 1931, played in eight games, and hung them up at age 33.

Dugan owned a bar and grill, scouted briefly for the Red Sox, and held odd jobs. He had no firm post-baseball career, and was a favorite and picturesque source of Yankee and general baseball information for reporters.

Dugan died at 85 in Norwood, Massachusetts.

Durst, Cedric Montgomery   **Outfielder**
Born: August 23, 1896, Austin, Texas
BL, TL, 5' 11", 160 lbs.
Died: February 16, 1971

	G	AB	H	2B	3B	HR	HR %	R	RBI	BB	SO	SB	BA	SA	Pinch AB	Hit H	G by POS
1927	65	129	32	4	3	0	0.0	18	25	6	7	0	.248	.326	21	4	OF-36
																	1B-2

Durst was brought up and schooled in Austin, Texas. He broke into organized baseball in 1921 with Beaumont of the Texas League, was then sold to the St. Louis Browns in late 1921. He was with the Browns for 1922 and 1923, then farmed to Los Angeles of the Pacific Coast League (PCL) in 1924. In 1925 Durst went to St. Paul of the American Association and returned to the Browns in 1926.

He came to the Yankees in 1927, played in 65 games, hit .248. and remained with the Yanks into the 1930 season. When Earle Combs was injured Durst replaced him in the 1928 series, and hit a solid .375 for the four games. Cedric was traded to the Boston Red Sox at the end of 1929 for Red Ruffing, who became a great Yankee pitcher. He remained a Red Sox through 1931, his last major league season.

Durst managed in the minors for San Diego, Rochester, and Omaha.

He died in San Diego at 71.

Gazella, Michael   **"Gazook"**   **Infielder**
Born: October 13, 1896, Olyphant, Pennsylvania
BR, TR, 5' 7-1/2", 165 lbs.
Died: September 11, 1978

	G	AB	H	2B	3B	HR	HR %	R	RBI	BB	SO	SB	BA	SA	Pinch AB	Hit H	G by POS
1927	54	115	32	8	4	0	0.0	17	9	23	16	4	.278	.417	0	0	3B-44
																	SS-6

Of Polish descent, Gazella was a utility infielder, but usually played third base. He was brought up and educated in Olyphant, Pennsylvania and attended Lafayette College on a scholarship. There he studied chemical engineering, was a backfield star on the football team, and also played baseball as a pitcher and third baseman. The Yankees signed him out of college and brought him to New York in 1923 where he played in eight games.

He was with Minneapolis in 1924 and Atlanta in 1925.

Upon returning to the Yanks in 1926, Gazella, a good fielder, was of crucial value as backup for Joe Dugan at third. In 1926 he appeared in one game of the World Series. His 1927 BA is .278, his lifetime is .241. Mike remained a Yankee through 1928.

Gazella played in the minors for Minneapolis, Newark, Hollywood, and Los Angeles. He also managed at Ponca City, Moline, Ventura, and Denver. In the late 1940s he scouted for the Yankees.

Mike Gazella was killed in an automobile accident in Odessa, Texas, a month short of age 82.

Gehrig, Henry Louis   **"The Iron Horse"**   **First Base**
Born: June 19, 1903, New York, New York
TL, BL, 6', 200 lbs.
Died: June 2, 1941   1927 salary: $8,000

	G	AB	H	2B	3B	HR	HR %	R	RBI	BB	SO	SB	BA	SA	Pinch Hit AB	Pinch Hit H	G by POS
1927	155	584	218	52	18	47	8.0	149	175	109	84	10	.373	.765	0	0	1B-155

Of German descent, Lou Gehrig was educated in the New York public school system. A graduate of the High School of Commerce, Lou played on their championship baseball team and was dubbed "Babe Ruth of the high schools."

He spent two years at Columbia University where he played outfield, first base, and pitcher on the baseball team. He also played tackle on the football team.

Gehrig, who was 6–3 as a pitcher, hit a famous homer which soared over the center field fence of South Field and smacked against the School of Journalism building at 116th and Broadway. He earned the nickname: the "Babe Ruth of Columbia."

Paul Krichell scouted Gehrig at Columbia. *Sport Magazine,* in October 1948, quoted Krichell as saying that with proper coaching Gehrig would have become a fine pitcher. "He would have learned control. He was the sort of boy who could learn anything." But the Yankees never had any notion of making a big league hurler out of Gehrig. A great hitter, Lou was destined to play every day.

He appeared in 13 games with the Yankees in 1923, 10 games in 1924, and spent the rest of those years with Hartford of the Eastern League. There Gehrig learned to play first base, hit .304 in 1923, and socked 24 home runs. In 1924 he hit .369 and had 37 homers. In 1925 he became a permanent Yankee.

On June 1, 1925, Lou was inserted as a pinch hitter; he remained in the lineup for 14 consecutive years, 2,130 games, a major league record.

Gehrig was voted most valuable player (MVP) in the AL in 1927 when he led the league with 52 doubles, 175 RBIs, hit .373, and had a .765 slugging average. He was the MVP again in 1936, when he led the league with 49 HRs, 167 RBIs, a .354 BA, and a .696 SA. In 1934, when he hit .363, Gehrig was the triple crown batting champ.

His 23 grand slams is the major league record. Lou hit three or more homers in one game on four occasions, an AL record. His 184 RBIs in 1931 is the AL per-season record. His 493 HRs are the most hit by a first baseman. Gehrig's 30 homers at Yankee Stadium are the most hit in one season in the Bronx ballpark.

Lou is third in career RBIs with 1,990; stands third in SA with .632; fifth in extra base hits at 1,190, seventh in runs with 1,888, 10th in bases on balls at 1,508. He has a lifetime .340 BA; an SA of .632; 493 homers; a World Series BA of .361.

Gehrig smacked four consecutive homers on June 3, 1932, against the Philadelphia A's, a record tied only once (by Rocky Colavito in 1959). Surprisingly, for a man his size and never considered a speedster, he stole home 14 times, the Yankee record.

Gehrig's Yankee marks include: hits (2,721); extra-base hits (1,190); singles (1,531); doubles (535); triples (162). Lou is second in Yankee RBIs with 1,990; second as a Yankee with 8,001 at-bats. He played in 2,164 games; his 1,888 runs scored is seventh in the ML.

What else Gehrig might have accomplished, if he had not been struck down by disease after 14 seasons, is an interesting speculation. Given his commitment to keeping in shape, and assuming a reasonable 20 seasons or so of play, he would surely have added significantly to his already fabulous stats.

Gehrig's number was retired on his "Day," and his locker permanently closed. The inscription on his plaque and monument at Yankee Stadium reads:

HENRY LOUIS GEHRIG
June 19, 1903–June 2, 1941
A MAN, A GENTLEMAN
and
A Great Ball Player
Whose amazing record
of 2130 Consecutive Games
Should stand for all Time
This Memorial is a Tribute
From the
Yankee Players
To their beloved Captain and Team Mate
July the Fourth
1941

Giard, Joseph Oscar   **"Peco"**   **Pitcher**
Born: October 7, 1898, Ware, Massachusetts
BL, TL, 5' 10-1/2", 170 lbs.
Died: July 10, 1956

	W	L	PCT	ERA	G	GS	CG	IP	H	BB	SO	ShO	Relief Pitching W	L	SV	BA
1927	0	0	-	8.00	16	0	0	27	38	19	10	0	0	0	0	.286

Giard was raised and educated in Ware, Massachusetts. He broke into pro ball in 1921 with Spartanburg of the South Atlantic (Sally) League, went to Toledo of the American Association in 1922, and remained with Toledo until the end of 1924.

He was sold to the Yankees but was soon traded to the St. Louis Browns where he played in 1925 and 1926. Giard had a 13–15 record with the Browns before being traded to the Yanks.

A Yankee in 1927, he appeared in 16 games, had a 0–0 record, and an 8.00 ERA.

Joe Giard died in Worcester, Massachusetts, at age 57.

Grabowski, John Patrick   **Catcher**
Born: January 7, 1900, Ware, Massachusetts
BR, TR, 5' 10", 185 lbs.
Died: May 23, 1946

	G	AB	H	2B	3B	HR	HR %	R	RBI	BB	SO	SB	BA	SA	Pinch Hit AB	H	G by POS
1927	70	195	54	2	4	0	0.0	29	25	20	15	0	.277	.328	2	0	C-68

John Grabowski attended elementary school at St. Mary's Parochial School in Schenectady, New York, then went to Mt. Pleasant High School in Schenectady. He signed with Minneapolis in 1921, then went to Saskatoon in 1921. After playing with St. Joseph in 1922, he was with the Minneapolis Millers in 1923 and 1924. John was sold to the Chicago White Sox in 1924, and played for them through 1926.

Grabowski came to the Yankees in 1927, and remained with them until the close of the 1929 season. He was then sent to St. Paul where he played until going to the Detroit Tigers in 1931. He caught for Montreal from 1932 until he retired in 1934.

Grabowski was strictly a backup catcher, appearing in 70 games with the 1927 Yankees, 75 games with 1928 Yankees, and 22 in 1929.

He umpired in the International League in 1935, in the Eastern League from 1938 to 1940, then returned to the International for the 1941–43 seasons.

After leaving baseball, he became a toolmaker in Schenectady. Johnny died at age 46 from burns resulting from a fire which destroyed his home in Guilderland, near Albany.

Hoyt, Waite Charles   "The Schoolboy"   Pitcher

Born: September 9, 1899, Brooklyn, New York
TR, BR, 5' 11-1/2", 185 lbs.
Died: August 25, 1984

1927 salary: $12,000

	W	L	PCT	ERA	G	GS	CG	IP	H	BB	SO	ShO	Relief Pitching W	L	SV	BA
1927	22	7	.759	2.63	36	32	23	256.1	242	54	86	3	0	1	1	.222

Hoyt was of English-German descent. Raised in Brooklyn, Waite was educated in the New York public schools. A star pitcher at Erasmus High School and with the sandlot Wyandottes, Hoyt attracted the attention of scouts before he was 16.

He was under option with the New York Giants in 1915, his first pay contract was signed in 1916. Waite was sent by the Giants to Mt. Carmel of the Penn State League where he was 5-1. Then he went to Hartford (1916), Memphis (1917), and Montreal (1917). Hoyt credited Montreal manager Dan Howley with teaching him more about pitching than "all the other minor league managers I worked for combined."

With the New York Giants in 1918, he pitched one inning, and was sent to Newark where he was 2-3. When ordered to Rochester Hoyt refused to go. Rochester sold his contract to New Orleans; instead he joined the semipro Baltimore Dry Docks. When he pitched a one-hitter against the Cincinnati Reds in an exhibition game, the Boston Red Sox signed him. With Boston in 1919 and 1920 his record was 10-12. Hoyt was traded to the Yankees in 1921.

He became the righty mainstay of the Yankees from 1921 to 1930, a smart, hard-throwing clutch pitcher. His best seasons were 1927 (22-7), and 1928 (23-7). He was traded by the Yanks to Detroit in 1930. From Detroit he went to Philadelphia Athletics in 1931, to Brooklyn in 1932, then to the Giants that same year. Pittsburgh got him in late 1933; he remained a Pirate from 1933 to 1937.

In June 1937 he was released to the Brooklyn Dodgers where he pitched until May 5, 1938, when he was released, ending his playing career. In his 21 years in the majors Hoyt won 237 games and lost 182, for a .566 PCT. His lifetime ERA is 3.59. He is 6-4 in World Series competition, with an exceptional 1.83 ERA.

Hoyt became a popular radio and TV sports announcer in Cincinnati, and was elected to the Baseball Hall of Fame in 1969.

He died in Cincinnati, Ohio, at age 84.

Koenig, Mark Anthony   Shortstop

Born: July 19, 1902, San Francisco, California
TR, Switch Hitter, 6', 180 lbs.
Died: April 22, 1993   1927 salary: $7,000

	G	AB	H	2B	3B	HR	HR %	R	RBI	BB	SO	SB	BA	SA	Pinch AB	Hit H	G by POS
1927	123	526	150	20	11	3	0.6	99	62	25	21	3	.285	.382	1	0	SS-122

Koenig was educated in San Francisco. He broke into pro ball with Moose Jaw, Canada, in the summer of 1921, and went to St. Paul of the American Association the same year. St. Paul sent him to Jamestown, South Dakota, in 1922. Mark was with Des Moines in 1923, then went back to St. Paul. He played little in 1924 until the regular shortstop was hurt; Koenig took over the position, starred in the Little World Series against Baltimore, and became the regular in 1925.

The Yanks bought him in 1925 for $35,000. He came to them near the end of 1925, and played in 28 games. Koenig was the regular shortstop on the flag-winning 1926–29 years. When he developed eye trouble and a severe sinus condition the Yankees dealt him to Detroit in May 1930. Waived out of majors in 1931, Mark was with the San Francisco Missions (PCL) for part of 1932, then went to the Chicago Cubs in late 1932. He was a Cub in 1933, and with Cincinnati in 1934. Koenig played for the Giants in 1935 and 1936, then went to the Missions in 1937, retiring after 39 games.

Koenig's lifetime BA is .279, his Yankee career BA is .268. Mark appeared in five World Series, three with the Yanks, one with the Cubs, one with the Giants.

The last survivor of the 1927 Yankees, Koenig died at age 90 in Orland, California.

Lazzeri, Anthony Michael   "Poosh 'em up"   Second Base

Born: December 6, 1903, San Francisco, California
TR, BR, 5' 11-1/2", 170 lbs.
Died: August 6, 1946   Salary: $8,000

	G	AB	H	2B	3B	HR	HR %	R	RBI	BB	SO	SB	BA	SA	Pinch AB	Hit H	G by POS
1927	153	570	176	29	8	18	3.2	92	102	69	82	22	.309	.482	0	0	2B-113
																	SS-38
																	3B-9

Lazzeri, of Italian descent, was raised in San Francisco. He had minimal formal education. After playing sandlot ball in the San Francisco area, he played with Salt Lake City of the Pacific Coast League in 1922–23 as a utility infielder. With Peoria in 1923, he played second base, then split the 1924 season with Salt Lake and Lincoln of the Western League, playing 3B, SS, and 2B. Tony went back to Salt Lake for 1925, where he played short.

In 1925, with Salt Lake, he hit 60 HRs and drove in 222 runs, both Pacific Coast League (PCL) records. Tony also scored a record 202 runs in 1925.

He came to the Yankees in 1926 as a second baseman. Under Huggins's coaching he became an immediate star. In his rookie year he hit .275, slammed 18 HRs, and drove in 114 runs. In each of the next four seasons he hit over .300. Tony drove in over 100 runs in seven seasons. He was an excellent clutch hitter. His career-high BA was a smashing, team leading .354 in 1929. He tailed off as he aged, but his lifetime BA is an estimable .292. Lazzeri was an excellent fielder who sometimes shifted to third. He was also a good base stealer, and a steadying influence on the occasionally erratic Mark Koenig. Knowledgeable pros and fans rated him as a very smart, tough player.

Lazzeri was chosen by the *Sporting News* in 1932 as the best second baseman in baseball. He was a member of the first All-Star Game team in 1933. Tony played in seven World Series, and hit .400 in 1937 in his final series as a Yankee. His lifetime World Series BA is .262. Lazzeri was released at the end of 1937.

He signed with the Chicago Cubs and helped them win the 1938 NL pennant. Lazzeri was with Brooklyn and the Giants in 1939, and played his final big league game on June 7, 1939.

Lazzeri managed Toronto, then of the International League, for one season before retiring and going home to San Francisco. He died at 42 of a heart attack in San Francisco.

He was elected to the Hall of Fame in 1991.

Meusel, Robert William   **"Long Bob"**   **Left Fielder**
Born: July 19, 1896, San Jose, California
TR, BR, 6' 3", 190 lbs.
Died: November 28, 1977   1927 salary: $13,000

	G	AB	H	2B	3B	HR	HR %	R	RBI	BB	SO	SB	BA	SA	Pinch Hit AB	H	G by POS
1927	135	516	174	47	9	8	1.6	75	103	45	58	24	.337	.510	3	1	OF-131

Meusel was of German descent. He was educated in the Los Angeles public schools, served in the U.S. Navy (1918–19), then played minor league ball with Vernon of the Pacific Coast League where he batted .337 in 1919. He came to the Yankees in 1920 where he remained as the regular left fielder for 10 years.

Bob was a solid hitter with a great arm and a surly disposition. A charter member of "Murderers' Row," he was also a roisterer with Babe Ruth, but with a personality the opposite of Babe's affinity for people, kids, reporters.

Meusel drove in more than 100 runs in five Yank seasons, and led the league with 138 RBIs and 33 homers in 1925. (Ruth was ill and out of the lineup for part of that year.) He hit for the cycle (in one game a single, double, triple, and homer), three times in his career ('21, '22, '28), an AL record. Meusel stole home twice in series games, the only player to do so.

He was no ascetic during his 10 Yank years; he paid a price for late hours shenanigans. After the 1927 season he lost a step or two, his BA tailed off. Let go by the Yankees at the close of 1929, Meusel played with the Cincinnati Reds in 1930, then exited the majors. At age of 34, nobody wanted him in the big leagues. Meusel played for minor league Minneapolis in 1931, Hollywood in 1932, then quit.

He spent his post-playing years out of baseball. Bob Meusel was 81 when he passed away in Downey, California.

Moore, William Wilcy   **"Cy"**   **Pitcher**
Born: May 20, 1897, Bonita, Texas
TR, BR, 6', 198 lbs.
Died: March 29, 1963   1927 salary: $1,800
(plus $2,500 post-season bonus)

	W	L	PCT	ERA	G	GS	CG	IP	H	BB	SO	ShO	Relief Pitching W	L	SV	BA
1927	19	7	.731	2.28	50	12	6	213	185	59	75	1	13	3	13	.080

Wilcy was the first of the great Yankee relievers. A sinker ball specialist, he had great control. Brought up in Oklahoma, Moore pitched in the semipros before entering organized baseball with Fort Worth of the Texas-Oklahoma League. Cy compiled excellent records in the minors (19–9 with Ardmore of Western Association, 17–6 with Okmulgee of same league), but attracted little attention from major league scouts. Good natured, of a mild disposition, Moore was a constant target of bench jockeys. But his sinker, now part of baseball lore, made batters ground out, and choked off rallies.

He came to the Yanks in 1927 from Greenville in the South Atlantic (Sally) League where his won-lost was an exceptional 30–4. As a Yankee in 1927 Moore was 19–7, a sensation and stopper. In the World Series against the Pirates he saved the first game for Hoyt, and won the final of the four game sweep, 4–3. Altogether, it was a magnificent season for Wilcy, and an unexpected boon to the Yankees.

After the 1927 season Moore developed a sore arm, was 4–4 in 1928, 6–4 in 1929. The Yankees sent him to St. Paul where he got his stuff back and was 22–9 in 1930. Sold to the Red Sox in 1931, Wilcy went 11–13, mostly in relief, a good record with a sixth place team. He appeared in 37 games for the last place Red Sox in 1932, and was 4–10. Traded back to the Yankees towards the end of the '32 season, he appeared in 10 games for a 2–0 mark to delight of his old 1927 chums (Ruth, Gehrig, Lazzeri, Combs, etc.).

In the fourth and final game of the 1932 World Series against the Chicago Cubs, after Yank starter Johnny Allen was bombed for four runs in the first, Moore came in to squelch the Cubs. He held them in check until the seventh as the Yanks caught up and went ahead. Then, in a kind of poetic justice, Herb Pennock, a pitcher Moore had often relieved in the '20s, took over to finish the 13–6 Yank win. Moore's World Series record now a perfect 1.000 (two games, two wins).

After a 5–5 season with the Yanks in 1933 Wilcy was through in majors—but not in organized baseball. He moved around the minors with his still effective sinker for seven more years. He pitched for Kansas City (American Association), Oakland (Pacific Coast League), Oklahoma City (Texas League), and Borger (West Texas-New Mexico League). By the time he retired to full-time farming, Wilcy had spent 13 of his 20 ball-playing years in the minors.

In his post-baseball years Moore farmed, attended an occasional Old Timers game, and reminisced about his Yankee buddies. He had traveled the minors until the age of 43, but no matter which club he was with he was always thought of as a 1927 Yankee.

Wilcy died at home, in Hollis, Oklahoma, at 65.

Morehart, Raymond Anderson   Infielder
Born: December 2, 1899, Abner, Texas
BL, TR, 5' 9", 157 lbs.
Died: January 13, 1989

	G	AB	H	2B	3B	HR	HR %	R	RBI	BB	SO	SB	BA	SA	Pinch Hit AB	Hit H	G by POS
1927	73	195	50	7	2	1	0.5	45	20	29	18	4	.256	.328	14	2	2B-53

Ray Morehart was brought up and educated in Texas. After graduating from Austin College with a degree in languages, Ray played in the minors with Flint of the Ontario League from 1922 to 1924. He went to the Chicago White Sox near the end of 1924, and played 31 games with the White Sox that season. Morehart was with Wichita for the 1925 season, went back to the White Sox in 1926. He was traded to the Yankees, along with catcher Johnny Grabowski, for Aaron Ward on January 13, 1927.

Morehart was a reliable utility infielder, filling in at second base for Tony Lazzeri. When Koenig was hurt and Lazzeri moved to short, Morehart played a strong second. At the end of the 1927 season he was traded to St. Paul. Years after that trade Morehart still spoke bitterly of Ed Barrow for sending him away from the Yankees and the majors. But Morehart always considered himself a Yankee, and was proud of having been a player on the great team. He remembered Huggins as a great manager: "Nobody better," he said in a phone interview with the author, December 26, 1984.

Ray played in the minors until 1933, then worked for the Sun Oil Company until he retired. He batted .256 in 1927; his lifetime major league BA is .269.

He died at 89 in Dallas, Texas.

Paschal, Benjamin Edwin   Outfielder

Born: October 13, 1895, Enterprise, Alabama
BR, TR, 5' 11", 185 lbs.
Died: November 10, 1974

	G	AB	H	2B	3B	HR	HR %	R	RBI	BB	SO	SB	BA	SA	Pinch Hit AB	Pinch Hit H	G by POS
1927	50	82	26	9	2	2	2.4	16	16	4	10	0	.317	.549	22	5	OF-27

Paschal was raised and educated in Alabama and attended the University of Alabama. He broke into organized baseball in 1915 with Dothan of the Georgia State League, hit .290, then signed with Cleveland. The Indians sent him to New Orleans in 1916, then to Charlotte. He was with Muskegon of the Central League in 1917, then went back to Charlotte where he remained until 1924 except for a brief stint with the Boston Red Sox in 1920. Ben played for Atlanta of the Southern League in 1924, scored 136 runs, and hit an eye-catching .341. In late 1924 he came to the Yankees and played four games.

In 1925 Paschal replaced Ruth during Babe's famous "bellyache heard 'round the world" season, played 89 games and hit .360. He remained with the Yankees until the end of 1929, the last year of his major league career. A consistently good hitter, an excellent pinch hitter and substitute outfielder, Paschal has a .309 lifetime BA. Ben appeared in the 1926 and 1928 World Series.

Paschal was a quiet, sometimes brooding, colorless player on a team famous for its frolicsome personalities. But he was a reliable and valuable substitute for the likes of Ruth, Meusel, Combs, a key performer on the Yankee teams of the middle and late 1920s.

Ben Paschal died at 79 in Charlotte, North Carolina.

Pennock, Herbert Jefferis   **"Squire of Kennett Square"**   **Pitcher**
Born: February 10, 1894, Kennett Square, Pennsylvania
TL, BL, 6', 160 lbs.
Died: January 30, 1948   1927 salary: $17,500

	W	L	PCT	ERA	G	GS	CG	IP	H	BB	SO	ShO	Relief Pitching W	L	SV	BA
1927	19	8	.704	3.00	34	26	18	209.2	225	48	51	1	2	0	2	.217

Born to a middle-class farm family south of Philadelphia, Pennock was a birthright Quaker. His family traced its roots to seventeenth-century settlers under William Penn. Herb was educated in private schools and loved to play baseball; at age 16, while at Cedar Croft School, he pitched a no-hitter. Connie Mack grabbed Pennock and sent him to the semipro Atlantic City team of the Seashore League.

At 18, in 1912, he went to the Philadelphia Athletics where he was 1–2 his first year, 2–1 his second year, and 11–4 in 1914. Herb pitched three innings in the 1914 series for no decision. In 1915 he was 3–6 with the A's, was dealt to the Boston Red Sox in midseason and was 0–0. He had a 0–2 mark with the Sox in 1916, 5–5 in 1917. Pennock was with the U.S Navy in 1917 during World War II. He went back to the Sox in 1919 for a 16–8 mark. With the Red Sox through 1922 he compiled an estimable 59–59 record with second-rate teams.

Herb came to New York in 1923 and became the star Yankee lefty throughout the '20s. His won-lost as a Yankee is 162–90, his lifetime mark is 240–162. His World Series mark, all with the Yankees, is a perfect 5–0, a record surpassed only by Lefty Gomez with 6–0. Herb saved the last two games of the 1932 series in the Yankees' 4–0 victory over the Cubs. He went to the Red Sox in 1934, and quit that year after 22 years in the major leagues.

Pennock died in New York in 1948 of a stroke, ten days short of 54. He was elected to the Baseball Hall of Fame in 1948.

Pipgras, George William   **"The Danish Viking"**   **Pitcher**
Born: December 20, 1899, Ida Grove, Iowa
BR, TR, 6' 1 1/2", 185 lbs.
Died: October 19, 1986

	W	L	PCT	ERA	G	GS	CG	IP	H	BB	SO	ShO	Relief Pitching W	L	SV	BA
1927	10	3	.769	4.11	29	21	9	166.1	148	77	81	1	0	0	0	.239

Pipgras was born in Iowa but grew up and was educated in Minnesota where his family owned a farm. He pitched for the Slayton High School team. He enlisted in the Army at 17 by falsifying his age, and served in France during World War I. Upon returning to the farm in 1919 he played with local semipros.

Pipgras first played in organized ball in 1920, with Joplin of the Western League. He was sent by Joplin to Saginaw where he stayed for two weeks before being released because of wildness. He pitched for Madison of the Dakota League in 1921 (12–6); and Charleston of the South Atlantic League in 1922 (19–9).

As a Yankee in 1923 he had a 1–3 record, in 1924 he was 0–1. George was sent to Atlanta and Nashville in 1925 (19–15); to St. Paul in 1926 (22–19), then returned to the Yankees in 1927. In midseason 1927 he became a regular and finished at 10–3, plus a series win over Pittsburgh. Pipgras, a strong, workhorse pitcher, went on to a notable Yankee career.

His league-leading 24 wins in 1928 are the most for a Yankee right hander. It was his 11–6 win over the Tigers that clinched the pennant that year. He is 93–64 as a Yankee; his lifetime is 102–73 with a 4.09 ERA. Pipgras is 3–0 in series competition, all with the Yankees.

After his playing days he umpired in the New York Penn League from 1936 to 1938, then umpired in the AL from 1939 to 1945. He was judged one of the best umpires in the business. After quitting as an active umpire, he became the minor league supervisor of umpires from 1946 to 1949.

George Pipgras died at 86 in Gainesville, Florida.

Ruether, Walter Henry   "Dutch"   Pitcher
Born: September 13, 1893, Alameda, California
BL, TL, 6' 1-1/2", 180 lbs.
Died: May 16, 1970

	W	L	PCT	ERA	G	GS	CG	IP	H	BB	SO	ShO	Relief Pitching W	L	SV	BA
1927	13	6	.684	3.38	27	26	12	184	202	52	45	3	0	0	0	.263

Brought up and educated in California. Dutch attended St. Ignatius College (now San Francisco University). He pitched for the college team, and attracted scouts during a March 10, 1913, exhibition game against the Chicago White Sox when he held the big leaguers to one hit and one run. Ruether signed with the Pittsburgh Pirates for a $500 bonus.

He was with Vancouver in 1914, then moved around to Salt Lake City, Portland, and Spokane before coming to the majors with the Chicago Cubs in 1917. He was 3–2 with them. With the Cincinnati Reds in 1917 he was 1–2 his first year, but an impressive 19–6 with a league-leading .760 PCT and a superb 1.82 ERA in 1919.

He remained with the Reds through 1920 when he was 16–12. In 1920 with the Brooklyn Dodgers he compiled a 54–52 won-loss by the end of the 1924 season. Dealt to the Washington Senators, Ruether had an excellent 18–7 mark in 1925.

In mid-1926 he came to the Yankees in a surprise deal after six clubs had waived him—unusual for a winning pitcher of Ruether's stature. There was much behind the scenes maneuvering by Ed Barrow on this transaction. Dutch finished the Yankee season with a 2–3 mark. At 34, and something of a drinker, he was a chancy addition to the Yanks. But Huggins spotted him carefully, and Ruether's 13–6 was an admirable farewell to the bigs. A good hitter, he often pinch hit. His lifetime BA is .259.

After leaving the majors Ruether spent eight years in the Pacific Coast League, and a final year in the Southern League with Nashville.

Down on his luck in the deep depression year of 1934, Dutch made an unusual deal to manage Seattle. He did not sign a contract and didn't earn a salary, but he did get living expenses. If the club showed a profit at the end of the season the owner, William Klepper, would pay him whatever he felt was fair. "I merely want to show you that I can manage the team and get results," said Ruether.

Ruether did well enough to manage Seattle for three years. He scouted for the Cubs and Giants before retiring from 56 years in pro ball.

Ruether died in Phoenix, Arizona, at age 76.

Ruth, George Herman "Babe"   "The Sultan of Swat"   Outfielder
Born: February 6, 1895, Baltimore, Maryland
TL, BL, 6' 2", 215 lbs.
Died: August 16, 1948   1927 salary: $70,000

	G	AB	H	2B	3B	HR	HR %	R	RBI	BB	SO	SB	BA	SA	Pinch Hit AB	Pinch Hit H	G by POS
1927	151	540	192	29	8	60	11.1	158	164	138	89	7	.356	.772	0	0	OF-151

Ruth was of Pennsylvania Dutch-German ancestry. An outfielder, and early in his career a pitcher, Babe was arguably the greatest ballplayer the game has seen; certainly, the most colorful and most famous. Even those with no interest in baseball, with no understanding of the game—in the United States and countries around the world—knew who he was.

His parents were George and Kate Ruth, and Babe was one of eight children. An ungovernable child, he was sent to St. Mary's Industrial Home for Boys in Baltimore to be disciplined and educated by the Catholic Xaverian Brothers. There he learned to play baseball, first as a catcher, then as an outstanding pitcher.

He left St. Mary's in 1914 when signed by Jack Dunn, owner of the then minor league Baltimore Orioles. Ruth was 14–6 with the Orioles, before being sold to the Boston Red Sox where he was 1–1 before being sent to Providence where he won 9 lost 2. He returned to Boston to win 1. In 1914 his major league mark was 2–1, his minor league mark 23–8.

Ruth's AL pitching record extends from 1914 to 1933. With the Red Sox from 1914 to 1919 his mark was 89-46. As a Yankee he was 5-0 (1 in 1920, 2 in 1921, 1 in 1930, 1 in 1933). Babe's lifetime as a pitcher is 94-46 for a .671 PCT, a 2.28 ERA. His World Series mark is 3-0 for a 1.000 PCT, a 0.87 ERA.

Ruth was traded by Boston to the Yanks in late 1919, becoming the home run hitting sensation of baseball, with 54 homers in 1920, 59 in 1921. His 60 homers in the 1927 season was unmatched until Roger Maris broke that record with 61 in 1961.

Ruth's 714 lifetime homers is second only to Henry Aaron's 755. But Babe is No. 1 in HR% with an 8.5 mark. His 17 homers in September 1927 is the most ever hit by a player in one month. On opening day 1923 he hit the first homer in the newly constructed Yankee Stadium. In 1933 he hit the first homer in the newly inaugurated All-Star Game.

In the record books Babe is first in slugging average (.690); first in bases on balls (2,056); second in RBIs (2,211); second in runs (2,174); third in extra-base hits (1,356); fifth in total bases (5,793); eleventh in BA (.342).

Babe scored more than 150 runs in six different seasons; 12 times he led the American League in home runs; 11 times in walks. All are major league records. His 1923 mark of 170 walks is the ML record. He led the AL in runs scored in eight seasons, a major league record. For six seasons Ruth was the RBI leader, a ML record. From 1918 to 1921 he topped the league in extra-base hits, an American League record.

His slugging averages for 1920 (.847), 1921 (.846), and 1927 (.772) are the three highest SAs ever in major league baseball. His .847 SA in 1920 and .846 in 1921 were the only times a player reached or exceeded the .800 mark. In a record seven consecutive seasons (1918–24) he led the AL in slugging percentage. And for a total of 13 seasons he led the league in slugging.

Ruth scored 177 runs in 1921 for a modern major league record. In 1923, the year he hit .393, the highest mark in Yankee history, he reached base 379 times, a major league record, and had a fabulous on-base PCT of .542.

From 1914 to 1918, he was played mostly as a pitcher. What his batting marks would have been had he played every day we can only surmise. Given his remarkable gift for slugging, his numbers would surely have been significantly higher.

Babe's World Series marks are outstanding. He is first in HR% with 11.6; second in bases on balls (33); second in home runs (15); second in slugging percentage (.744); third in runs scored (37); fourth in RBIs (33); 10th in hits (42). And, it is only fair to note, fourth in strike outs (30). His series BA is .326 over 10 World Series (three with Boston, seven with New York).

Babe played his final Yankee game on September 30, 1934. After an unconditional release, he signed with the Boston Braves as player and coach, played in 28 games in 1935 and quit. Except for a short 1938 coaching stint with the Dodgers, he never again was part of organized baseball.

He spent his last thirteen years in quiet retirement, occasionally going to ball games, seeing friends, hoping for a job in baseball. It never came.

Babe Ruth died on August 16, 1948.

The monument and plaque in the Yankees Memorial Park reads:

GEORGE HERMAN "BABE" RUTH
1895–1948
A Great Ball Player
A Great Man
A Great American
Erected By
THE YANKEES
And
The New York Baseball Writers
April 19, 1949

Shawkey, James Robert   **Pitcher**
Born: December 4, 1890, Brookville, Pennsylvania
BR, TR 5' 11", 168 lbs.
Died: December 31, 1980

	W	L	PCT	ERA	G	GS	CG	IP	H	BB	SO	ShO	Relief Pitching W	L	SV	BA
1927	02	3	400	2.89	19	2	0	43.2	44	16	23	0	2	2	4	.091

Shawkey, a great Yankee hurler, began working at the age of 14 after minimal formal education. He worked with a logging crew for several years and was a fireman on the Pennsylvania Railroad. Being a professional ballplayer was not in his plans.

Seeking further education he entered Slippery Rock Normal School. There the athletic coach noticed Shawkey's ballplaying talent and in 1910 encouraged him to join Bloomsburg, a semipro club in the local Mountain League. From there he moved to Harrisburg, a pro team in the Tri-States League where he went 10–10. Connie Mack looked at young Bob, signed him, and placed him with the Baltimore Orioles of the International League for seasoning.

In 1913 Mack brought him to the Athletics. He was 6–5 that year, and 16–8 with the 1914 pennant-winning A's. But Mack was a disenchanted man after losing the 1914 series in four straight, to the "Miracle Braves."

Systematically Mack sold off his star players: in the middle of the 1915 season Shawkey was waived to the Yanks for the waiver price of $2,500. It turned out to be a coup for Jake Ruppert, a source of ongoing chagrin to Connie Mack.

Shawkey, with his zipping fast ball and elusive curve, became a mainstay of the Yankee pitching staff. In 1916 he was 24–14. For four seasons he won 20 or more games. He holds the Yankee record for 1–0 shutouts, seven. When the Yanks inaugurated Yankee Stadium in April 18, 1923, Shawkey pitched and won the 4–1 three-hitter against the Red Sox. He slammed a homer after Ruth had hit the first ever in the new ballpark.

By the time he retired at the close of the 1927 season, Shawkey had won 196 games while losing 150. His lifetime ERA is 3.09. Only his World Series record is undistinguished: he is 1–2 as a Yankee, 1–3 lifetime.

Shawkey coached with the Yankees in 1928 and 1929. After Miller Huggins died, Bob was appointed manager, a post he held through 1930, after which he was replaced by Joe McCarthy.

Shawkey managed a number of minor league teams after leaving the Yanks: Jersey City in 1931, Scranton from 1932 to 1933, Newark in 1934 and 1935, Watertown in 1947, Tallahassee in 1949.

When the Golden Anniversary of Yankee Stadium was celebrated on September 30, 1973, Shawkey had the honor of throwing out the first ball. And in the reconstructed Yankee Stadium, on April 15, 1976, he again threw out the first ball.

Shawkey had served in the U.S. Navy in 1918 during World War I. He died at 90 in the Veterans Administration Hospital in Syracuse, New York.

Shocker, Urban James   Pitcher
Born: August 22, 1890, Cleveland, Ohio
TR, BR, 5' 10", 170 lbs.
Died: September 9, 1928

	W	L	PCT	ERA	G	GS	CG	IP	H	BB	SO	ShO	Relief Pitching W	L	SV	BA
1927	18	6	.750	2.84	31	27	13	200	207	41	35	2	1	0	0	.241

Shocker was born Urban Jacques Shockeor. He began as a catcher with semipro teams in Michigan and Canada, then switched to pitching and signed with Windsor of the Border League in 1913. After a 6–7 season he joined the Ottawa team where he won 20 and lost 8 for a .714 PCT. He pitched with Ottawa for most of 1915, was 19–10, then was sold to the Yankees for a reported $750 late in the 1915 season.

With the Yankees in 1916 he was 4–3, then was optioned to Toronto of the International League for most of the season. He was 15–3 with Toronto with a stunning 1.31 ERA. Recalled to the Yanks late in 1916, he remained in the majors for rest of his career.

In 1917 Shocker was 8–5 for the Yankees with a 2.61 ERA. He was traded by Yankees to the St. Louis Browns in 1918. With the Browns, Shocker became one of the best pitchers in the American League, compiling a 126–80 record with a usually mediocre club. In 1921 his 27–12 mark led the league. Traded back to the Yanks in 1925, he was 12–12, the best mark of the Yankee pitchers in that disastrous seventh place season for New York. Urban was 19–ll in 1926; 18–6 in 1927, his final season. An excellent fielding pitcher, he had a career .980 fielding average. His lifetime won-lost is 187–117 for a PCT of .615. His lifetime ERA is a fine 3.17.

When the spitball was outlawed in 1920, Shocker was one of 17 pitchers permitted to throw the spitter until they retired.

His death at 38 during the Yankee pennant-winning year stunned his teammates and fans, none of whom knew how very ill he was.

Thomas, Myles Lewis   **Pitcher**
Born: October 22, 1897, State College, Pennnsylvania
BR, TR, 5' 9", 170 lbs.
Died: December 12, 1963

													Relief Pitching			
	W	L	PCT	ERA	G	GS	CG	IP	H	BB	SO	ShO	W	L	SV	BA
1927	7	4	.636	4.87	21	9	1	88.2	111	43	25	0	4	1	0	.333

Thomas was brought up and educated in Pennsylvania. He attended Penn State College, and signed with the Yankee organization in 1921. With Hartford of the Eastern League he pitched a no-hitter against Springfield in his rookie year. He pitched for Reading of the International League in 1922, then went to Toronto of the International League. Thomas joined the Yankees in 1926.

He was 6–6 in 1926 with a 4.23 ERA. In 1927 Myles was 7–4, often in relief. He remained a Yankee in 1928 when he was 1–0. In 1929 he was 0–2 before being traded to the Senators in June. His combined record for 1929 is 7–10. Thomas's last season in the majors was 1930 when he went 2–2 for Washington.

Thomas pitched in the minors with Newark (1931), Hollywood (1932), St. Paul (1933 and 1934); he went to Toledo as pitcher and coach from 1935 to 1939. He managed Tiffin in the Ohio State League in 1940.

Myles Thomas died at 64 of a heart attack in Toledo, Ohio.

Wera, Julian Valentine   **Third Base**
Born: February 9, 1902, Winona, Minnesota
BR, TR, 5' 8", 164 lbs.
Died: December 12, 1975

	G	AB	H	2B	3B	HR	HR %	R	RBI	BB	SO	SB	BA	SA	Pinch Hit AB	Hit H	G by POS
1927	38	42	10	3	0	1	2.4	7	8	1	5	0	.238	.381	4	0	3B-19

Wera was raised and educated in Winona where he starred in baseball, football, and basketball at Winona High School. He played sandlot ball in Minnesota.

He joined St. Paul in late 1924, then went to Peoria in 1925, and back to St. Paul in 1926. He was a Yankee in 1927 and 1929, his only years in the majors. Wera played a total of 43 games in major leagues, had a lifetime .278 BA, then spent the rest of his career in the minors.

Julian Wera died at 73 in Rochester, Minnesota.

1927 New York Yankees Staff

Krichell, Paul Bernard   "Krich"   **Scout**
Born: December 19, 1882, New York, New York
Died: June 4, 1957

Paul Krichell failed as a big league catcher, but was an outstanding success as a big league scout.

He entered baseball in 1903 as a catcher with Ossining of the lowly Hudson River League, and in 1911 made it to the majors with the St. Louis Browns. In Krichell's two major league years he appeared in only 85 games, and hit a paltry .222. But in 1920, while coaching for the Boston Red Sox, he found his true metier when he was hired as a scout by Yankee business manager Ed Barrow.

Krichell's success as a Yankee scout became legendary. Not only did he scout Lou Gehrig when the future Iron Man was attending Columbia University, but he also scouted many other Yankee notables. The list of Krichell's signed players—whom he bird-dogged with the help of associate Bob Connery and 20 other scouts—included 1927 Yankees Tony Lazzeri, Mark Koenig, Benny Bengough, and, of course, Gehrig. His future signees included Phil Rizzuto, Charlie Keller, Red Rolfe, Whitey Ford, Leo Durocher, George Selkirk, and George Sternweiss. Of the above famous names five are Hall of Famers.

Surely, without Krichell's astute appraisal of ballplayers the 1927 Yankees would have been just another moderately good baseball team. He began his scouting career by signing Hinky Haines in 1921, and ended it by bird-dogging Tom Carroll in 1954, both of whom soon sank to oblivion. But in between these washouts Krich gave baseball some of its greatest players, and a true immortal in Lou Gehrig.

Paul Krichell died at 74 in the Bronx, New York.

Fletcher, Art   **Coach**
Born: January 5, 1885, Collinsville, Illinois
BR, TR, 5' 10-1/2", 170 lbs.
Died: February 6, 1950

Fletcher was brought up in Collinsville by English immigrant parents. He pitched for the Collinsville High School team, then attended Draughton's Practical Business College, and took a job as a stenographer and shipping clerk with Ingersoll Rand Co. Art played weekend ball for $8 per game with Staunton, Illinois, team of the semipro Trolley League. He had no desire to play baseball for a living: an assured $60 a month at Ingersoll Rand seemed preferable to a chancy ball-playing life.

In 1906 the Staunton club of the Dallas, Texas, League offered Fletcher $125 per month to play shortstop. Art refused; it was the first of many refusals Fletcher would make in his baseball career. The same club offered him $135 to play in 1907; again Art said no, and went home. In spring of 1908 the hard-to-get Fletcher took his vacation with the Dallas club. His playing became the talk of the training camp.

Owner Joe Gardner thought he now had a good shortstop, but Art still resisted. When his Illinois boss informed Fletcher that business was bad and he could remain with the club until the fall, the reluctant shortstop finally said O.K. He played ball with Texas—and did not leave the game until he retired in 1945.

In 1909 Fletcher was bought by the New York Giants, where he played occasionally for two seasons; then he became regular shortstop in 1911. Art was a Giant until 1920, playing on four flag winners, and was McGraw's team captain for last three of those years.

An animated fellow, the lantern-jawed Fletcher was a fine, aggressive shortstop, a fair hitter (his lifetime is .277), a master bench jockey. Traded to the Philadelphia Phillies midseason of the 1920 season, he played there through 1922, and was made manager in 1923. He managed the Phillies for four years; the highest finish under him was sixth.

He came to the Yankees as Huggins's principal coach in 1927, and remained a Yankee coach for 14 years, serving under Huggins, Bob Shawkey, and Joe McCarthy. Art was offered the manager's job with the Yankees after Huggins died, but, to Colonel Ruppert's astonishment, he turned it down. He had seen the toll that managing took from Huggins, and he wanted no part of the job. And that went for offers from the St. Louis Browns, the Detroit Tigers, and the Chicago White Sox.

A shrewd baseball man, a tough competitor on the field, a gentleman in his private life, Art Fletcher is remembered as one of the great Yankee coaches.

He died of a heart attack at 65 while driving a car in Los Angeles.

O'Leary, Charles Timothy   **Coach**
Born: October 15, 1882, Chicago, Illinois
BR, TR, 5' 7", 165 lbs.
Died: January 6, 1941

Charley O'Leary was one of 16 children, 11 of them boys. His parents were Irish immigrants. Raised in Chicago, Charley went to All Saints

Parochial School. At 16 he quit, and went to work for the Mandel Brothers Clothing Company. He played ball for the company team in the local Sunday League, where he was spotted by a scout for the Chicago White Sox.

When White Sox shortstop Frank Shugart broke his leg in the middle of a tight pennant race 17-year-old Charley took over, played 26 games, hit .163 and fielded .876. Chicago won the AL pennant in 1900, though O'Leary finished the season on the bench with a broken arm.

In 1904 Charley caught on with Detroit and remained with them through 1911. During that time the Tigers won three straight pennants (1907–09). O'Leary played for Indianapolis in 1912, and with the St. Louis Cards in 1913, where he covered short alongside second baseman Miller Huggins. In 1914 he was with San Francisco, 1915–16 with St. Paul, and 1917—as a player/manager—with San Antonio.

Out of baseball in 1918 and 1919 when he worked in Chicago's city hall and played semipro ball on Sundays. In 1920 he answered the call from Miller Huggins and joined the Yankees as a coach. He remained in New York through 1930.

Charley was trusted and reliable, a valuable assistant and friend to Huggins. He was respected by players, well-liked by the press, and his Irish wit was an enlivening feature of the club. He was a colorful source of information about players' life in early days of the pro game.

Retorting to complaints by contemporary players, on May 22, 1927, Charley told John Kieran of the *New York Times,* "Hear that now. Do they know that in the early days a player had to pay for his own uniform and was charged fifty cents a day for his board while he was on the road?...When I was a lad we stopped at hotels that nobody else would go into except the police. Now they have taxicabs, baggage trunks, and everything except a valet. We had to walk from the train...and carry everything except the manager. And," he snorted, "sometimes we'd have to carry him."

As for what Charley perceived as excessive propriety among players in the '20s, he told Kieran, "Remember that old Detroit club?...We had a fight every day in the clubhouse.... Sometimes we had two. We fought the other players on the field or under the grandstand, and we fought each other.... I never won anything except some fine black eyes, but I was always in there trying."

After Huggins's death O'Leary coached for Hug's replacement, Bob Shawkey. He left the Yankees after the 1930 season to coach with the Chicago Cubs in 1931 and 1932, and the St. Louis Browns from 1934 to 1937.

Charley O'Leary died in Chicago at the age of 58.

Woods, Doc   **Trainer**
Born: Date unknown
Died: Date unknown
     Little information exists on the career of Doc Woods. It's certain he
was the trainer on most of the 1920s Yankees; in the team photo of the 1927
club he stands in the top row on the extreme right.
     Milt Gaston, a 1924 Yankee pitcher still remarkably spirited and clear-
minded during a 1995 interview, remembered Woods as "a nice fellow, and
a good trainer." According to a surviving business card, in off-season Doc
Woods worked from an office in New York treating people afflicted with
"Sciatic, Muscular, and Inflammatory Rheumatism." His speciality was
"Corrective Manipulations," and he advertised himself as a "Trainer of Big
League Baseball Clubs for twenty-three years. For the past six years and
present Trainer of the NEW YORK YANKEES."
     The *Yankee Encyclopedia*, states that Babe Ruth asked Woods to forge
Babe's signature on baseballs because Ruth couldn't keep up with the
requests. This makes suspect many surviving autographs on baseballs
supposedly signed by Ruth.

Sheehy, Michael Joseph   **"Pete"**   **Gofer**
Born: 1910, New York, New York
Died: August 13, 1985
     Pete came to the Yanks as clubhouse boy, messenger, gofer, in
midseason 1927. He worked as assistant to clubhouse man Fred Logan,
then served in the U.S. Army in the Pacific Theatre during World War II.
He became head clubhouse man in 1945, a job he held for the rest of his
life.
     Pete was the longest-serving Yankee employee ever, beloved and
respected by players, management, the press, by everyone who knew him.
In 1977, 50 years after he appeared on the scene, the Stadium clubhouse
was named the "Pete Sheehy Clubhouse" in his honor. It was a suitable
distinction for a man who became a Yankee living legend.
     Pete remained at his clubhouse post until shortly before he died, 58
years after he had been asked to help out for a day in return for a free entry
to the game.

Eddie Bennett   **Batboy/Mascot**
Born: Probably 1904, Brooklyn, New York
Died: January 16, 1935
     Wiz, hex-artist, Eddie was of uncertain parentage. He was batboy for
the Chicago White Sox in 1919, batboy for the Brooklyn Dodgers in 1920,
and came to the Yankees as batboy/mascot in 1921.

Eddie, a hunchback, remained a Yankee through the '20s, and into the '30s. A familiar figure on the field among the great Yankee players, he was popular with the team and management.

Crippled in a cab accident in 1932, Eddie had to give up his job, but was kept on payroll by Jake Ruppert. An alcoholic, he died alone in a New York rooming house, January 16, 1935.

Bibliography

Archival Resources

Waite Hoyt Papers, Cincinnati Historical Society, Cincinnati, Ohio.

Player, Manager, and Owner File, National Baseball Library, Cooperstown, New York.

Personal Communications

Glenn, Joe. Telephone interview, 1985.

Gould, David. Telephone interview, February 1987.

Hoyt, Waite Charles. Letter to Jim Ogle, Yankee Alumni Association, (undated).

Koenig, Mark A. Telephone interview, 26 December 1984.

Pipgras, George W. Telephone interview, 10 December 1984.

Pipgras, George W. Telephone interview, 28 January 1985.

Sheehy, Michael J. (Pete). Interview at Yankee Stadium, 3 October 1984.

Smith, Ken. Telephone interview, 17 March 1987.

Wells, Edwin Lee. Telephone interview, 1985.

Books

Barrow, Edward Grant, with James M. Kahn. *My Fifty Years in Baseball.* New York: Coward-McCann, 1951.

Creamer, Robert W. *Babe: The Legend Comes to Life.* New York: Simon and Schuster, 1974

Durocher, Leo Ernest, with Ed Linn. *Nice Guys Finish Last.* New York: Simon and Schuster, 1975.

Emerson, Ralph Waldo. "New England Reformers." Essays: Second Series. 1844. Vol. 3 of *The Collected Works of Ralph Waldo Emerson.* Cambridge: Harvard University Press, 1983.

Fitzgerald, F. Scott. *The Crack-Up.* New York: New Directions, 1956.

Johnson, Paul. *Modern Times.* New York: Harper and Row, 1983.

Levine, Peter. *A.G. Spalding and the Rise of Baseball.* New York: Oxford University Press, 1985.

Lieb, Fred. *Baseball As I Have Known It.* New York: Coward, McCann, Geoghegan 1977.

Riess, Steven A. *Touching Base.* Westport: Greenwood Press, 1980.

Ruth, Babe, as told to Bob Considine. *The Babe Ruth Story.* New York: Penguin, 1992.

Seymour, Harold. *Baseball: The Early Years.* New York: Oxford University Press, 1960.

Thoreau, Henry D. *Walden.* Ed. J. Lyndon Shanley. Princeton: Princeton University Press, 1971.

Gallagher, Mark. *Yankee Encyclopedia.* New York: Leisure Press, 1982.

Magazines and Journals

Gallico, Paul. "Reign of Terror." *Sport Magazine,* May 1951: 26.

Lane, F.C. "Urban Shocker One of the Great Pitchers of 1920." *Baseball Magazine,* January 1921: 381-82.

——. "Can Flawless Skill Prove a Handicap?" *Baseball Magazine,* August 1926: 409-20.

——. "The Season's Sensation." *Baseball Magazine,* October 1918: 472.

Meany, Tom. "The Merry Mortician of the Mound." *Baseball Digest,* January 1952: 89.

Sher, Jack. "Lou Gehrig; The Man and the Legend." *Sport Magazine,* October 1948: 60.

Spalding Official Base Ball Guide, 1929: 349.

Vance, David M. "The Success of Earle B. Combs." *Eastern Kentucky Alumnus,* Spring 1970: 11.

"Taps for Huggins: A Great Little Bear-Tamer." *Literary Digest,* 12 October 1929: 40.

Ward, John J. "The Coming Southpaw." *Baseball Magazine,* July 1916: 41.

——. "The Hero of the Hot Corner." *Baseball Magazine,* November 1927: 306.

Newspapers

Baton Rouge State-Times, 1987.

New York Herald-Tribune, 1927.

New York Journal-American, 1957, 1964.

New York Sun, 1927.

New York Times, The, 1920, 1927, 1930, 1939, 1965, 1976.

New York Tribune, 1923.

New York World, 1923.

New York World-Telegram, 1933.

Spalding Official Base Ball Guide, 1929.

Sporting News, 1914, 1917, 1918, 1919, 1922, 1927, 1930, 1933, 1939, 1948, 1963, 1965, 1971, 1977, 1979, 1980.

Williamson Sun-Sentinel, 1981.

Worcester Evening Gazette, 1970.

Index